The Meaning of Addiction

The Meaning of Addiction

Compulsive Experience and Its Interpretation

Stanton Peele

Lexington Books
D.C. Heath and Company/Lexington, Massachusetts/Toronto

Library of Congress Cataloging in Publication Data

Peele, Stanton.
  The meaning of addiction.

  Bibliography: p. 159
  Includes indexes.
  1. Substance abuse. 2. Alcoholism. 3. Compulsive
behavior 4. Substance abuse—Treatment—United States.
5. Substance abuse—Government policy—United States.
I. Title.
RC564.P45   1985   616.86   84-54208
ISBN 0-669-02952-1 (alk. paper)
ISBN 0-669-13835-5 (pbk.: alk. paper)

Fifth printing, December 1986

Published simultaneously in Canada
Printed in the United States of America on acid-free paper
Casebound International Standard Book Number: 0-669-02952-1
Paperbound International Standard Book Number: 0-669-13835-5
Library of Congress Catalog Card Number: 84-54208

To Isidor Chein and David McClelland—
two who showed the way

Contents

Figures

Preface

The conventional idea of addiction—that a substance or activity can produce a compulsion to act that is beyond the individual's self-control—is a powerful one. In *The Meaning of Addiction*, I explore the social and personal meanings of this idea and its relevance to human behavior. This exploration includes histories of narcotic addiction (chapter 1) and alcoholism (chapter 2) in the United States, histories that explain recent theoretical developments in these fields. I judge the efficacy of prominent theories of drug and alcohol addiction—along with current models of overeating, smoking, and even running and love addictions—and analyze their flaws in a larger intellectual and psychological context (chapter 3).

In the course of this book I review a large body of epidemiological, historical, experimental, life-span, and clinical research about human drug use. I also address the literature on animal drug use studies, along with ideas about infant addiction, because these hold such a large place in contemporary views of addiction (chapter 4). In addition, I present the results of systematic experimentation on animal opiate use conducted by Dr. Bruce Alexander and his colleagues, which correct inaccurate popular notions about how animals respond to drugs. The purpose of these animal data, in common with much of the material in this book, is to puncture simplistic, often magical visions about the nature of addiction.

My major endeavor, after establishing a suitable level of analysis for addiction, is to create a framework for understanding addictive behavior (chapter 5). I evaluate the factors that cause addiction and describe the nature of self-perpetuating, self-destructive behavior. I construct a model of the relationships among cultural, social, psychological, pharmacological, and other components of addictive motivation, based on the idea that addiction is a response to socially and individually conditioned needs for specific psychophysiological, or experiential, states. This model is designed to apply equally well to *all* areas of repetitive, compulsive behavior, from self-destructive running to narcotic addiction.

I draw further implications from my analysis (chapter 6), including an understanding of the current high levels of addiction and of the failures of treatment and public policies for addiction, and I propose a direction for reasonable therapeutic and prevention efforts. Moreover, my analysis offers insights into the process of scientific definition and into some core social and psychological themes of our times: namely, the designation of new categories of psychic disease and their impact on our image of the sources of human conduct. The idea of addiction, I make clear, has always expressed central cultural conceptions about motivation and behavior. Now, in an age when science and health magazines have become our bibles, ill-founded psychological generalizations presented as scientific wisdom dictate our collective decisions about children, criminals, and ourselves.

Our conventional view of addiction—aided and abetted by science—does nothing so much as convince people of their vulnerability. It is one more element in a pervasive sense of loss of control that is the major contributor to drug and alcohol abuse, along with a host of other maladies of our age. We feel we must warn people against the dangers of the substances our society has banned, or attempted to curtail, but cannot eradicate. This book argues that our best hope is to convey these dangers realistically, by rationally pointing out the costs of excess and, more importantly, by convincing people of the benefits of health and of positive life experience. Otherwise, the idea of addiction can only become another burden to the psyche. Science cannot increase our understanding of ourselves and our world—nor can it show us the way to freedom—if it is held captive by our fears.

Acknowledgments

Beginning any book is a daunting project. I found the work on this book—extending over three years—to be particularly so. Although I was well familiar with and in constant touch with much of the material, organizing and expressing my ideas to achieve the force I hoped proved a formidable task. To the extent that I accomplished my goal, I am indebted to Archie Brodsky for the assistance he gave in discussing ideas, restructuring chapters, contributing original insights (chapter 4), and correcting phraseology and syntax. Bruce Alexander, as well as contributing original material to chapter 3 and (along with his colleagues Patricia Hadaway and Bruce Beyerstein) conducting, analyzing, and presenting the animal research in chapter 4, commented on drafts of chapters 1 and 5 and made available to me reference materials used throughout this book. Stanley Morse, as he has so often done before, selflessly read and critiqued several of these chapters, making particularly invaluable contributions to chapters 1 and 4. Without the help of any of these people, I would not have been able to give the book the form it has.

In addition, a number of people over the years made me aware of information and ideas that have helped shape this book. These people include John Falk, Nick Heather, Alan Marlatt, Harold Kalant, William Miller, Norman Zinberg, Peter Nathan, Griffith Edwards, James Woods, Harriet Braiker, Mark and Linda Sobell, Robin Room, Constance Weisner, Dan Waldorf, Martha Sanchez-Craig, Larry Gaines, David Funder, David McClelland, Robert Allen, and Judd Allen. Needless to say, although this book has been enriched by my contact with all these people, the responsibility for the ideas I express is strictly my own. I have also received great assistance in retrieving source materials from the staffs of the libraries of Fairleigh Dickinson University, Drew University, Sandoz Corporation, and the Institute for the Study of Drug Dependence (particularly the ISDD's ever-helpful information officers, Mike Ashton and Harry Shapiro). Paula Ives, for her typing, and Paula Cloutier, for her help in duplicating my manuscripts, get my special thanks. Finally, Dan Barmettler of the Institute for

Integral Development enabled me to present and sharpen my ideas during these years by offering me a continuing forum at the conferences he organized around the United States, and Mary Arnold, my wife, provided the financial support needed to complete this work.

1
The Concept of Addiction

The conventional concept of addiction this book confronts—the one accepted not only by the media and popular audiences, but by researchers whose work does little to support it—derives more from magic than from science. The core of this concept is that an entire set of feelings and behaviors is the unique result of one biological process. No other scientific formulation attributes a complex human phenomenon to the nature of a particular stimulus: statements such as "He ate all the ice cream because it was so good" or "She watches so much television because it's fun" are understood to call for a greater understanding of the actors' motivations (except, ironically, as these activities are now considered analogous to narcotic addiction). Even reductionist theories of mental illness such as of depression and schizophrenia (Peele 1981b) seek to account for a general state of mind, not specific behavior. Only compulsive consumption of narcotics and alcohol—conceived of as addictions (and now, other addictions that are seen to operate in the same way)—is believed to be the result of a spell that no effort of will can break.

Addiction is defined by tolerance, withdrawal, and craving. We recognize addiction by a person's heightened and habituated need for a substance; by the intense suffering that results from discontinuation of its use; and by the person's willingness to sacrifice all (to the point of self-destructiveness) for drug taking. The inadequacy of the conventional concept lies not in the identification of these signs of addiction—they do occur—but in the processes that are imagined to account for them. Tolerance, withdrawal, and craving are thought to be properties of particular drugs, and sufficient use of these substances is believed to give the organism no choice but to behave in these stereotypical ways. This process is thought to be inexorable, universal, and irreversible and to be independent of individual, group, cultural, or situational variation; it is even thought to be essentially the same for animals and for human beings, whether infant or adult.

Observers of addictive behavior and scientists studying it in the laboratory or in natural settings have uniformly noted that this pure model of addiction does not exist in reality, and that the behavior of people said to be addicted is far more variable than conventional notions allow. Yet unexamined, disabling residues of this inaccurate concept are present even in the work of those who have most astutely exposed the inadequacy of conventional models for describing addictive behavior. Such residues include the persistent view that complex behaviors like craving and withdrawal are straightforward physiological reactions to drugs or are biological processes—even when they appear with nondrug involvements. Although these beliefs have been shown to be unfounded in the context in which they first arose—that of heroin use and heroin addiction—they have been rearranged into new notions such as drug dependence, or used as the basis for conditioning models that assume that drugs produce invariant physiological responses in humans.

It is the burden of this book to show that exclusively biological concepts of addiction (or drug dependence) are ad hoc and superfluous and that addictive behavior is no different from all other human feeling and action in being subject to social and cognitive influences. To establish how such factors affect the dynamics of addiction is the ultimate purpose of this analysis. In this reformulation, addiction is seen not to depend on the effects of specific drugs. Moreover, it is not limited to drug use at all. Rather, addiction is best understood as an individual's adjustment, albeit a self-defeating one, to his or her environment. It represents an habitual style of coping, albeit one that the individual is capable of modifying with changing psychological and life circumstances.

While in some cases addiction achieves a devastating pathological extremity, it actually represents a continuum of feeling and behavior more than it does a distinct disease state. Neither traumatic drug withdrawal nor a person's craving for a drug is exclusively determined by physiology. Rather, the experience both of a felt need (or craving) for and of withdrawal from an object or involvement engages a person's expectations, values, and self-concept, as well as the person's sense of alternative opportunities for gratification. These complications are introduced not out of disillusionment with the notion of addiction but out of respect for its potential power and utility. Suitably broadened and strengthened, the concept of addiction provides a powerful description of human behavior, one that opens up important opportunities for understanding not only drug abuse, but compulsive and self-destructive behaviors of all kinds. This book proposes such a comprehensive concept and demonstrates its application to drugs, alcohol, and other contexts of addictive behavior.

Since narcotic addiction has been, for better or worse, our primary model for understanding other addictions, the analysis of prevailing ideas about addiction and their shortcomings involves us in the history of narcotics, particularly in the United States in the last hundred years. This history shows that styles of opiate use and our very conception of opiate addiction are historically and culturally determined. Data revealing regular nonaddictive narcotic use have consistently complicated the effort to define addiction, as have revelations of the addictive use of nonnarcotic drugs. Alcohol is one drug whose equivocal relationship to prevailing conceptions of addiction has confused the study of substance abuse for well over a century. Because the United States has had a different—though no less destructive and disturbing—experience with alcohol than it has had with opiates, this cultural experience is analyzed separately in chapter 2. This emphasis notwithstanding, alcohol is understood in this book to be addictive in exactly the same sense that heroin and other powerful drug and nondrug experiences are.

Cultural and historical variations in ideas about drugs and addiction are examples of the range of factors that influence people's reactions to drugs and susceptibility to addiction. These and other salient nonpharmacological factors are outlined and discussed in this chapter. Taken together, they offer a strong prod to reconceive of addiction as being more than a physiological response to drug use. Drug theorists, psychologists, pharmacologists, and others have been attempting such reconceptualizations for some time; yet their efforts remain curiously bound to past, disproven ideas. The resilience of these wrongheaded ideas is discussed in an effort to understand their persistence in the face of disconfirming information. Some of the factors that explain their persistence are popular prejudices, deficiences in research strategies, and issues of the legality and illegality of various substances. At the bottom, however, our inability to conceive of addiction realistically is tied to our reluctance to formulate scientific concepts about behavior that include subjective perceptions, cultural and individual values, and notions of self-control and other personality-based differences (Peele 1983e). This chapter shows that any concept of addiction that bypasses these factors is fundamentally inadequate.

Opiate Addiction in the United States and the Western World

Contemporary scientific and clinical concepts of addiction are inextricably connected with social developments surrounding the use of narcotics, especially in the United States, early in this century. Before that time, from the late sixteenth through the nineteenth centuries, the term "addicted" was generally used to mean "given over to a habit or vice." Although withdrawal and craving had been noted over the centuries with the opiates, the latter were not singled out as substances that produced a distinctive brand of dependence. Indeed, morphine addiction as a disease state was first noted in 1877 by a German physician, Levenstein, who "still saw addiction as a human passion 'such as smoking, gambling, greediness for profit, sexual excesses, etc.'" (Berridge and Edwards 1981: 142–143). As late as the twentieth century, American physicians and pharmacists were as likely to apply the term "addiction" to the use of coffee, tobacco, alcohol, and bromides as they were to opiate use (Sonnedecker 1958).

Opiates were widespread and legal in the United States during the nineteenth century, most commonly in tincturated form in potions such as laudanum and paregoric. Yet they were not considered a menace, and little concern was displayed about their negative effects (Brecher 1972). Furthermore, there was no indication that opiate addiction was a significant problem in nineteenth–century America. This was true even in connection with the enthusiastic medical deployment of morphine—a concentrated opiate prepared for injection—during the U.S. Civil War (Musto 1973). The situation in England, while comparable to that in the United States, may have been even more extreme. Berridge and Edwards (1981) found that use of standard opium preparations was massive and indiscriminate in England throughout much of the nineteenth century as was use of hypodermic morphine at the end of the century. Yet these investigators found little evidence of serious narcotic addiction problems at the time. Instead, they noted that later in the century, "The quite small number of morphine addicts who happened to be obvious to the [medical] profession assumed the dimensions of a pressing problem—at a time when, as general consumption and mortality data indicate, usage and addiction to opium in general was tending to decline, not increase" (p.149).

Although middle-class consumption of opiates was considerable in the United States (Courtwright 1982), it was only the smoking of opium in illicit dens both in Asia and by Chinese in the United States that was widely conceived to be a disreputable and debilitating practice (Blum et al. 1969). Opium smoking among immigrant Asian laborers and other social outcasts presaged changes in the use of opiates that were greatly to modify the image of narcotics and their effects after the turn of the century. These developments included:

1. A shift in the populations using narcotics from a largely middle-class and female clientele for laudanum to mostly male, urban, minority, and lower-class users of heroin—an opiate that had been developed in Europe in 1898 (Clausen 1961; Courtwright 1982);
2. Both as an exaggerated response to this shift and as an impetus to its acceleration, the passage in 1914 of the Harrison Act, which was later interpreted to outlaw medical maintenance of narcotic addicts (King 1972; Trebach 1982); and

3. A widely held vision of narcotic users and their habits as being alien to American lifestyles and of narcotic use as being debased, immoral, and uncontrollable (Kolb 1958).

The Harrison Act and subsequent actions by the Federal Bureau of Narcotics led to the classification of narcotic use as a legal problem. These developments were supported by the American Medical Association (Kolb 1958). This support seems paradoxical, since it contributed to the loss of a historical medical prerogative—the dispensing of opiates. However, the actual changes that were taking place in America's vision of narcotics and their role in society were more complex than this. Opiates first had been removed from the list of accepted pharmaceuticals, then their use was labeled as a social problem, and finally they were characterized as producing a specific medical syndrome. It was only with this last step that the word "addiction" came to be employed with its present meaning. "From 1870 to 1900, most physicians regarded addiction as a morbid appetite, a habit, or a vice. After the turn of the century, medical interest in the problem increased. Various physicians began to speak of the condition as a disease" (Isbell 1958: 115). Thus, organized medicine accepted the loss of narcotic use as a treatment in return for the rewards of seeing it incorporated into the medical model in another way.

In Britain, the situation was somewhat different inasmuch as opium consumption was a lower-class phenomenon that aroused official concern in the nineteenth century. However, the medical view of opiate addiction as a disease arose as doctors observed more middle-class patients injecting morphine later in the century (Berridge and Edwards 1981: 149–150):

> The profession, by its enthusiastic advocacy of a new and more "scientific" remedy and method, had itself contributed to an increase in addiction. . . . Disease entities were being established in definitely recognizible physical conditions such as typhoid and cholera. The belief in scientific progress encouraged medical intervention in less definable conditions [as well] . . . . [S]uch views were never, however, scientifically autonomous. Their putative objectivity disguised class and moral concerns which precluded a wider understanding of the social and cultural roots of opium [and later morphine] use.

The evolution of the idea of narcotic—and particularly heroin—addiction was part of a larger process that medicalized what were previously regarded as moral, spiritual, or emotional problems (Foucault 1973; Szasz 1961). The idea central to the modern definition of addiction is that of the individual's inability to choose: that addicted behavior is outside the realm of ordinary consideration and evaluation (Levine 1978). This idea was connected to a belief in the existence of biological mechanisms—not yet discovered—that caused the use of opiates to create a further need for opiates. In this process the work of such early heroin investigators as Philadelphia physicians Light and Torrance (1929), who were inclined to see the abstaining addict wheedling for more drugs as a malcontent demanding satisfaction and reassurance, was replaced by deterministic models of craving and withdrawal. These models, which viewed the need for a drug as qualitatively different from other kinds of human desires, came to dominate the field, even though the behavior of narcotic users approximated them no better than it had in Light and Torrance's day.

However, self-defined and treated addicts did increasingly conform to the prescribed models, in part because addicts mimicked the behavior described by the sociomedical category of addiction and in part because of an unconscious selection process that determined which addicts became visible to clinicians and researchers. The image of the addict as powerless, unable to make choices, and invariably in need of professional treatment ruled out (in the minds of the experts) the possibility of a natural evolution out of addiction brought on by changes in life circumstances, in the person's set and setting, and in simple individual resolve. Treatment professionals did not look for the addicts who did achieve this sort of spontaneous remission and who, for their part, had no wish to call attention to themselves. Meanwhile, the treatment rolls filled up with addicts whose ineptitude in coping with the drug brought them to the attention of the authorities and who, in their highly dramatized withdrawal agonies and predictable relapses, were simply doing what they had been told they could not help but do. In turn, the professionals found their dire prophecies confirmed by what was in fact a context–limited sample of addictive behavior.

Divergent Evidence about Narcotic Addiction

The view that addiction is the result of a specific biological mechanism that locks the body into an invariant pattern of behavior—one marked by superordinate craving and traumatic withdrawal when a given drug is not available—is disputed by a vast array of evidence. Indeed, this concept of addiction has never provided a good description either of drug-related behavior or of the behavior of the addicted individual. In particular, the early twentieth-century concept of addiction (which forms the basis of most scientific as well as popular thinking about addiction today) equated it with opiate use. This is (and was at the time of its inception) disproven both by the phenomenon of controlled opiate use even by regular and heavy users and by the appearance of addictive symptomatology for users of nonnarcotic substances.

Nonaddicted Narcotics Use

Courtwright (1982) and others typically cloud the significance of the massive nonaddicted use of opiates in the nineteenth century by claiming local observers were unaware of the genuine nature of addiction and thus missed the large numbers who manifested withdrawal and other addictive symptomatology. He struggles to explain how the commonplace administration of opiates to babies "was unlikely to develop into a full-blown addiction, for the infant would not have comprehended the nature of its withdrawal distress, not could it have done anything about it" (p. 58). In any case, Courtwright agrees that by the time addiction was being defined and opiates outlawed at the turn of the century, narcotic use was a minor public health phenomenon. An energetic campaign undertaken in the United States by the Federal Bureau of Narcotics and—in England as well as the United States—by organized medicine and the media changed irrevocably conceptions of the nature of opiate use. In particular, the campaign eradicated the awareness that people could employ opiates moderately or as a part of normal lifestyle. In the early twentiety century, "the climate . . . was such that an individual might work for 10 years beside an industrious law-abiding person and then feel a sense of revulsion toward him upon discovering that he secretly used an opiate" (Kolb 1958: 25). Today, our awareness of the existence of opiate users from that time who maintained normal lives is based on the recorded cases of "eminent narcotics addicts" (Brecher 1972: 33).

The use of narcotics by people whose lives are not obviously disturbed by their habit has continued into the present. Many of these users have been identified among physicians and other medical personnel. In our contemporary prohibitionist society, these users are often dismissed as addicts who are protected from disclosure and from the degradation of addiction by their privileged positions and easy access to narcotics. Yet substantial numbers of them do not appear to be addicted, and it is their control over their habit that, more than anything else, protects them from disclosure. Winick (1961) conducted a major study of a body of physician narcotic users, most of whom had been found out because of suspicious prescription activities. Nearly all these doctors had stabilized their dosages of a narcotic (in most cases Demerol) over the years, did not suffer diminished capacities, and were able to fit their narcotic use into successful medical practices and what appeared to be rewarding lives overall.

Zinberg and Lewis (1964) identified a range of patterns of narcotic use, among which the classic addictive pattern was only one variant that appeared in a minority of cases. One subject in this study, a physician, took morphine four times a day but abstained on weekends and two months a year during vacations. Tracked for over a decade, this man neither increased his dosage nor suffered withdrawal during his periods of abstinence (Zinberg and Jacobson 1976). On the basis of two decades of investigation of such cases, Zinberg (1984) analyzed the factors that separate the addicted from the nonaddicted drug user. Primarily, controlled users, like Winick's physicians, subordinate their desire for a drug to other values, activities, and personal relationships, so that the narcotic or other drug does not dominate their lives. When engaged in other pursuits that they value, these users do not crave the drug or manifest withdrawal on discontinuing their drug use. Furthermore, controlled use of narcotics is not limited to physicians or to middle-class drug users. Lukoff and Brook (1974) found that a majority of ghetto users of heroin had stable home and work involvements, which would hardly be possible in the presence of uncontrollable craving.

If life circumstances affect people's drug use, we would expect patterns of use to vary over time. Every naturalistic study of heroin use has confirmed such fluctuations, including switching among drugs, voluntary and involuntary periods of abstinence, and spontaneous remission of heroin addiction (Maddux and Desmond 1981; Nurco et al. 1981; Robins and Murphy 1967; Waldorf 1973, 1983; Zinberg and Jacobson 1976). In these studies, heroin does not appear to differ significantly in the potential range of its use from other types of involvements, and even compulsive users cannot be distinguished from those given to other habitual involvements in the ease with which they desist or shift their patterns of use. These variations make it difficult to define a point at which a person can be said to be addicted. In a typical study (in this case of former addicts who quit without treatment), Waldorf (1983) defined addiction as daily use for a year along with the appearance of significant withdrawal symptoms during that period. In fact, such definitions are operationally equivalent to simply asking people whether they are or were addicted (Robins et al. 1975).

A finding with immense theoretical importance is that some former narcotics addicts become controlled users. The most comprehensive demonstration of this phenomenon was Robins et al.'s (1975) research on Vietnam veterans who had been addicted to narcotics in Asia. Of this group, only 14 percent became readdicted after their return home, although fully half used heroin—some regularly—in the United States. Not all these men used heroin in Vietnam (some used opium), and some relied on other drugs in the United States (most often alcohol). This finding of controlled use by former addicts may also be limited by the extreme alteration in the environments of the soldiers from Vietnam to the United States. Harding et al. (1980), however, reported on a group of addicts in the United States who had all used heroin more than once a day, some as often as ten times a day, who were now controlled heroin users. None of these subjects was currently alcoholic or addicted to barbiturates. Waldorf (1983) found that former addicts who quit on their own frequently—in a ceremonial proof of their escape from their habit—used the drug at a later point without becoming readdicted.

Although widely circulated, the data showing that the vast majority of soldiers using heroin in Vietnam readily gave up their habits (Jaffe and Harris 1973; Peele 1978) and that "contrary to conventional belief, the occasional use of narcotics without becoming addicted appears possible even for men who have previously been dependent on narcotics" (Robins et al. 1974: 236) have not been assimilated either into popular conceptions of heroin use or into theories of addiction. Indeed, the media and drug commentators in the United States seemingly feel obligated to conceal the existence of controlled heroin users, as in the case of the television film made of baseball player Ron LeFlore's life. Growing up in a Detroit ghetto, LeFlore acquired a heroin habit. He reported using the drug daily for nine months before abruptly withdrawing without experiencing any negative effects (LeFlore and Hawkins 1978). It proved impossible to depict this set of circumstances on American television, and the TV movie ignored LeFlore's personal experience with heroin, showing instead his brother being chained to a bed while undergoing agonizing heroin withdrawal. By portraying heroin use in the most dire light at all times, the media apparently hope to discourage heroin use and addiction. The fact that the United States has long been the most active propagandizer against recreational narcotic use—and drug use of all kinds—and yet has by far the largest heroin and other drug problems of any Western nation indicates the limitations of this strategy (see chapter 6).

The failure to take into account the varieties of narcotic use goes beyond media hype, however. Pharmacologists and other scientists simply cannot face the evidence in this area. Consider the tone of disbelief and resistance with which several expert discussants greeted a presentation by Zinberg and his colleagues on controlled heroin use (see Kissin et al. 1978: 23–24). Yet a similar reluctance to acknowledge the consequences of non-addictive narcotics use is evident even in the writings of the very investigators who have demonstrated that such use occurs. Robins (1980) equated the use of illicit drugs with drug abuse, primarily because previous studies had done so, and maintained that among all drugs heroin creates the greatest dependency (Robins et al. 1980). At the same time, she noted that "heroin as used in the streets of the United States does not differ from other drugs in its liability to being used regularly or on a daily basis" (Robins 1980: 370) and that "heroin is 'worse' than amphetamines or barbiturates only because 'worse' people use it" (Robins et al. 1980: 229). In this way controlled use of narcotics—and of all illicit substances—and compulsive use of legal drugs are both disguised, obscuring the personality and social factors that actually distinguish styles of using any kind of drug (Zinberg and Harding 1982). Under these circumstances, it is perhaps not surprising that the major predictors of illicit use (irrespective of degree of harmfulness of such use) are nonconformity and independence (Jessor and Jessor 1977).

One final research and conceptual bias that has colored our ideas about heroin addiction has been that, more than with other drugs, our knowledge about heroin has come mainly from those users who cannot control their habits. These subjects make up the clinical populations on which prevailing notions of addiction have been based. Naturalistic studies reveal not only less harmful use but also more variation in the behavior of those who are addicted. It seems to be primarily those who report for treatment who have a lifetime of difficulty in overcoming their addictions (cf. Califano 1983). The same appears true for alcoholics: For example, an ability to shift to controlled drinking shows up regularly in field studies of alcoholics, although it is denied as a possibility by clinicians (Peele 1983a; Vaillant 1983). (See chapter 2.)

Nonnarcotic Addiction

The prevailing twentieth-century concept of addiction considers addiction to be a byproduct of the chemical structure of a specific drug (or family of drugs). Consequently, pharmacologists and others have believed that an effective pain-reliever, or analgesic, could be synthesized that would not have addictive properties. The search for such a nonaddictive analgesic has been a dominant theme of twentieth-century pharmacology (cf. Clausen 1961; Cohen 1983; Eddy and May 1973; Peele 1977). Indeed, heroin was introduced in 1898 as offering pain relief without the disquieting side effects sometimes noted with morphine. Since that time, the early synthetic narcotics such as Demerol and the synthetic sedative family, the barbiturates, have been marketed with the same claims. Later, new groups of sedatives and narcotic-like substances, such as Valium and Darvon, were introduced as having more focused anti-anxiety and pain-relieving effects that would not be addictive. All such drugs have been found to lead to addiction in some, perhaps many, cases (cf. Hooper and Santo 1980; Smith and Wesson 1983; Solomon et al. 1979). Similarly, some have argued that analgesics based on the structures of endorphins—opiate peptides produced endogenously by the body—can be used without fear of addiction (Kosterlitz 1979). It is hardly believable that these substances will be different from every other narcotic with respect to addictive potential.

Alcohol is a nonnarcotic drug that, like the narcotics and sedatives, is a depressant. Since alcohol is legal and almost universally available, the possibility that it can be used in a controlled manner is generally accepted. At the same time, alcohol is also recognized to be an addicting substance.

The divergent histories and differing contemporary visions of alcohol and narcotics in the United States have produced two different versions of the addiction concept (see chapter 2). Whereas narcotics have been considered to be universally addictive, the modern disease concept of alcoholism has emphasized a genetic susceptibility that predisposes only some individuals to become addicted to alcohol (Goodwin 1976; Schuckit 1984). In recent years, however, there has been some convergence in these conceptions. Goldstein (1976b) has accounted for the discovery that only a minority of narcotic users go on to be addicts by postulating constitutional biological differences between individuals. Coming from the opposite direction, some observers oppose the disease theory of alcoholism by maintaining that alcoholism is simply the inevitable result of a certain threshold level of consumption (cf. Beauchamp 1980; Kendell 1979). (See chapter 3.)

Observations of the defining traits of addiction have been made not only with the broader family of sedative-analgesic drugs and alcohol but also with stimulants. Goldstein et al. (1969) have noted craving and withdrawal among habitual coffee drinkers that are not qualitatively different from the craving and withdrawal observed in cases of narcotics use. This discovery serves to remind us that at the turn of the century, prominent British pharmacologists could say of the excessive coffee drinker, "the sufferer is tremulous and loses his self-command. . . . As with other such agents, a renewed dose of the poison gives temporary relief, but at the cost of future misery" (quoted in Lewis 1969: 10). Schachter (1978), meanwhile, has forcefully presented the case that cigarettes are addicting in the typical pharmacological sense and that their continued use by the addict is maintained by the avoidance of withdrawal (cf. Krasnegor 1979).

Nicotine and caffeine are stimulants that are consumed indirectly, through their presence in cigarettes and coffee. Surprisingly, pharmacologists have classified stimulants that users self-administer directly—such as amphetamines and cocaine—as nonaddictive because, according to their research, these drugs do not produce withdrawal (Eddy et al. 1965). Why milder stimulant use like that manifested by coffee and cigarette habitués should be more potent than cocaine and amphetamine habits is mystifying. In fact, as cocaine has become a popular recreational drug in the United States, severe withdrawal is now regularly noted among individuals calling a hot line for counseling about the drug (Washton 1983). In order to preserve traditional categories of thought, those commenting on observations of compulsive cocaine use claim it produces "psychological dependence whose effects are not all that different from addiction" because cocaine "is the most psychologically tenacious drug available" ("Cocaine: Middle Class High" 1981: 57, 61).

In response to the observation of an increasing number of involvements that can lead to addiction-like behavior, two conflicting trends have appeared in addiction theorizing. One, found mainly in popular writing (Oates 1971; Slater 1980) but also in serious theorizing (Peele and Brodsky 1975), has been to return to the pre-twentieth-century usage of the term "addiction" and to apply this term to all types of compulsive, self-destructive activities. The other refuses to certify as addictive any involvement other than with narcotics or drugs thought to be more or less similar to narcotics. One unsatisfactory attempt at a synthesis of these positions has been to relate all addictive behavior to changes in the organism's neurological functioning. Thus biological mechanisms have been hypothesized to account for self-destructive running (Morgan 1979), overeating (Weisz and Thompson 1983), and love relationships (Liebowitz 1983; Tennov 1979). This wishful thinking is associated with a continuing failure to make sense of the experiential, environmental, and social factors that are integrally related to addictive phenomena.

Nonbiological Factors in Addiction

A concept that aims to describe the full reality of addiction must incorporate nonbiological factors as *essential ingredients* in addiction—up to and including the appearance of craving, withdrawal, and tolerance effects. Following is a summary of these factors in addiction.

Cultural

Different cultures regard, use, and react to substances in different ways, which in turn influence the likelihood of addiction. Thus, opium was never proscribed or considered a dangerous substance in India, where it was grown and used indigenously, but it quickly became a major social problem in China when it was brought there by the British (Blum et al. 1969). The external introduction of a substance into a culture that does not have established social mechanisms for regulating its use is common in the history of drug abuse. The appearance of widespread abuse of and addiction to a substance may also take place after indigenous customs regarding its use are overwhelmed by a dominant foreign power. Thus the Hopi and Zuni Indians drank alcohol in a ritualistic and regulated manner prior to the coming of the Spanish, but in a destructive and generally addictive manner thereafter (Bales 1946). Sometimes a drug takes root as an addictive substance in one culture but not in other cultures that are exposed to it at the same time. Heroin was transported to the United States through European countries no more familiar with opiate use than was the United States (Solomon 1977). Yet heroin addiction, while considered a vicious social menace here, was regarded as a purely American disease in those European countries where the raw opium was processed (Epstein 1977).

It is crucial to recognize that—as in the case of nineteenth-and twentieth-century opiate use—addictive patterns of drug use do not depend solely, or even largely, on the *amount* of the substance in use at a given time and place. Per capita alcohol consumption was several times its current level in the United States during the colonial period, yet both problem drinking and alcoholism were at far lower levels than they are today (Lender and Martin 1982; Zinberg and Fraser 1979). Indeed, colonial Americans did not comprehend alcoholism as an uncontrollable disease or addiction (Levine 1978). Because alcohol is so commonly used throughout the world, it offers the best illustration of how the effects of a substance are interpreted in widely divergent ways that influence its addictive potential. As a prime example, the belief that drunkenness excuses aggressive, escapist, and other antisocial behavior is much more pronounced in some cultures than in others (Falk 1983; MacAndrew and Edgerton 1969). Such beliefs translate into cultural visions of alcohol and its effects that are strongly associated with the appearance of alcoholism. That is, the displays of antisocial aggression and loss of control that define alcoholism among American Indians and Eskimos and in Scandinavia, Eastern Europe, and the United States are notably absent in the drinking of Greeks and Italians, and American Jews, Chinese, and Japanese (Barnett 1955; Blum and Blum 1969; Glassner and Berg 1980; Vaillant 1983).

Social

Drug use is closely tied to the social and peer groups a person belongs to. Jessor and Jessor (1977) and Kandel (1978), among others, have identified the power of peer pressure on the initiation and continuation of drug use among adolescents. Styles of drinking, from moderate to excessive, are strongly influenced by the immediate social group (Cahalan and Room 1974; Clark 1982). Zinberg (1984) has been the main proponent of the view that the way a person uses heroin is likewise a function of group membership—controlled use is supported by knowing controlled users (and also by simultaneously belonging to groups where heroin is not used). At the same time that groups affect *patterns* of usage, they affect the way drug use is *experienced.* Drug effects give rise to internal states that the individual seeks to label cognitively, often by noting the reactions of others (Schachter and Singer 1962).

Becker (1953) described this process in the case of marijuana. Initiates to the fringe groups that used the drug in the 1950s had to learn not only how to smoke it but how to recognize and anticipate the drug's effects. The group process extended to defining for the individual why this intoxicated state was a desirable one. Such social learning is present in all types and all stages of drug use. In the case of narcotics, Zinberg (1972) noted that the way withdrawal was experienced—including its degree of severity—varied among military units in Vietnam. Zinberg and Robertson (1972) reported that addicts who had undergone traumatic withdrawal in prison manifested milder symptoms or suppressed them altogether in a therapeutic community whose norms forbade the expression of withdrawal. Similar observations have been made with respect to alcohol withdrawal (Oki 1974; cf. Gilbert 1981).

Situational

A person's desire for a drug cannot be separated from the situation in which the person takes the drug. Falk (1983) and Falk et al. (1983) argue, primarily on the basis of animal experimentation, that an organism's environment influences drug-taking behavior more than do the supposedly inherently reinforcing properties of the drug itself. For example, animals who have alcohol dependence induced by intermittent feeding schedules cut their alcohol intake as soon as feeding schedules are normalized (Tang et al. 1982). Particularly important to the organism's readiness to overindulge is the absence of alternative behavioral opportunities (see chapter 4). For human subjects the presence of such alternatives ordinarily outweighs even positive mood changes brought on by drugs in motivating decisions about continuing drug use (Johanson and Uhlenhuth 1981). The situational basis of narcotic addiction, for example, was made evident by the finding (cited above) that the majority of U.S. servicemen who were addicted in Vietnam did not become readdicted when they used narcotics at home (Robins et al. 1974; Robins et al. 1975).

Ritualistic

The rituals that accompany drug use and addiction are important elements in continued use, so much so that to eliminate essential rituals can cause an addiction to lose its appeal. In the case of heroin, powerful parts of the experience are provided by the rite of self-injection and even the overall lifestyle involved in the pursuit and use of the drug. In the early 1960s, when Canadian policies concerning heroin became more stringent and illicit supplies of the drug became scarce, ninety-one Canadian addicts emigrated to Britain to enroll in heroin maintenance programs. Only twenty-five of these addicts found the British system satisfactory and remained. Those who returned to Canada often reported missing the excitement of the street scene. For them the pure heroin administered in a medical setting did not produce the kick they got from the adulterated street variety they self-administered (Solomon 1977).

The essential role of ritual was shown in the earliest systematic studies of narcotic addicts. Light and Torrance (1929) reported that addicts could often have their withdrawal symptoms relieved by "the single prick of a needle" or a "hypodermic injection of sterile water." They noted, "paradoxic as it may seem, we believe that the greater the craving of the addict and the severity of the withdrawal symptoms the better are the chances of substituting a hypodermic injection of sterile water to obtain temporary relief" (p. 15). Similar findings hold true for nonnarcotic addiction. For example, nicotine administered directly does not have nearly the impact that inhaled nicotine does for habitual smokers (Jarvik 1973) who continue to smoke even when they have achieved their accustomed levels of cellular nicotine via capsule (Jarvik et al. 1970).

Developmental

People's reactions to, need for, and style of using a drug change as they progress through the life cycle. The classic form of this phenomenon is "maturing out." Winick (1962) originally hypothesized that a majority of young addicts leave their heroin habits behind when they accept an adult role in life. Waldorf (1983) affirmed the occurrence of substantial natural remission in heroin addiction, emphasizing the different forms it assumes and the different ages when people achieve it. It does appear, however, that heroin use is most often a youthful habit. O'Donnell et al. (1976) found, in a nationwide sample of young men, that more than two-thirds of the subjects who had ever used heroin (note these were not necessarily addicts) had not touched the drug in the previous year. Heroin is harder to obtain, and its use is less compatible with standard adult roles, than most other drugs of abuse. However, abusers of alcohol—a drug more readily assimilated into a normal lifestyle—likewise show a tendency to mature out (Cahalan and Room 1974).

O'Donnell et al. (1976) found that the greatest continuity in drug use among young men occurs with cigarette smoking. Such findings, together with indications that those seeking treatment for obesity only rarely succeed at losing weight and keeping it off (Stunkard 1958; Schachter and Rodin 1974), have suggested that remission may be unlikely for smokers and the obese, perhaps because their self-destructive habits are the ones most easily assimilated into a normal lifestyle. For this same reason remission would be expected to take place all through the life cycle rather than just in early adulthood. More recently, Schachter (1982) has found that a majority of those in two community populations who attempted to cease smoking or to lose weight were in remission from obesity or cigarette addiction.

While the peak period for natural recovery may differ for these various compulsive behaviors, there may be common remission processes that hold for all of them (Peele 1983d).

Personality

The idea that opiate use caused personality defects was challenged as early as the 1920s by Kolb (1962), who found that the personality traits observed among addicts preceded their drug use. Kolb's view was summarized in his statement that "The neurotic and the psychopath receive from narcotics a pleasurable sense of relief from the realities of life that normal persons do not receive because life is no special burden to them" (p. 85). Chein et al. (1964) gave this view its most comprehensive modern expression when they concluded that ghetto adolescent addicts were characterized by low self-esteem, learned incompetence, passivity, a negative outlook, and a history of dependency relationships. A major difficulty in assessing personality correlates of addiction lies in determining whether the traits found in a group of addicts are actually characteristics of a social group (Cahalan and Room 1974; Robins et al. 1980). On the other hand, addictive personality traits are obscured by lumping together controlled users of a drug such as heroin and those addicted to it. Similarly, the same traits may go unnoted in addicts whose different ethnic backgrounds or current settings predispose them toward different types of involvements, drug or otherwise (Peele 1983c).

Personality may both predispose people toward the use of some types of drugs rather than others and also affect how deeply they become involved with drugs at all (including whether they become addicted). Spotts and Shontz (1982) found that chronic users of different drugs represent distinct Jungian personality types. On the other hand, Lang (1983) claimed that efforts to discover an overall addictive personality type have generally failed. Lang does, however, report some similarities that generalize to abusers of a range of substances. These include placing a low value on achievement, a desire for instant gratification, and habitual feelings of heightened stress. The strongest argument for addictiveness as an individual personality disposition comes from repeated findings that the same individuals become addicted to many things, either simultaneously, sequentially, or alternately (Peele 1983c; Peele and Brodsky 1975). There is a high carry-over for addiction to one depressant substance to addiction to others—for example, turning from narcotics to alcohol (O'Donnell 1969; Robins et al. 1975). Alcohol, barbiturates, and narcotics show cross-tolerance (addicted users of one substance may substitute another) even though the drugs do not act the same way neurologically (Kalant 1982), while cocaine and Valium addicts have unusually high rates of alcohol abuse and frequently have family histories of alcoholism ("Many addicts . . ." 1983; Smith 1981). Gilbert

(1981) found that excessive use of a wide variety of substances was corre-lated—for example, smoking with coffee drinking and both with alcohol use. What is more, as Vaillant (1983) noted for alcoholics and Wishnie (1977) for heroin addicts, reformed substance abusers often form strong compulsions toward eating, prayer, and other nondrug involvements.

Cognitive

People's expectations and beliefs about drugs, or their mental set, and the beliefs and behavior of those around them that determine this set strongly influence reactions to drugs. These factors can, in fact, entirely reverse what are thought to be the specific pharmacological properties of a drug (Lennard et al. 1971; Schachter and Singer 1962). The efficacy of placebos demonstrates that cognitions can *create* expected drug effects. Placebo ef-fects can match those of even the most powerful pain killers, such as mor-phine, although more so for some people than others (Lasagna et al. 1954). It is not surprising, then, that cognitive sets and settings are strong deter-minants of addiction, including the experience of craving and withdrawal (Zinberg 1972). Zinberg (1974) found that only one of a hundred patients receiving continuous dosages of a narcotic craved the drug after release from the hospital. Lindesmith (1968) noted such patients are seemingly protected from addiction because they do not see themselves as addicts.

The central role of cognitions and self-labeling in addiction has been demonstrated in laboratory experiments that balance the effects of expec-tations against the actual pharmacological effects of alcohol. Male subjects become aggressive and sexually aroused when they incorrectly believe they have been drinking liquor, but not when they actually drink alcohol in a disguised form (Marlatt and Rohsenow 1980; Wilson 1981). Similarly, al-coholic subjects lose control of their drinking when they are misinformed that they are drinking alcohol, but not in the disguised alcohol condition (Engle and Williams 1972; Marlatt et al. 1973). Subjective beliefs by clinical patients about their alcoholism are better predictors of their likelihood of relapse than are assessments of their previous drinking patterns and degree of alcohol dependence (Heather et al. 1983; Rollnick and Heather 1982). Marlatt (1982) has identified cognitive and emotional factors as the major determinants in relapse in narcotic addiction, alcoholism, smoking, over-eating, and gambling.

The Nature of Addiction

Studies showing that craving and relapse have more to do with subjective factors (feelings and beliefs) than with chemical properties or with a per-son's history of drinking or drug dependence call for a reinterpretation of the essential nature of addiction. How do we know a given individual is addicted? No biological indicators can give us this information. We decide the person is addicted when he acts addicted—when he pursues a drug's effects no matter what the negative consequences for his life. We cannot detect addiction in the absence of its defining behaviors. In general, we believe a person is addicted when he says that he is. No more reliable indicator exists (cf. Robins et al. 1975). Clinicians are regularly confused when patients identify themselves as addicts or evince addicted lifestyles but do not display the expected physical symptoms of addiction (Gay et al. 1973; Glaser 1974; Primm 1977).

While claiming that alcoholism is a genetically transmitted disease, the director of the National Institute on Alcohol Abuse and Alcoholism (NIAAA), a physician, noted there are not yet reliable genetic "markers" that predict the onset of alcoholism and that "the most sensitive instruments for identifying alcoholics and problem drinkers are questionnaires and inventories of psychological and behavioral variables" (Mayer 1983: 1118). He referred to one such test (the Michigan Alcohol Screening Test) that contains twenty questions regarding the person's concerns about his or her drinking behavior. Skinner et al. (1980) found that three subjective items from this larger test provide a reliable indication of the degree of a person's drinking problems. Sanchez-Craig (1983) has further shown that a single subjective assessment—in essence, asking the subject how many problems his or her drinking is causing—describes level of alcoholism better than does impairment of cognitive functioning or other biological measures. Withdrawal seizures are not related to neurological impairments in alcoholics, and those with even severe impairment may or may not undergo such seizures (Tarter et al. 1983). Taken together, these studies support the conclusions that the physiological and behavioral indicators of alcoholism do not correlate well with each other (Miller and Saucedo 1983), and that the latter correlate better than the former with clinical assessments of alcoholism (Fisher et al. 1976). This failure to find biological markers is not simply a question of currently incomplete knowledge. Signs of alcoholism such as blackout, tremors, and loss of control that are presumed to be biological have already been shown to be inferior to psychological and subjective assessments in predicting future alcoholic behavior (Heather et al. 1982; Heather et al. 1983).

When medical or public health organizations that subscribe to biological assumptions about addiction have attempted to define the term, they have relied primarily on the hallmark behaviors of addiction, such as "an overpowering desire or need (compulsion) to continue taking the drug and to obtain it by any means" (WHO Expert Committee on Mental Health 1957) or, for alcoholism, "impairment of social or occupational functioning such as violence while intoxicated, absence from work, loss of job, traffic accidents while intoxicated, arrested for intoxicated behavior, familial arguments or difficulties with family or friends related to drinking" (American Psychiatric Association 1980). However, they then tie these behavior syndromes to other constructs, namely tolerance (the need for an increasingly high dosage of a drug) and withdrawal, that are presumed to be biological in nature. Yet tolerance and withdrawal are not themselves measured physiologically. Rather, they are delineated entirely by how addicts are observed to act and what they say about their states of being. Light and Torrance (1929) failed in their comprehensive effort to correlate narcotic withdrawal with gross metabolic, nervous, or circulatory disturbance. Instead, they were forced to turn to the addict—like the one whose complaints were most intense and who most readily responded to saline solution injections—in assessing withdrawal severity. Since that time, addict self-reports have remained the generally accepted measure of withdrawal distress.

Withdrawal is a term for which meaning has been heaped upon meaning. Withdrawal is, first, the cessation of drug administration. The term "withdrawal" is also applied to the condition of the individual who experiences this cessation. In this sense, withdrawal is nothing more than a homeostatic readjustment to the removal of any substance—or stimulation—that has had a notable impact on the body. Narcotic withdrawal (and withdrawal from drugs also thought to be addictive, such as alcohol) has been assumed to be a qualitatively distinct, more malignant order of withdrawal adjustment. Yet studies of withdrawal from narcotics and alcohol offer regular testimony, often from investigators surprised by their observations, of the variability, mildness, and often nonappearance of the syndrome (cf. Jaffe and Harris 1973; Jones and Jones 1977; Keller 1969; Light and Torrance 1929; Oki 1974; Zinberg 1972). The range of withdrawal discomfort, from the more common moderate variety to the occasional overwhelming distress, that characterizes narcotic use appears also with cocaine (van Dyke and Byck 1982; Washton 1983), cigarettes (Lear 1974; Schachter 1978), coffee (Allbutt and Dixon, quoted in Lewis 1969: 10; Goldstein et al. 1969), and sedatives and sleeping pills (Gordon 1979; Kales et al. 1974; Smith 1983). We might anticipate the investigations of laxatives, antidepressants, and other drugs—such as L-Dopa (to control Parkinson's disease)—that are prescribed to maintain physical and psychic functioning will reveal a comparable range of withdrawal responses.

In all cases, what is identified as pathological withdrawal is actually a complex self-labeling process that requires users to detect adjustments taking place in their bodies, to note this process as problematic, and to express their discomfort and translate it into a desire for more drugs. Along with the amount of a drug that a person uses (the sign of tolerance), the degree of suffering experienced when drug use ceases is—as shown in the previous section—a function of setting and social milieu, expectation and cultural attitudes, personality and self-image, and, especially, lifestyle and available alternative opportunities. That the labeling and prediction of addictive behavior cannot occur without referring to these subjective and social-psychological factors means that addiction exists fully only at a cultural, a social, a psychological, and an experiental level. We cannot descend to a purely biological level in our scientific understanding of addiction. Any effort to do so must result in omitting crucial determinants of addiction, so that what is left cannot adequately describe the phenomenon about which we are concerned.

Physical and Psychic Dependence

The vast array of information disconfirming the conventional view of addiction as a biochemical process has led to some uneasy reevaluations of the concept. In 1964 the World Health Organization (WHO) Expert Committee on Addiction-Producing Drugs changed its name by replacing "Addiction" with "Dependence." At that time, these pharmacologists identified two kinds of drug dependence, physical and psychic. "Physical dependence is an inevitable result of the pharmacological action of some drugs with sufficient amount and time of administration. Psychic dependence, while also related to pharmacological action, is more particularly a manifestation of the individual's reaction to the effects of a specific drug and varies with the individual as well as the drug." In this formulation, psychic dependence "is the most powerful of all factors involved in chronic intoxication with psychotropic drugs . . . even in the case of most intense craving and perpetuation of compulsive abuse" (Eddy et al. 1965: 723). Cameron (1971a), another WHO pharmacologist, specified that psychic dependence is ascertained by "how far the use of drugs appears (1) to be an important life-organizing factor and (2) to take precedence over the use of other coping mechanisms" (p. 10).

Psychic dependence, as defined here, is central to the manifestations of drug abuse that were formerly called addiction. Indeed, it forms the basis of Jaffe's (1980: 536) definition of addiction, which appears in an authoritative basic pharmacology textbook:

> It is possible to describe all known patterns of drug use without employing the terms *addict* or *addiction.* In many respects this would be advantageous, for the term *addiction,* like the term *abuse,* has been used in so many ways that it can no longer be employed without further qualification or elaboration. . . . In this chapter, the term *addiction* will be used to mean *a behavioral pattern of drug use, characterized by overwhelming involvement with the use of a drug (compulsive use), the securing of its supply, and a high tendency to relapse after withdrawal.* Addiction is thus viewed as an extreme on a continuum of involvement with drug use . . .

[based on] the degree to which drug use pervades the total life activity of the user. . . . [*T*]*he term* addiction *cannot be used interchangeably with* physical dependence. [italics in original]

While Jaffe's terminology improves upon previous pharmacological usage by recognizing that addiction is a behavioral pattern, it perpetuates other misconceptions. Jaffe describes addiction as a pattern of drug use even though he defines it in behavioral terms—that is, craving and relapse—that are not limited to drug use. He devalues addiction as a construct because of its inexactness, in contrast with physical dependence, which he incorrectly sees as a well-delineated physiological mechanism. Echoing the WHO Expert Committee, he defines physical dependence as "an altered physiological state produced by the repeated administration of a drug which necessitates the continued administration of the drug to prevent the appearance of . . . withdrawal" (p. 536).

The WHO committee's efforts to redefine addiction were impelled by two forces. One was the desire to highlight the harmful use of substances popularly employed by young people in the 1960s and thereafter that were not generally regarded as addictive—including marijuana, amphetamines, and hallucinogenic drugs. These drugs could now be labeled as dangerous because they were reputed to cause psychic dependence. Charts like one titled "A Guide to the Jungle of Drugs," compiled by a WHO pharmacologist (Cameron 1971b), classified LSD, peyote, marijuana, psilocybin, alcohol, cocaine, amphetamines, and narcotics (that is, every drug included in the chart) as causing psychic dependence (see figure 1–1). What is the value of a pharmacological concept that applies indiscriminately to the entire range of pharmacological agents, so long as they are used in socially disapproved ways? Clearly, the WHO committee wished to discourage certain types of drug use and dressed up this aim in scientific terminology. Wouldn't the construct describe as well the habitual use of nicotine, caffeine, tranquilizers, and sleeping pills? Indeed, the discovery of this simple truism about socially accepted drugs has been an emerging theme of pharmacological thought in the 1970s and 1980s. Furthermore, the concept of psychic dependence cannot distinguish compulsive drug involvements—those that become "life organizing" and "take precedence over . . . other coping mechanisms"—from compulsive overeating, gambling, and television viewing.

The WHO committee, while perpetuating prejudices about drugs, claimed to be resolving the confusion brought on by the data showing that addiction was not the biochemically invariant process that it had been thought to be. Thus, the committee labeled the psychic-dependence-producing properties of drugs as being the major determinant of craving and of compulsive abuse. In addition, they maintained, some drugs cause physical dependence. In "A Guide to the Jungle of Drugs" and the philosophy it rep-

A GUIDE TO THE JUNGLE OF DRUGS

	Drug	Medical use	Dependence		Tolerance
			Physical	Psychic	
1	Hallucinogenic cactus (mescalin, peyote)	None	No	Yes	Yes
2	Hallucinogenic mushrooms (psilocybin)	None	No	Yes	Yes
3	Cocaine (from coca bush)	Anaesthesia	No	Yes	No
	Amphetamines* (synthetic, not derived from coca)	Treatment of narcolepsy and behavioural disorders	No	Yes	Yes
4	Alcohol (in many forms)	Antisepsis	Yes	Yes	Yes
5	Cannabis (marihuana, hashish)	None in modern medicine	Little if any	Yes	Little if any
6	Narcotics (opium, heroin, morphine, codeine)	Relief of pain and cough	Yes	Yes	Yes
7	LSD (synthetic, derived from fungus on grain)	Essentially none	No	Yes	Yes
8	Hallucinogenic morning glory seeds	None	No	Yes	Uncertain

* Taken intravenously, cocaine and amphetamines have quite similar effects.

Source: Cameron 1971b. With acknowledgments to *World Health*.

Figure 1–1. A Guide to the Jungle of Drugs

resented, two drugs were designated as creating physical dependence. These drugs were narcotics and alcohol. This effort to improve the accuracy of drug classifications simply transposed erroneous propositions previously associated with addiction to the new idea of physical dependence. Narcotics and alcohol do not produce qualitatively greater tolerance or withdrawal—whether these are imputed to physical dependence or addiction— than do other powerful drugs and stimulants of all kinds. As Kalant (1982) makes clear, physical dependence and tolerance "are two manifestations of the same phenomenon, a biologically adaptive phenomenon which occurs in all living organisms and many types of stimuli, not just drug stimuli" (p. 12).

What the WHO pharmacologists, Jaffe, and others are clinging to by retaining the category of physical dependence is the idea that there is a purely physiological process associated with specific drugs that will describe the behavior that results from their use. It is as though they were saying: "Yes, we understand that what has been referred to as addiction is a complex syndrome into which more enters than just the effects of a given drug. What we want to isolate, however, is the addiction-like state that stems from these drug effects if we could somehow remove extraneous psychological and social considerations." This is impossible because what are being identified as pharmacological characteristics exist only in the drug user's sensations and interactions with his environment. Dependence is, after all, a characteristic of people and not of drugs.

The Persistence of Mistaken Categories

While there has been some movement in addiction theorizing toward more realistic explanations of drug-related behavior in terms of people's life circumstances and nonbiological needs, old patterns of thought persist, even where they don't agree with the data or offer helpful ways of conceptualizing drug abuse problems. This is nowhere more apparent than in the writing of investigators whose work has effectively undermined prevailing drug categorizations and yet who rely on categories and terminology that their own iconoclastic findings have discredited.

Zinberg and his colleagues (Apsler 1978; Zinberg et al. 1978) have been among the most discerning critics of the WHO committee's definitions of drug dependence, pointing out that "these definitions employ terms that are virtually indefinable and heavily value-laden" (Zinberg et al. 1978: 20). In their understandable desire to avoid the ambiguities of moral categories of behavior, these investigators seek to restrict the term "addiction" to the most limited physiological phenomena. Thus they claim that "physical dependence is a straightforward measure of addiction" (p. 20). However, this retrenchment is inimical to their purpose of satisfactorily conceptualizing and operationalizing addictive behavior. It is also irreconcilable with their own observation that the effort to separate psychological habituation and physical dependence is futile, as well as with their forceful objections to the idea that psychic dependence is "less inevitable and more susceptible to the elements of set and setting" than is physical dependence (p. 21). At the same time that they complain that "The capacity of different individuals to deal with different amounts of substances without development of tolerance is sufficiently obvious . . . [that] one must question how the complexity of this phenomenon could have been missed" (p. 15), they trumpet "the inevitable physical dependence which occurs following the continued and heavy use of substances such as the opiates, barbiturates, or alcohol, that contain certain pharmacological properties" (p. 14). They then contradict this principle by citing the case, described earlier by Zinberg and Jacobson (1976), of the doctor who injected himself with morphine four times a day for over a decade but who never underwent withdrawal while abstaining on weekends and vacations.

Zinberg et al. (1978) find that "the behavior resulting from the wish for a desired object, whether chemical or human," is not the result of "differentiation between a physiological or psychological attachment. . . . Nor does the presence of physical symptoms per se serve to separate these two types of dependence" (p. 21). Yet they themselves maintain exactly this distinction in terminology. While noting that people may be just as wedded to amphetamines as to heroin, they claim that the former are not "psychologically addicting." (Probably the authors meant to say that amphetamines are not "physiologically addicting." They employ "psychological addiction" elsewhere in this article to describe nondrug or nonnarcotic involvements and "physiological addiction" to describe heavy heroin use characterized by withdrawal. Their use of both phrases, of course, adds to the confusion of terms.) Zinberg et al. claim without supporting citations that "if naloxone, a narcotic antagonist, is administered to someone who is physically dependent on a narcotic, he will immediately develop withdrawal symptoms" (p. 20). It is puzzling to compare this declaration with their statement that it "is now evident many of the symptoms of withdrawal are strongly influenced by expectations and culture" (p. 21). In fact, many people who identify themselves in treatment as narcotic addicts do not manifest withdrawal even when treated by naloxone challenge (Gay et al. 1973; Glaser 1974; O'Brien 1975; Primm 1977).

The Zinberg et al. formulation leaves unexplained the hospital patients Zinberg (1974) studied who, having received greater than street level dosage of narcotics for ten days or more, almost never reported craving the drug. If these people are physically dependent, as Zinberg et al. (1978) seem to suggest they would be, it amounts to saying that people can depend on what they can't detect and don't care about. Surely this is the reductio ad absurdum of the concept of physical dependence. That amphetamines and co-caine are labeled as not physical-dependence inducing or addictive (see discussion above), despite the fact that users can be wedded to them in ways that are indistinguishable from addiction, invalidates these distinctions among drugs from the opposite direction. Apparently, those pharmacological effects of a given drug that *are* unique and invariant are irrelevant to human functioning. Here scientific terminology approaches the mystical by identifying distinctions that are unmeasurable and unrepresented in thought, feeling, and action.

Finally, Zinberg et al.'s illustrations of the "difficulty of separating physical dependence from psychic dependence and of differentiating both from overpowering desire" (p. 21) go to show the futility of using different terms to describe drug-related and nondrug-related variants of the same process. A primitive logic dictates that a chemical introduced into the body should be conceived to exert its effects biochemically. However, any other experience a person has will also possess biochemical concomitants (Leventhal 1980). Zinberg et al. emphasize that craving and withdrawal associated with intimate relationships are substantial and unmistakable. In detecting withdrawal symptoms on the order of those reported for barbiturates and alcohol among compulsive gamblers, Wray and Dickerson (1981) noted that "any repetitive, stereotyped behavior that is associated with repeated experiences of physiological arousal or change, *whether induced by a psychoactive agent or not,* may be difficult for the individual to choose to discontinue and should he so choose, then it may well be associated with disturbances of mood and behavior" (p. 405, italics in original). Why do these states and activities not have the same capacity to produce physical dependence?

The Science of Addictive Experiences

What has held science back from acknowledging commonalities in addiction and what now impedes our ability to analyze these is a habit of thought that separates the action of the mind and the body. Furthermore, it is for concrete physical entities and processes that the label of science is usually reserved (Peele 1983e). The mind–body duality (which long antedates current debates about drugs and addiction) has hidden the fact that addiction has always been defined phenomenologically in terms of the experiences of the sentient human being and observations of the person's feelings and behavior. Addiction may occur with any potent experience. In addition, the number and variability of the factors that influence addiction cause it to occur along a continuum. The delineation of a particular involvement as addictive for a particular person thus entails a degree of arbitrariness. Yet this designation is a useful one. It is far superior to the rela-beling of addictive phenomena in some roundabout way.

Addiction, at its extreme, is an overwhelming pathological involve-ment. The object of addiction is the addicted person's experience of the combined physical, emotional, and environmental elements that make up the involvement for that person. Addiction is often characterized by a trau-matic withdrawal reaction to the deprivation of this state or experience. Tolerance—or the increasingly high level of need for the experience—and craving are measured by how willing the person is to sacrifice other rewards or sources of well-being in life to the pursuit of the involvement. The key to addiction, seen in this light, is its persistence in the face of harmful con-sequences for the individual. This book embraces rather than evades the complicated and multifactorial nature of addiction. Only by accepting this complexity is it possible to put together a meaningful picture of addiction, to say something useful about drug use as well as about other compulsions, and to comprehend the ways in which people hurt themselves through their own behavior as well as grow beyond self-destructive involvements.

2
The American Image of Alcohol: Does Liquor Have the Power to Corrupt and Control?

A lcohol is the substance, along with heroin, with which addiction is most strongly associated. Yet addiction has been studied separately for the two substances because of their disparate cultural histories. The concepts of addiction for each do have commonalities—perhaps more now than at any time previously in this century. However, cultural perceptions of the drugs and of their abuse still differ widely. This book approaches both substances as being addictive in the same way, although the process of addiction in each case is influenced by distinct cultural attitudes toward its use.

It seems strange to us today that in the nineteenth century, narcotics use was legal and accepted, while strong movements arose to ban all consumption of alcohol. In the early nineteenth century, problem drinking was rampant in the United States, while opium and morphine addiction presented a negligible problem. Even as heroin came to be regarded as the most sinister drug of abuse in the United States in the 1910s and 1920s and public officials claimed narcotics addicts numbered in the millions, there were probably no more than 100,000 such addicts in the United States (Clausen 1961; Courtwright 1982). Concepts of drug use as a disease first appeared in the eighteenth century in the United States and concerned alcoholism (Levine 1978). Early versions of the disease theory of alcoholism were predicated solely on the idea of exposure to the drug. That is, alcoholism appeared in the individual who drank habitually and chronically became intoxicated. This kind of exposure model eventually was applied to narcotics addiction; today heroin is viewed as being inherently addicting—independent of the physical and psychological make-up of the person using the drug—both popularly and by addiction theorists (see chapter 3).

Conceptions of alcoholism meanwhile took a different direction following the repeal of Prohibition in 1933. The failure of national temperance led the alcoholism movement instead to propose that alcoholics were a special group of people with an inbred susceptibility to alcohol's effects (Beauchamp 1980). The differences in the views of narcotic and alcohol addiction are inextricably entwined with the social realities of their use. Controlled users of heroin form a distinct majority of those taking the drug (Lukoff and Brook 1974; Robins et al. 1975; Zinberg and Lewis 1964)—Trebach (1982) reported 500,000 regular users or addicts compared to 3.5 million occasional users. Yet such users, by definition, keep their illegal drug use hidden and are not part of public consciousness. It is obvious, on the other hand, that most people drink liquor—many regularly—without becoming addicted. What the prevailing disease notions of alcoholism and heroin addiction have in common is their physiological determinism and the belief in a stereotypical addiction syndrome that rules out controlled or variable use by the addict.

That prejudice and misinformation have formed the basis for much of what we think about heroin addiction can partially be explained by the minimal involvement most people have with the drug. Alcohol, on the other hand, is everywhere present in our society and is widely consumed. The emotional component of attitudes toward alcohol is thus more deeply engrained in people's experience and intrudes more into treatment policies. The American approach to drinking has indeed been deeply contentious and problematic and has continued to distort our understanding of alcoholism (Room 1983). The cultural history of American drinking practices in the United States provides an immediate example of the ways in which larger social attitudes influence not only the views of addiction to a drug but a drug's very addictive potential.

The Disease of Alcoholism

Approximately 80 percent of the Americans responding to a Gallup poll conducted in August 1982 said that they thought alcoholism was a disease. This was the highest figure recorded since the question was first asked by Gallup in 1955. A collation of public surveys indicated that about one-fifth of the general population agreed that alcoholism was an illness in the 1946–1951 period, that about three-fifths thought so in 1955–1960, and that by the early 1960s the percentage agreeing with this view had risen to sixty-five percent (Room 1983). As Room pointed out, those who endorse this position simultaneously often hold many nondisease ideas, such as that the alcoholic is morally deficient. Yet the almost universal medical, public, and treatment community acceptance of the outlines of a disease theory and of the appropriateness of medical treatment for alcoholism, forged largely over the last thirty to forty years, represents a transition in cultural attitudes of formidable dimensions.

As the continued moralism in many people's conceptions of the disease of alcoholism indicates, the disease theory is broad and inclusive. Critics of the disease theory are often required to specify the theory's elements in order to dispute them (Pattison et al. 1977). The key element that emerges in the disease theory of alcoholism is the alcoholic's *loss of control,* or the inability to drink moderately that leads some regularly to drink until they become intoxicated. Only the true—or "gamma"—alcoholic manifests this inability, unlike some others who get drunk as a matter of "choice" (Alcoholics Anonymous 1939; Jellinek 1952; Mann 1970). At the same time, alcoholism is seen to be a progressive disease, meaning that it inexorably proceeds from its early stages to its ultimate true form. A contradiction appears here: How is it possible to know whether an individual who displays drinking problems is a true alcoholic at an early stage of the disease or whether the person simply has a mild or passing drinking problem?

The actual empirical basis for the current disease model was Jellinek's (1946) analysis of ninety-eight questionnaires from a mailing sent to about 1,600 Alcoholics Anonymous members. Certain uniformities in the experiences of this highly self-selected group led Jellinek (1952, 1960) to formulate a typology of alcoholism. However, practically every independent effort to test these categories has found that alcoholism does not necessarily follow any particular path in its development and is not a unitary entity (cf. Miller 1983b; Pattison et al. 1977; Room 1983). Of even greater import are studies showing that no internal mechanism (nor the failure of any such mechanism) accounts for the alcoholic's loss of control. Instead, laboratory studies in which priming dosages of liquor are given to alcoholics or in which alcoholics are simply observed while drinking find that alcoholics typically *do* regulate their drinking (Mello and Mendelson 1971; Nathan and O'Brien 1971; Heather and Robertson 1981: 122). Finally, contrary to the idea of an inevitable progression, alcoholics with every degree of severity of drinking problem have been found to recover without treatment and to return to nonproblematic drinking (Heather and Robertson 1981; Knupfer 1972; Polich et al. 1981).

The nonempirical basis of the disease concept of alcoholism is actually most apparent in a recent, widely heralded defense of the disease approach to alcoholism. In his study of both treated and untreated alcoholics, Vaillant (1983) presented data showing that alcoholism occurs along a continuum and includes a range of drinking disorders, that alcohol problems regularly reverse themselves without medical intervention or the support of Alcoholics Anonymous (AA), that a genetic basis for alcoholism is doubtful, and that alcoholics generally drink again without endangering their sobriety. As a result of such findings, Vaillant concluded that "in our attempts to *understand* and to *study* alcoholism, it behooves us to employ the models of the social scientist and of the learning theorist. But in order to *treat* alcoholics effectively we need to invoke the model of the medical practitioner" (p. 20). Compare this, however, with Vaillant's evaluation of his own success in treating alcoholics in a medical setting and requiring that they attend AA: "our results were no better than the natural history of the disorder" (p. 285).

Historical, Social, Ethnic, and Economic Factors in Alcoholism in the United States

The cultural variations in attitudes toward a substance—and particularly its addictiveness (see chapter 1)—are especially relevant to the history and variety of American drinking patterns. Both because of the ethnic diversity in the United States and because of changes in this ethnic balance and in other social factors, attitudes toward alcohol have undergone considerable historical shifts and have been the object of major social disagreements and conflict (Lender and Martin 1982). In the ethnically homogeneous American colonies, where the community and family were the major forces in regulating drinking, drinking problems were minimal. Although per capita consumption was several times its contemporary levels in the United States, excessive drinking was not regarded as a social problem, alcoholism rates were lower, and heavy drinkers did not report experiencing a compulsion to drink (Zinberg and Fraser 1979; Levine 1978).

In this cultural setting, alcohol was seen as a benign, even positive force (Lender and Martin 1982). The current idea of alcoholism did not exist and the person who became drunk was thought of as having chosen this state (Levine 1978). The idea of drunkenness as an uncontrollable disease was introduced late in the colonial period by the physician Benjamin Rush. It grew rapidly between 1790 and 1830 when expanding frontiers and new waves of immigration broke down the traditional social regulation of drinking. Instead of taking place in a family-oriented tavern, most drinking was now done in saloons where the only women likely to be present were prostitutes. Alcohol took on a new image—drinking became a male prerogative that symbolized assertive independence and high spiritedness. Simultaneously liquor began to be seen by many as "demon rum."

Alcoholism rates rose precipitously during this period, and the temperance movement was born and flourished in response. Many former drunkards took the pledge of abstinence, forming self-help groups such as the Washingtonians to assist their resolve. The concept of alcoholism and the behavior of alcoholics reinforced each other, with the new kind of inebriate swearing that it was only by dint of total abstinence that he could forestall drunkenness. Meanwhile, the entire nation became polarized around the issue of temperance. Wet and dry forces began a century-long battle that ended when national Prohibition went into effect in 1920 (at a point, paradoxically, when drinking patterns had moderated substantially compared to the first half of the nineteenth century). The dry and wet sides of the issue divided up variously (cf. Gusfield 1963) according to region (the South and the Midwest versus the East and the West), religion (Protestant versus Catholic), sophistication (the less-well educated versus the better educated), and ethnicity (older versus newer Americans).

When Prohibition was repealed in 1933, the goal of national temperance was permanently laid to rest. In its place grew the modern disease theory of alcoholism, as defined and defended by the Alcoholics Anonymous self-help fellowship. Both the disease theory and AA achieved prominence in the late 1930s and early 1940s with the assistance of researchers at the Yale University Center of Alcohol Studies (most notably Jellinek and Keller), and through the energetic efforts of several recovered alcoholics who formed the progenitor of the National Council on Alcoholism (NCA) and its many state and local chapters (Beauchamp 1980; Room 1983; Wiener 1981). Whereas the nineteenth-century version of the disease theory focused on the substance itself, claiming that the disease befell anyone who drank regularly and who frequently became intoxicated, the modern version of the theory emphasized that only a small group of habitual inebriates had the disease. This group of people was characterized by a peculiar sensitivity or allergy to alcohol that caused them to crave it without bounds— that is, to lose control of their drinking—once they began to drink (cf. Alcoholics Anonymous 1939: 55).

Nonetheless, the AA vision of alcoholism had important commonalities with the temperance vision of demon rum. The chief of these was the utter necessity of abstinence (Roizen 1978). This point of view was forwarded by AA adherents with a religious fervor strongly reminiscent of the temperance movement. AA borrowed much in style from the nineteenth-century temperance brotherhoods like the Washingtonians. As they did in the earlier organization, reformed drinkers in AA meet in a highly charged atmosphere to relate their struggles with alcohol and to support each other's continued abstinence (as well as to convince others to join them). Both types of groups descend from the Protestant revival meeting, where the sinner seeks salvation through personal testimony, public contrition, and submission to a higher power (Trice and Roman 1970). The issue of abstinence for the alcoholic has thus always been a deeply emotional one in the United States, not one that has rested on a body of evidence.

AA-based groups and recovered alcoholics have been involved in formulating treatment policy in the United States in a way unmatched by any other Western nation (Miller 1983b). However, the current dominance of the disease model rests on more than the outlook of such groups and individuals. It has been supported by the general trend toward the medicalization of emotional and moral problems that has occurred in Western societies (Foucault 1973; Levine 1978). When it was formally endorsed by the American Medical Association in 1956, the disease model was given biomedical legitimacy. At the same time, the alliance between grass-roots self-help movements and the medical profession is often uneasy. A typical treatment apparatus will be under nominal medical supervision, while actual contact and counseling with clients is carried out by paraprofessionals who are themselves recovered alcoholics.

The identification and treatment of alcohol abusers who are not gamma alcoholics has always presented a problem for the disease model. In practice, the same abstinence orientation and overall approach to alcoholism have been utilized for all those who manifest drinking problems (cf. Hansen and Emrick 1983). The group of people for whom the disease approach has been applied seems consistently to have expanded as acceptance of the disease theory has grown. Room (1980) estimated that there was a twentyfold increase in the number of alcoholics in treatment between 1942 and 1976. The rate of growth has accelerated dramatically in the last fifteen years, as changes in the financing of treatment have placed a premium on the aggressive marketing of alcohol services (Weisner 1983; Weisner and Room 1984).

The result has been an explosion in the scope of alcohol services and those deemed to need it. These developments have included: (1) the proliferation of private treatment facilities, (2) the definition of new populations as requiring special attention, such as the young, women, minorities, (3) the creation of compulsory treatment referrals through such agencies as employee-assistance programs and the traffic court system, (4) the designation of certain social problems or crimes as being inescapably linked to alcohol abuse—including wife battering and child abuse and other crimes against people and property, (5) the identification of families of alcoholics as a whole new group with problems equivalent to the alcoholic's, and (6) the encouragement of confrontational interventions to reach those who do not recognize their own drinking problems. A theme for the alcoholism movement in the United States since the 1940s has been the public's lack of awareness of the nature and the extent of the alcohol problem. The ascendance of the disease theory has changed our entire culture's concept of the nature of its problems with alcohol. (The implications of these developments are treated in chapter 6.)

The Social Science Challenge to the Disease Theory

Psychological and other social scientific studies refuting the disease theory are of four types: (1) laboratory studies showing that alcoholics' patterns of drinking do not conform to the loss-of-control model (Marlatt et al. 1973;

Merry 1966; Paredes et al. 1973), (2) clinical research demonstrating the efficacy of techniques aimed at moderating problem drinking and alcoholism (Miller and Hester 1980; Sobell and Sobell 1973, 1976), (3) longitudinal studies both of the natural course of alcoholism and of outcomes for treated populations (Cahalan and Room 1974; Gerard and Saenger 1966; Polich et al. 1981; Vaillant 1983), (4) cross-ethnic and cultural studies demonstrating that social and belief systems are a principal component in alcoholism (Blum and Blum 1969; MacAndrew and Edgerton 1969; McClelland et al. 1972).

The last category of study has special relevance in America where so many divergent drinking traditions are present. Greeley et al. (1980) continued a tradition of finding distinct "ethnic drinking subcultures" in the United States with Irish, Slavic, and Protestant populations having a high incidence of drinking problems among white ethnic groups, while Jews and Italians have a low incidence. Perhaps even more noteworthy is the dichotomy among Oriental groups' drinking habits in the United States: the widespread chronic disabling alcoholism of Native Americans and Eskimos and the deeply engrained moderate drinking of Chinese and Japanese Americans (Stewart 1964). These data seem to indicate how readily culturally inculcated patterns of drinking overcome genetic differences in the rate of metabolizing alcohol (Mendelson and Mello 1979a). (See chapter 3.) The mechanisms by which moderate drinking is socialized in the young and maintained by the social group have been studied for Italians (Lolli et al. 1958), Jews (Glassner and Berg 1980), Chinese (Barnett 1955), and Greeks (Blum and Blum 1969). In these groups, children are gradually introduced to drinking in the family setting, where alcohol is not made to seem a rite of passage into adulthood or associated with masculinity and power. Adult drinking is also controlled by group attitudes about both the proper amount of drinking and the person's behavior when drinking. Strong disapproval is expressed when an individual violates these standards and acts in an antisocial manner. Wilkinson (1970) reported very similar dimensions to characterize the different ways alcoholics and nonproblem drinkers were taught to drink at home, regardless of their cultural heritage.

Group differences in alcoholism rates run counter to the emphasis of disease theorists on inbred and unalterable alcoholic mechanisms. There seems little reason why groups should differ in terms of biological susceptibility. Thus the movement in the field of alcoholism has been toward revealing greater-than-suspected numbers of alcoholics among such groups as women and Jews on the assumption that their apparently lower alcoholism rates are due simply to underreporting. Yet even studies conducted to substantiate hidden numbers of Jewish and women alcoholics continue to turn up distinctly lower rates for them than for the society at large (Efron et al. 1974; Glassner and Berg 1980). Moreover, the studies of general or community populations (cf. Cahalan and Room 1974) have revealed that drinking problems vary (increase) with such traditional demographic traits as age (younger), socioeconomic status (lower), ethnicity and race (black and hispanic). Not only drinking problems, but actual diagnoses of alcohol dependence or alcoholism are strongly associated with such demographic factors. Vaillant (1983) found his working-class, core-city sample had three times the percentage of alcoholics that his college sample had. Similarly, Irish-Americans in Vaillant's study were seven times as likely to be alcohol dependent as were those from Mediterranean backgrounds.

Cahalan and Room (1974) found the most important factor in predicting drinking problems for both a national and a community sample was an individual's immediate social context: how much his companions drank and how much of his social life revolved around drinking. A contextual framework for drinking is supported by a number of studies that find that people imitate the type of drinking going on around them (Caudill and Marlatt 1975; Jessor and Jessor 1975; Harford 1979). These findings strongly suggest the value (in both prevention and treatment) of creating moderate-drinking atmospheres for both young people and adults (Kraft 1982; Wilkinson 1970; Zinberg and Fraser 1979). The elements in these settings generally reproduce the ones found in moderate-drinking ethnic groups: serving wine and beer rather than distilled spirits, drinking where food is served and where those of all ages and both sexes participate, explicitly presenting values for responsible drinking. This approach conflicts with the growing trend in the alcoholism movement to identify young people with drinking problems as being alcohol dependent—an allegedly permanent condition like alcoholism—or to label those from families in which there is alcohol abuse as having a high risk for alcoholism. In both these cases, the proposed remedy is enrollment in abstinence-oriented groups to prevent the likely or inevitable development of alcoholism (see chapter 6).

The concept of problem drinking that Cahalan and Room (1974) employed is fundamentally different from the disease idea of alcoholism because it sees alcohol abuse as a function of time and situation rather than as a clinical problem; that is, it focuses on the ground rather than the figure in problem drinking. This viewpoint is supported by the observation that problem drinking is an extremely changeable and complicated behavior (Clark and Cahalan 1976; Room 1977). Various measures of alcohol abuse show little connection to each other (Clark 1976; Miller and Saucedo 1983) and seem instead to be situation-specific. Not only do young people often grow out of their drinking problems, but even older drinkers with long histories of abuse frequently abstain or drink without problems. Indeed, laboratory studies of diagnosed alcoholics support this view of drinking as a highly situation-specific behavior (Mello and Mendelson 1972).

This social-setting or sociological perspective is most at odds with the disease model when it regards alcoholism itself as a social construct (Beauchamp 1980; Gusfield 1981; Room 1983; Shaw 1979). What is defined as alcoholism at any time or place is a social convention at the same time that social policies have a great impact on the amount of alcohol abuse in a society. Keller, (1981, quoted in Room 1983: 53) directed a particularly pointed attack on this point of view:

> [If] it is a social problem, . . . the social scientists are the ones to take charge of it! . . . They freely use words they have invented—like medicalization, clinicization, with obvious implications that these are bad—socially undesirable—practices. . . . It is no accident but a logical coincidence that the proponents of legal measures to combat alcohol problems are the same people who decry, deny and denigrate the disease concept of alcoholism. . . . The solution of the problem should not be left to the medicalists—biologists. The solution should be put into the hands of us all-knowing social scientists, the expert formulators of social policy.

Although the social constructivist point of view is totally incompatible with disease notions, the full fury of the disease movement has been reserved for findings that alcoholics can control their drinking. It is here that disease advocates and social scientific researchers and clinicians clash over issues of treatment. Prior to 1960, controlled drinking was often regarded matter of factly as one potential outcome of therapy for alcoholism in the United States (Miller 1983a; see Wallerstein et al. 1957). In some European countries, such as Norway, this attitude still holds, and clinicians do not even consider the question of controlled drinking versus abstinence to be a primary one in treatment, but focus simply on the reduction of an individual's drinking problems (Duckert, cited in "The Behaviorists," 1984). This outlook is so foreign to current policies in the United States that we must comprehend contemporary attitudes toward controlled-drinking treatment as having undergone a culturewide shift induced by disease conceptions.

The first research to be attacked for uncovering a return to social drinking by alcoholics was by Davies (1962) in England. Davies was a clinician who found safely moderated drinking among seven of a group of ninety-three alcoholics who had been followed up for about ten years following treatment. The challenge to these findings appeared principally in the pages of the American *Quarterly Journal of Studies on Alcohol*. That disease adherents felt the capability and necessity of attacking this research was due to the consolidation of their power over the treatment of alcoholism at this time. Numerous confirmations of the possibility of a return to controlled drinking by a range of alcoholics appeared in the years following the Davies study. These are documented and summarized in detail in Heather and Robertson's (1981) thorough review, *Controlled Drinking* (these authors also point out studies prior to Davies's that uncovered controlled drinking outcomes). It thus requires some explanation to account for the uproar raised by the Rand Reports, the first of which appeared in 1976 (Armor et al. 1978).

The Rand investigators were under contract to the National Institute on Alcohol Abuse and Alcoholism (NIAAA) to evaluate the results of NIAAA treatment programs. They did so for 2,339 alcoholics at six months and for 597 at eighteen months. At the eighteenth-month point, 24 percent of the treated alcoholics were abstaining while 22 percent were drinking normally. Among those the investigators identified as definitely alcoholic, the figures were 25 percent abstaining and 16 percent drinking normally. The report was immediately assailed, principally by the National Council on Alcoholism, which made an effort to have the report delayed and its results reinterpreted (see Roizen 1978). Amidst many wild and unfounded allegations about the report, there were genuine methodological criticisms raised (although none that would obviate the thrust of the results). In response to these, the investigators conducted a follow-up study (Polich et al. 1981) in which they extended the period over which treated patients were observed to four years, checked self-reports of drinking with breathalyzer tests, carefully divided the subjects into groups based on how severely dependent on alcohol they were at admission, and toughened their definitions of controlled drinking—which was called nonproblem drinking. Nonproblem drinking was defined as the absence of any alcohol dependence symptoms (e.g., tremors, blackout, morning drinking) or negative consequences from drinking (e.g., arrest, missing work). The second of the Rand Reports found that nearly 40 percent of the subjects who were free from drinking problems were drinking, including a distinct portion of those most severely alcoholic initially.

Opposition to the second Rand Report continued to be both substantial and emotional. Despite the success of its authors in affirming and solidifying their results (see Beauchamp et al. 1980), most practitioners in the field and disease researchers have felt safe in simply ignoring the Rand data (see Vaillant 1983). The directors of the NIAAA at the time of both of the reports reiterated that abstinence remained the "appropriate goal in the treatment of alcoholism" (see Armor et al. 1978: 230; "Drinking Problem Dispute" 1980). Thus the ultimate significance of the reports rests in the cultural response to them rather than their actual findings. Ernest Noble, the director of the NIAAA, solicited reviews from impartial scientific sources when the first Rand Report was issued. While the comments were inherently reasonable, they appear ironic in light of the current atmosphere toward alcoholism in America. From Gerald L. Klerman, Professor of Psychiatry, Harvard Medical School (in Armor et al. 1978: 223):

This is a very important document. I think the conclusions are highly justified. I understand you are under great political pressure. . . . I would strongly urge you and the NIAAA to stand firm wherever possible.

From Samuel B. Guze, Head of the Department of Psychiatry, Washington University School of Medicine (in Armor et al. 1978: 221):

What the data do demonstrate is that remission is possible for many alcoholics and that many of these are able to drink normally for extended periods. These points deserve emphasis, because they offer encouragement to patients, to their families, and to relevant professionals.

Controlled-Drinking Therapy for Alcoholism

The reaction to the Rand Reports indicated that rejection of the idea of controlled drinking for alcoholics was beyond questions of evidence. The Rand investigators, in reporting these outcomes, were attempting to describe how clients at NIAAA treatment centers behaved following treatment. They were not advocates or practitioners of controlled-drinking therapy nor were their subjects encouraged to become moderate drinkers at the abstinence-oriented NIAAA centers where they were treated. The Rand Reports were in fact a part of a different tradition in alcoholism research, one that has repeatedly emphasized how variable and responsive to life and situational cues drinking of any kind is (Polich et al. 1981: 214):

We found a great deal of change in individual status, with some persons continuing to improve, some persons deteriorating, and most moving back and forth between relatively improved and unimproved statuses.

Another body of work has applied behavioral modification techniques to the task of teaching alcoholics to drink moderately. Success for this approach was reported in the early 1970s by several research teams (Lovibund and Caddy 1970; Schaefer 1972; Vogler et al. 1975). In 1982, a study published in the prestigious journal *Science* by Pendery et al. attacked one of these seminal studies, by Sobell and Sobell (1973, 1976), which had found that alcoholics who received behavior therapy aimed at moderating drinking patterns fared better than did a comparable group who underwent standard hospital abstinence treatment. In their reinvestigation of the controlled-drinking subjects from the original study, Pendery et al. reported that most had difficulty moderating their drinking years later and that nearly all had reported instances of relapse very soon after treatment. The

Science study was highly publicized, usually accompanied by accusations by the investigators that the Sobells had falsified their results. Media depictions of the case generally assumed that abstinence had been shown to be the only possible alternative for alcoholics (see Peele 1984c).

The Pendery et al. investigation was by any standards an unusual one. It focused solely on the experimental, controlled-drinking group without reporting any follow-up on the comparison, abstinence group. The data were primarily recollections by subjects, in some cases nine years after the events, and descriptions of individual episodes of relapse. The only summary data in the paper were in the form of the amount of hospitalization controlled-drinking subjects underwent after treatment. The Addiction Research Foundation of Toronto, which at the time of the *Science* article employed the Sobells, convened an investigation of the controversy by an independent panel of distinguished academics not previously involved in alcoholism policy. The panel's report (Dickens et al. 1982) found that Pendery et al. had presented no new data, since the Sobells' published papers had already noted more hospitalizations for the experimental subjects than were reported in the *Science* article. Moreover, the committee chastized the Pendery group for failing to reexamine the subjects treated with abstinence techniques and to take into account the body of evidence about controlled drinking (Peele 1983f).

It is impossible to understand this controversy without considering, as all the media failed to do, the history of the debate about alcoholism in the United States. For example, the senior author of the *Science* article was a prominent critic of the Rand Reports and a spokesperson for the National Council on Alcoholism in its effort to suppress the first report (Roizen 1978: 266). That the Pendery et al. article does not present a balanced perspective on alcoholism research has gone unrecognized by the public; indeed, the article has been invested with importance beyond its dubious value precisely because it is one of the few answers to an avalanche of studies contradicting disease notions. As such, however, it fits in with dominant views about alcoholism that trace back to nineteenth-century America and that are buttressed by effective control of public information about alcoholism by medical, AA, and other disease proponents.

One consequence of this near-unanimity in the United States has been the almost complete extinction of controlled drinking as a treatment goal. The director of the Rutgers Center of Alcohol Studies, who has himself endorsed controlled-drinking treatment, announced: "There is no alcoholism center in the United States using the technique as official policy" ("Debate Rages . . ." 1982). This certainly contrasts with other countries, such as Britain, where a survey of treatment centers revealed that 93 percent consider controlled drinking an appropriate goal and 76 percent offer it as one alternative (Robertson and Heather 1982). What may be more important than the erosion in controlled-drinking therapy in the United States is that the assault on the idea has influenced approaches to and theories of alcoholism even among those who explicitly oppose the disease viewpoint.

Clinical Approaches to Controlled-Drinking Therapy

The Pendery et al. (1982) attack on one controlled-drinking study for alcoholics paradoxically occurred at a time of retrenchment for those practicing the approach. In nearly all cases, behavior therapists have indicated that the goal of controlled drinking should be employed with problem drinkers rather than alcoholics or alcohol-dependent clients (Marlatt 1983). This new consensus began to emerge in the mid-1970s after the publication of the first Rand Report. Thus, controlled-drinking studies and books authored before that time are less guarded or more optimistic about the prospects for treating alcoholics (Miller and Muñoz 1976; Sobell and Sobell 1976; Steiner 1971; Vogler et al. 1975), while later works by the same authors tred that ground cautiously or even deny the possibility (Miller and Muñoz 1982; Sobell and Sobell 1982; Vogler and Bartz 1982). No clinician in the United States today actively speaks for the controlled-drinking option for alcoholics. This is again in contrast with Britain, where some observers "regret the tendency to relegate the new methods to a minor and ancillary role . . . as being applicable, for example, to *only* those with less serious problems" (Heather and Robertson 1981: viii).

The evidence for taking into account the level of alcoholism when applying controlled-drinking goals is that the more severe a person's drinking problems the more likely are abstinence outcomes relative to moderation outcomes (Miller 1983a). However, the investigations of clinical psychologists agree with survey researchers in finding no distinct point where a line between alcoholics and others with drinking problems can be drawn. Instead, drinking problems occur along a continuum to which a number of factors contribute (Clark and Cahalan 1976; Miller and Saucedo 1983), and some drinkers at even the most severe levels of alcohol dependence successfully adopt controlled drinking. While fewer of the most dependent subjects (those with eleven or more signs of dependence on admission) in the Rand Study were drinking without problems at four years than were those who had been less dependent, still over one-quarter of those in remission were doing so.

Longitudinal studies likewise find it uncommon for heavily alcoholic subjects to become normal social drinkers. The Davies finding of between 5 and 10 percent who did so over a period from seven to eleven years appears typical (Vaillant 1983). However, only about the same 5 to 10 percent range of alcoholics achieve complete abstinence following treatment (Emrick and Hansen 1983; Polich et al. 1981). For the 80 to 90 percent of alcoholics who do not abstain totally or return to normal drinking, the issue is the relative frequency of the person's drunken binges. Thus clearcut outcome categories have little meaning for the majority of alcoholics. Vaillant (1983) observed that among 110 alcohol abusers in his study who were tracked for over thirty years, 20 percent became moderate drinkers (no signs of dependence in the previous year) and 34 percent became abstinent. However, Vaillant assigned to the abstinence category those *drinking less than once a month* as well as those who had *drinking binges of less than a week's duration once a year.*

There seems quite a bit of leeway in the definition of controlled drinking and abstinence. Some, unlike Vaillant, might call a person who drank only occasionally to be a controlled rather than an abstinent drinker. Some (including, paradoxically, the Rand investigators, whom Vaillant derided for their leniency in defining controlled drinking) would label those who had drinking binges of any duration to be problem drinkers. In noting that occasional drinkers may for all intents and purposes be considered abstinent, Vaillant identified a crucial issue in therapy: how an alcoholic who has had one drink avoids a full-blown alcoholic relapse. Marlatt (1982) has developed an overall strategy for relapse prevention that includes teaching the alcoholic that a single slip is not necessarily a precursor to an episode of drunkenness. Alcoholics given practice in relapse prevention abstained no less than a comparison group of treated alcoholics (almost two-thirds of all subjects drank within a year), but they did show significantly less drunkenness (Chaney et al. 1978).

Abstinence philosophers argue that the danger of relapse is overwhelming for the alcoholic who is told he may take another drink. Yet there is an equivalent danger that those trying to adhere to strict abstinence will be more likely to abandon self-control entirely when they have a single drink (Heather et al. 1982; Marlatt 1978; Peele and Brodsky 1975; Schaefer 1971). This occurs because they believe they are powerless after they taste alcohol, as AA teaches them. The Rand Reports found relapses between eighteen months and four years had occurred for both those abstaining and those drinking without problems. In general, lower levels of dependence favored efforts to limit drinking and higher levels favored abstinence. However, other factors such as age and marital status were also important in this equation: For example, highly alcohol-dependent single men under age 40 were more likely to relapse if they were abstaining at eighteen months than if they were drinking moderately. It would seem that these alcoholics confront more drinking opportunities that may break their resolve to abstain, after which they are likely to drink excessively.

An understanding of the concept of relapse and a recognition of its frequency are necessary to make sense out of the Sobells' study and its critique by Pendery et al. The central finding in the original study was that abstinence subjects relapsed more than did controlled-drinking subjects. Pendery et al. pointed out that debilitating drinking was not uncommon for the controlled-drinking group following treatment. In the absence of any information about the abstinence group, it is possible to imagine that abstinence treatment successfully eliminated relapse. In fact, Pendery et al. (1982) noted about this group that "all agree (they) fared badly" (p. 173). Vaillant (1983) found a 95 percent relapse rate for a comparable group of patients he treated with hospital detoxification, compulsory AA attendance, and an active follow-up program.

Vaillant's strenuous insistence on the value of such medical and abstinence treatment is remarkable considering his own treatment group showed no better progress at two and eight years than did comparable groups of untreated alcoholics. This finding reflects a general absence of definitive results from therapeutic interventions for alcoholism (cf. Emrick 1975; Orford and Edwards 1977). On what grounds, then, have psychologists come to agree with medical practitioners that controlled-drinking approaches are not feasible for more seriously alcoholic clients? Miller (1983a, 1983b) maintains this position while reporting that twenty-three out of twenty-four studies have found reduced drinking techniques superior to other treatments for a range of alcohol abuse and "no study has demonstrated moderation training to be less effective than abstinence overall (that is, for any group of alcoholics)" (Miller 1983b: 15). It is not the evidence that has led to the total rejection of this technique for alcoholics. Rather, it is the current cultural climate toward alcoholism, one in which an alcoholism expert is quoted in a national magazine as saying "the suggestion that an alcoholic might be able to return to social drinking safely is 'a serious ethical problem, because at least 97% of alcoholics, if you let them drink, could die'" ("New Insights into Alcoholism" 1983: 69). Compare this with Vaillant's forlorn finding for his clinical sample that, "Tragically, abstinence does little to reduce the increased mortality of alcoholics" (1983: 164). Still, the risk to the therapist whose client fails at controlled drinking—since sooner or later nearly all alcoholics will relapse under any treatment condition—is that he or she will be accused of causing the client's death.

In this vein, several of the media depictions of the Sobells–Pendery et al. case visited graves or sites where controlled-drinking clients died. Yet the Addiction Research Foundation investigation actually found fewer deaths among subjects in the controlled-drinking group than in the abstinence group. The Sobells (1984) reported a detailed analysis of all subject deaths. They found the death rate for controlled-drinking subjects was lower than that regularly reported in alcoholism studies (none of these subjects died in the first six years following treatment and the last two died ten years later, while intoxicated, shortly after leaving abstinence treatment clinics). In their rebuttal to Pendery et al., the Sobells (1984: 413) concluded that reinvestigations of their work "actually strengthen the validity of our original reports and conclusions." In the strange environment of controlled-drinking research, the publication of the Rand Reports—which found non-problem drinking among those with the most severe alcoholism—contributed to the rejection of controlled-drinking approaches for alcoholics in the United States. Then a fervid attack on a study of controlled-drinking therapy for severe alcoholics by researchers who no longer maintained this position reopened the question, at least for those interested in the truth.

Given that the two principal parties in the controlled-drinking debate had agreed by the late 1970s that this therapy was inapplicable to gamma (physically dependent) alcoholics, there seems little reason for argument. In the area of controlled drinking for alcoholics, however, broad outward agreement fails to obviate mutual suspicion and antagonism. There is, in addition, a practical side to the continuing battle: the competition over the less severely alcoholic person, labeled the problem drinker by psychologists (cf. Marlatt 1983). Every available comparative study has found that controlled-drinking therapy is the superior treatment for such clients (Miller and Hester 1980). Yet therapy with a goal of moderating drinking is just as unavailable for these types of drinkers as for those termed alcoholics. While abstinence proponents painstakingly evaluate whether those who return to social drinking were ever genuine alcoholics (see discussion of such a case in Pendery et al. 1982: 173), in practice abstinence treatment is offered to anyone with a noticeable drinking problem. In one highly publicized study in Denver, subjects who reported to alcoholism clinics with any type of concern about their drinking were invariably welcomed for treatment as alcoholics (Hansen and Emrick 1983).

The theoretical loophole in the disease approach that permits abstinence to be urged for all is the putative progressive nature of the disease. A more important Catch-22 concept in disease treatment is "denial." Alcoholics are defined as having an innate proclivity for denying their true condition, and this provides a justification for coercing clients to acknowledge that they are alcoholics and that therefore they need to abstain (see chapter 6). In fact, the second Rand Report discovered alcoholics were very aware of the negative consequences of their drinking (Polich et al. 1981). Those whose drinking problems obviously do not qualify them as alcoholic frequently refuse this label and with it, treatment (Miller 1983c). A Canadian study that offered stable, employed problem drinkers an abstinence therapy found that two-thirds rejected this goal at the outset while nearly all of a comparable group accepted treatment aimed at moderation (Sanchez-Craig 1980).

The Self-Selection of Treatment and Treatment Goals

It is clear, however, that not only those with milder drinking problems reject the idea that they are alcoholic, the need for lifelong abstinence, or both. All the Rand subjects underwent traditional alcoholism treatment, and yet very many of them, including a portion of those displaying a large number of symptoms of dependence, chose moderation as their own standard for improvement. These clients were not likely to be ones who enrolled in AA as an adjunct to treatment. Still, quite a few of them *were* able to demonstrate improved functioning and the elimination of drinking problems. A similar process occurred for the less severely impaired subjects who were told to abstain in the Canadian study. A solid majority of these actually moderated their drinking, so that there were not differences in the diminution of drinking problems between this group and those taught controlled drinking after two years (Sanchez-Craig et al. 1984). The finding that just as many people moderate their drinking no matter how extensive—or nonexistent—the controlled-drinking therapy they receive suggests that the primary determinant of moderation as a treatment outcome is a client's motivation to control his drinking (Nathan 1980).

Miller (1983a), Heather and Robertson (1981), Hodgson et al. (1979), and other behavior therapists have emphasized the need to classify alcoholics for treatment according to how potentially able they are to control their drinking. The primary criterion used is the severity of the individual's dependence on alcohol. A drinker's self-conception of being alcoholic also plays a role, however (Skinner et al. 1982). For example, subjects who believe that they are alcoholic and that abstinence is the only possible answer for their problem do better with an abstinence regimen (Miller 1983a). They are more likely to relapse following treatment after having had just one drink (Heather et al. 1983). These are examples of clients for whom abstinence is undoubtedly the preferred treatment modality. On the other hand, there may be just as much risk in contradicting the alcoholic who believes he can control his drinking as there is in convincing an alcoholic who believes abstinence will work that he should drink.

The more basic issue is in assuming an alcoholic's self-diagnosis is unreliable and that instead the therapist should determine the goal of treatment. It is not surprising that, as in the Rand Reports, we find human beings defiantly pursuing their own agendas for improvement. Alcoholics may avoid not only disease treatments but therapy of any kind. Tuchfeld (1981) interviewed people who had had significant drinking problems (e.g., blackout, tremors) and who had quit or moderated drinking on their own. These people often explicitly rejected the value of therapy for them. Instead, they changed their behavior when their drinking patterns became intolerable in line with other values, relationships, or desires (Peele 1983d). Untreated alcoholics and problem drinkers are often identified by both disease theorists and psychologists as needing their attention. However, those who refuse to seek treatment for their abuse of alcohol remain in the majority. Vaillant (1983), while championing the effectiveness of AA, found that only about one-fifth of the 54 percent of alcohol abusers in his sample who were in remission were assisted by AA. Nor did many turn to other therapies. Not only did the 20 percent of those drinking without problems go it on their own, but so too did the majority of the 34 percent who were abstaining. One wonders if those Vaillant defined as abstinent but who continued to drink less than once a month were those who did not attend AA and who were thus less dogmatic about abstinence. In their national and community surveys, Cahalan (1970) and Roizen et al. (1978) uncovered large percentages of their samples whose drinking problems mitigated in the natural course of their lives, hardly any of whom became abstinent.

We have no evidence that those people who eschew treatment would be better off to admit their problem openly to others and to enlist in therapy (see chapter 5). Even when alcoholics show improvement through therapy the impetus is often provided by events outside the therapy setting (Gerard and Saenger 1966; Moos and Finney 1982). The kind of change involved in becoming a social drinker would seem especially to entail a substantial change in environment and outlook (Peele 1983a). For this reason, young drinkers show the greatest capacity to outgrow drinking problems (Cahalan and Room 1974), even when they have manifested symptoms of serious alcoholism (Fillmore 1975).

The disease theory of alcoholism—with its emphasis on lifelong abstinence, the need to confront people actively about their denial, and the treatable nature of alcoholism—has become firmly ensconced in American lore and social services. At the same time, success rates from typical abstinence programs seem to center in the 5 to 10 percent range (Emrick and Hansen 1983), with one massive study of a hospital-based program reporting less than 10 percent abstaining by the end of a year (Gordis et al. 1981). Treatment of any type strains to demonstrate a clearcut improvement in prognosis over the natural course of alcoholism (Baekeland et al. 1975; Emrick 1975; Orford and Edwards 1977; Vaillant 1983). Perhaps of most concern, the number of those with active alcohol problems does not seem to have decreased along with the ascendance of the disease theory, but rather has increased alarmingly (see chapter 6).

The growth of the disease theory is not due to its demonstrated efficacy, but instead represents the dominance of a set of attitudes about drinking. These attitudes paradoxically characterize those groups that are *most* likely to have alcohol problems. Vaillant found that not only were Irish-Americans in his sample seven times as likely to be alcoholic as those of

Mediterranean descent but that, in order to deal with a drinking problem, they were more likely to abstain. He notes that "It is consistent with Irish culture to see the use of alcohol in terms of black and white, good or evil, drunkenness or complete abstinence, while in Italian culture it is the distinction between moderate drinking and drunkenness that is most important" (1983: 226). This former view, from which the disease theory springs, is coming increasingly to inform our entire culture's conception of drinking. In noting the increasing incidence of drunkenness among U.S. high school students (by the end of the 1970s and the beginning of the 1980s, 40 percent of high school seniors reported having five drinks in one sitting at least once in the prior two weeks), Johnston et al. (1981) found a parallel rise in the acceptance of binge drinking on weekends in preference to mild daily consumption.

Theories about alcoholism reflect the same cultural influences. The strict version of the disease theory endorsed by AA and some physicians has found next to no empirical support. Meanwhile, however, medical investigators continue to emphasize genetic influences in alcoholism (cf. Schuckit 1984). More tellingly, the psychologists who most actively contest the disease theory have begun to formulate the problem in terms very reminiscent of those with whom they are arguing. Even within sociology today, the dominant view is that alcohol problems are solely a function of consumption (Room 1984).

3
Theories of Addiction

Stanton Peele and Bruce K. Alexander

I n many cases, addiction theorists have now progressed beyond stereotyped disease conceptions of alcoholism or the idea that narcotics are
inherently addictive to anyone who uses them. The two major areas of
addiction theory—those concerning alcohol and narcotics—have had a
chance to merge, along with theorizing about overeating, smoking, and
even running and interpersonal addictions. Yet this new theoretical synthesis is less than meets the eye: It mainly recycles discredited notions while
including piecemeal modifications that make the theories marginally more
realistic in their descriptions of addictive behavior. These theories are described and evaluated in this chapter as they apply to all kinds of addictions. They are organized into sections on genetic theories (inherited mechanisms that cause or predispose people to be addicted), metabolic theories
(biological, cellular adaptation to chronic exposure to drugs), conditioning
theories (built on the idea of the cumulative reinforcement from drugs or
other activities), and adaptation theories (those exploring the social and
psychological functions performed by drug effects).

While most addiction theorizing has been too unidimensional and
mechanistic to begin to account for addictive behavior, adaptation theories
have typically had a different limitation. They do often correctly focus on
the way in which the addict's experience of a drug's effects fits into the
person's psychological and environmental ecology. In this way drugs are
seen as a way to cope, however dysfunctionally, with personal and social
needs and changing situational demands. Yet these adaptation models,
while pointing in the right direction, fail because they do not directly explain the pharmacological role the substance plays in addiction. They are
often considered—even by those who formulate them—as adjuncts to biological models, as in the suggestion that the addict uses a substance to gain
a specific effect until, inexorably and irrevocably, physiological processes
take hold of the individual. At the same time their purview is not ambitious enough (not nearly so ambitious as that of some biological and conditioning models) to incorporate nonnarcotic or nondrug involvements.

They also miss the opportunity, readily available at the social-psychological level of analysis, to integrate individual and cultural experiences.

Genetic Theories

How Is Alcoholism Inherited?

Cigarette smoking, alcoholism, and overweight—like divorce, child abuse and religion—run in families. This addictive inheritance has been most studied in the case of alcoholism. Studies endeavoring to separate genetic from environmental factors, such as those in which adopted-away offspring of alcoholics were compared to adopted children with nonalcoholic biological parents, have claimed a three to four times greater alcoholism rate for those whose biologic parents were alcoholic (Goodwin et al. 1973). Vaillant (1983) approvingly cited the Goodwin et al. and other research indicating genetic causality in alcoholism (see especially Vaillant and Milofsky 1982), but his own research did not support this conclusion (cf. Peele 1983c). In the inner-city sample that formed the basis for Vaillant's primary analysis, those with alcoholic relatives were between three and four times as likely to be alcoholic as those without alcoholic relatives. Since these subjects were reared by their natural families, however, this finding does not distinguish effects of alcoholic environment from inherited dispositions. Vaillant did find that subjects with alcoholic relatives they did not live with were twice as likely to become alcoholic as subjects who had no alcoholic relatives at all.

Yet further nongenetic influences remain to be partialed out of Vaillant's results. The chief of these is ethnicity: Irish Americans in this Boston sample were seven times as likely to be alcohol dependent as were those of Mediterranean descent. Controlling for such large ethnicity effects would surely reduce the 2 to 1 ratio (for subjects with alcoholic relatives compared to those without) in alcoholism substantially even as other potential environmental factors that lead to alcoholism (besides ethnicity) would still remain to be controlled for. Vaillant reported two other tests of genetic causality in his sample. He disconfirmed Goodwin's (1979) hypothesis that alcoholics with alcoholic relatives—and hence a presumed inherited predisposition to alcoholism—inevitably develop problems with drinking earlier than do others. Finally, Vaillant found no tendency for the choice of moderate drinking versus abstinence as a resolution for drinking problems to be related to number of alcoholic relatives, although it was associated with the drinker's ethnic group.

Proposing genetic mechanisms in alcoholism on the basis of concordance rates does not provide a model of addiction. What are these mechanisms through which alcoholism is inherited and translated into alcoholic behavior? Not only has no biological mechanism been found to date to underlie alcoholism, but research on alcoholics' behavior indicates that one cannot be found in the case of the loss of control of drinking that defines alcoholism. Even the most severely alcoholic individuals "clearly demonstrate positive sources of control over drinking behavior" so that "extreme drunkenness cannot be accounted for on the basis of some internally located inability to stop" (Heather and Robertson 1981: 122). Intriguingly, controlled-drinking theorists like Heather and Robertson (1983) propose exceptions to their own analyses: Perhaps "some problem drinkers are born with a physiological abnormality, either genetically transmitted or as a result of intrauterine factors, which makes them react abnormally to alcohol from their first experience of it" (Heather and Robertson 1983: 141).

While it is certainly a fascinating possibility, no research of any type supports this suggestion. Vaillant (1983) found that self-reports by AA members that they immediately succumbed to alcoholism the first time they drank were false and that severe drinking problems developed over periods of years and decades. The exceptions to this generalization were psychopaths whose drinking problems were components of overall abnormal lifestyles and behavior patterns from an early age. However, these kinds of alcoholics showed a greater tendency to outgrow alcoholism by moderating their drinking (Goodwin et al. 1971), indicating they also do not conform to a putative biological model. Prospective studies of those from alcoholic families also have failed to reveal early alcoholic drinking (Knop et al. 1984).

Findings like these have led genetic theorists and researchers instead to propose that the inherited vulnerability to alcoholism takes the form of some probabilistically greater risk of developing drinking problems. In this view a genetic tendency—such as one that dictates a drinker will have an overwhelming response to alcohol—does not cause alcoholism. The emphasis is instead on such biological abnormalities as the inability to discriminate blood alcohol level (BAL), which leads alcoholics to show less effect from drinking and to drink more without sensing their condition (Goodwin 1980; Schuckit 1984). Alternately, Schuckit (1984) proposed that alcoholics inherit a different style of metabolizing alcohol, such as producing higher levels of acetaldehyde due to drinking. Finally, Begleiter and other theorists have proposed that alcoholics have abnormal brain waves prior to ever having drunk or that drinking creates unusual brain activity for them (Pollock et al. 1984; Porjesz and Begleiter 1982).

All these theorists have indicated that their results are preliminary and require replication, particularly through prospective studies of people who become alcoholics. Negative evidence, however, is already available. Several studies have found that sensitivity to BAL, peak BAL after drinking, and elimination of blood alcohol are unrelated to family histories of alcoholism (Lipscomb and Nathan 1980; Pollock et al. 1984). Other negative evidence for both BAL discrimination *and* metabolic hypotheses is provided by the case of American Indians and Eskimos. These groups are hyperresponsive to alcohol's effects (that is, they respond immediately and intensely to the alcohol in their systems) and yet have the highest alcoholism rates in the United States. The claim of inheritance of alcoholism from the opposite theoretical direction—that these groups succumb to alcoholism so readily because they metabolize alcohol so quickly—likewise does not succeed. Groups that share the hypermetabolism of alcohol that Eskimos and Indians display (called Oriental flush), such as the Chinese and Japanese, have among the lowest alcoholism rates in America. The disjunctive connection between obvious metabolic characteristics and drinking habits actually contraindicates significant biological determinism in alcoholism (Mendelson and Mello 1979a).

The basic problem with genetic models of alcoholism is the absence of a reasonable link to the drinking behaviors in question. Why do any of the proposed genetic mechanisms lead people to become compulsive imbibers? For example, in the case of an insensitivity to alcohol's effects, why wouldn't an individual who can't reliably detect that he has drunk too much simply learn from experience (in the absence of any proposed genetic compulsion to drink) to limit himself to a safer number of drinks? Do such drinkers simply choose to drink at unhealthy levels and to experience the extreme negative consequences of drinking that, after years, may lead to alcoholism (Vaillant 1983)? If so, why? That is the question.

On the other hand, the proposed differences in metabolizing alcohol and changes in brain functioning due to drinking are extremely subtle when compared with the gross effects of Oriental flush. Yet even groups characterized by Oriental flush, like the Indians and the Chinese, can show diametrically opposite responses to the same intense physiological changes. If a given individual did indeed have an extreme reaction to alcohol, why would he not become the type of drinker who announces, "I only have a drink or two because otherwise I become giddy and make a fool of myself"? For those drinkers for whom alcohol might produce a desirable change in brain waves, why does the person prefer this state over others or other ways of gaining the same effect? The variation in behavior that is left unaccounted for in the most optimistic of these models is such as to discount the potential gain from the pursuit of as yet unestablished links between genetically inherited reactions to alcohol and alcoholic behavior. Finally, since all studies have found that it is sons and not daughters who most often inherit the risk of alcoholism (Cloninger et al. 1978), in what comprehensible ways can any of the genetic mechanisms thus far suggested for alcoholism be sex-linked?

The Endorphin-Deficiency Explanation of Narcotic Addiction

Since the primary assumption about narcotics has been that the drugs are equally and inevitably addictive for everyone, pharmacological theories of narcotic addiction have rarely stressed individual biological proclivities to be addicted. It was only a matter of time, however, before pharmacological and biological theorists began to hypothesize inherited mechanisms to account for differences in addictive susceptibility. When Dole and Nyswander (1967) introduced the ideas that narcotic addiction was a "metabolic disease" and that the tendency to become addicted outlived the actual dependence on a drug, the way was opened to suggest that "metabolic disorder could precede as well as be precipitated by opiate use" (Goldstein, cited in Harding et al. 1980: 57). That is, not only might habitual narcotic use cause a chronic and residual need for drugs, but people conceivably might already have had such a need when they started taking drugs and came to rely on them.

The discovery that the body produces its own opiates, called endorphins, presented a plausible version of this mechanism. Endorphin theorists like Goldstein (1976b) and Snyder (1977) speculated that addicts may be characterized by an inbred endorphin deficiency that leaves them unusually sensitive to pain. Such people would then especially welcome— and might even require—the elevation of their pain threshhold brought on by narcotics. Heroin addicts have not yet been demonstrated to show unusual levels of endorphins. Moreover, this type of theorizing is badly strained—as are all metabolic theories of addiction—by the commonplace observations of drug abuse and addiction that were noted in chapter 1. Addicts do not in fact indicate a chronic, habitual need for narcotics. They regularly alter the type and amount of drug they use, sometimes abstaining or quitting altogether as they age. Most of the Vietnam veterans who were addicted in Asia and who then used narcotics in the United States did not become readdicted. Noting that almost none of the patients introduced to a narcotic in the hospital indicate a prolonged desire for the drug, we may wonder why so small a percentage of the general population displays this endorphin deficiency.

Endorphin deficiency and other metabolic models suggest a course of progressive and irreversible reliance on narcotics that actually occurs in only exceptional and abnormal cases of addiction. Those with inbred metabolic defects could conceivably account for only a small percentage of those who become addicted over their lifetimes. Why would the narcotic addiction that disappeared for most Vietnam veterans (or for the many other addicts who outgrow it) differ fundamentally from all other kinds of addiction, such as the kind that persists for some people? To accept this dichotomous view of addiction violates the basic principle of scientific parsimony, by which we should assume that the mechanisms at work in a large portion of cases are present in all cases. This is the same error made by psychologists who concede (without empirical provocation) that some alcoholics may indeed have constitutional traits that cause them to be alcoholic from their first drink even as research shows all alcoholics to be responsive to situational rewards and to subjective beliefs and expectations.

Preprogrammed Obesity

In his influential internal–external model of obesity, Schachter (1968) proposed that fat people had a different style of eating, one that depended on external cues to tell them when to eat or not. Unlike those of normal weight, Schachter's overweight subjects apparently could not rely on internal physiological signs to decide whether they were hungry. As a social psychologist, Schachter originally emphasized cognitive and environmental stimuli that encouraged the obese to eat. However, his model left open the question of the source of this insensitivity to somatic cues, suggesting the probability that this was an inherited trait. Schachter's (1971) view of the sources of overeating became increasingly physiological in nature when he began comparing the behavior of ventromedial-lesioned rats with obese humans. Several of Schachter's prominent students followed his lead in this direction. For example, Rodin (1981) eventually rejected the internal–external model (as most researchers have by now) with an eye toward locating a neurological basis for overeating. Meanwhile Nisbett (1972), another Schachter student, proposed an extremely popular model of body weight based on an internal regulatory mechanism, called set-point, which is inherited or determined by prenatal or early childhood eating habits.

Peele (1983e) analyzed Schachter's evolution into a purely biological theoretician in terms of biases Schachter and his students had shown all along against personality dynamics; against group, social, and cultural mechanisms; and against the role of values and complex cognitions in the choice of behavior. As a result, the Schachter group consistently failed to pick up discrepant indicators in their obesity research, some of which led eventually to the jettisoning of the internal–external model. For example, Schachter (1968) noted that normal-weight subjects did not eat more when they were hungry (as predicted) because they found the type of food and the time of day inappropriate for eating. In another study that had important implications, Nisbett (1968) discovered that formerly overweight subjects who were no longer obese behaved similarly to obese subjects in an eating experiment. That is, they ate more after having been forced to eat earlier than when they had not eaten before. Nisbett interpreted these results as showing that these subjects were unable to control their impulses to over-eat and could therefore not be expected to keep excess weight off.

This line of thinking was solidified in Nisbett's set-point hypothesis, which held that the hypothalamus was set to defend a specific body weight and that going below this weight stimulated a greater desire to eat. The idea that obese people could not lose weight, based on laboratory studies and the performance of clients in weight-loss programs, had been the central tenet in all of the Schachter group's work on obesity (cf. Schachter and Rodin 1974; Rodin 1981). Yet such pessimism seems an unlikely deduction from a study like Nisbett's (1968), in which subjects who had been obese and who continued to display an external eating style had indeed lost weight. When Schachter (1982) actually questioned people in the field about their weight-loss histories, he found remission was quite common in obesity: of all those interviewed who had ever been obese and who had tried to lose weight, 62.5 percent were currently at normal weight.

Schachter's serendipitous finding disputed the entire thrust of over a decade's research—namely, that people were locked into obesity by biological forces. The idea would not die easily, however. Another Schachter student and his colleague recorded Schachter's (1982) finding but dismissed its significance by indicating it was probably only those obese subjects who were above their set-points who had been able to lose weight in this study (Polivy and Herman 1983: 195–96). Polivy and Herman based this calculation on the estimate that from 60 to 70 percent of obese people were not obese in childhood. Their assertion requires that we believe that nearly all of the people in the Schachter study who have been overweight for reasons other than biological inheritance (and only these) had lost weight. Yet undoubtedly many in this category would remain fat for whatever presumably nonset-point reasons had caused them to become obese in the first place. Rather than being the underlying source of obesity its adherents had painted it to be, set-point now seemed not to be a major factor in most cases of overweight.

Polivy and Herman's (1983) description of their outlook did not reflect this understanding about set-point and obesity. Instead, they argued that "for the foreseeable future, we must resign ourselves to the fact that we have no reliable way to change the natural weight that an individual is blessed or cursed with" although "perhaps, as research progresses, we will be able to imagine such biological interventions—including even genetic manipulations" that will enable people to lose weight (p. 52). Polivy and Herman furthermore attributed binge overeating—the extreme of which is bulimia—to people's attempts to restrain their eating in the effort to go below their natural weight (see chapter 5). These researchers' work agrees with that of popular writers (Bennett and Gurin 1982) and the dominant research approaches in the field (Stunkard 1980) in maintaining a view of human eating and overeating that is essentially the same as that held by biological theorists of alcoholism and drug addiction toward drinking and drug consumption. In all cases, people are seen to be under the sway of invariant forces that, in the long run, they cannot hope to contravene.

Meanwhile, Garn and his coworkers (1979) have shown that similarities in weight levels among people who live together are a result of similar eating habits and energy expenditure. This "cohabitational effect" holds for husbands and wives and is the largest factor in weight similarities between parents and adopted offspring. People who live together who *become* fat do so together (Garn et al. 1979). The longer parents and their children live together (even when the children are age 40) the more they resemble each other in fatness. The longer parents and children live separately, the less pronounced such similarities become until they approach 0 at the extremes of separation (Garn, LaVelle, and Pilkington 1984). Garn, Pilkington, and LaVelle (1984), observing 2,500 people over two decades, found "those . . . who were lean to begin with generally increased in fatness level. Those who were obese to begin with generally decreased in fatness level" (pp. 90–91). "Natural weight" may be a very variable thing, influenced by the same social values and personal coping strategies that affect all behavior (Peele 1984a).

Interpersonal Addiction

The enormity of the implications of the genetic transmission of addictive impulses is driven home by several theories claiming that people are compelled by chemical imbalances to form unhealthy, compulsive, and self-destructive interpersonal relationships. Tennov (1979) maintained that such "limerent" people, who are in every other way indistinguishable from other people, have a biological propensity to fall head-over-heels in love and create disastrous romantic attachments. Liebowitz (1983) proposed that a failure in neurochemical regulation—similar to that hypothesized to cause manic-depressive reactions—leads people (almost exclusively women) to fall heatedly in love, often with inappropriate partners, and to become inordinately depressed when the relationships fail. These theories illustrate mainly the temptation to believe that compelling motivations must have a biological source and the desire to mechanize human differences, imperfections, and mysteries.

Global Biologic Theories of Addiction

Peele and Brodsky (1975), in the book *Love and Addiction*, also described interpersonal relationships as having addictive potential. The thrust of their version of interpersonal addiction, however, was exactly the opposite of that in Liebowitz (1983) and Tennov (1979): Peele and Brodsky's aim was to show that any powerful experience can form the object of an addiction for people predisposed by combinations of social and psychological factors. Their approach was antireductionist and rejected the deterministic force of inbred, biological, or other factors outside the realm of human consciousness and experience. Their work signaled a burst of addiction theorizing in areas other than substance abuse, the bulk of which—paradoxically— sought to analyze these phenomena at a biological level. The result has been the proliferation of biologic theories to account both for the range of compulsive involvements people form and for the tendency some people show to be addicted to a host of substances.

Smith (1981), a medical clinician, has posited the existence of an "addictive disease" to account for why so many of those who become addicted to one substance have prior histories of addiction to dissimilar substances (cf. "The Collision of Prevention and Treatment" 1984). It is impossible to explain—as Smith attempts to do—how innate, predetermined reactions could cause the same person to become excessively involved with substances as disparate as cocaine, alcohol, and Valium. In examining the generally strong positive correlations among tobacco, alcohol, and caffeine use, Istvan and Matarazzo (1984) explored the possibilities both that these substances are "linked by reciprocal activation mechanisms" and that they may be linked by their "pharmacologically antagonistic . . . effects" (p. 322). The evidence here is rather that substance abuse exceeds biological predictability. The fact of multiple addictions to myriad substances and nonsubstance-related involvements is *primary evidence against genetic and biological interpretations of addiction.*

Nonetheless, neuroscientists put forward biological theories of just this degree of universality. One researcher (Dunwiddie 1983: 17) noted that

> drugs of abuse such as opiates, amphetamine, and cocaine can pharmacologically stimulate many of the brain centers identified as reward centers. . . . On the other hand, there is considerable evidence that certain individuals have an enhanced liability for drug abuse, and frequently misuse a variety of seemingly unrelated drugs. It is interesting to speculate that for various reasons, perhaps genetic, perhaps developmental or environmental, the normal inputs to these hypothetical "reward pathways" function inadequately in such individuals. If this were the case, there may be a biological defect underlying poly-drug abuse.

While piling hypothesis upon hypothesis, Dunwiddie's description presents no actual research findings about drug abusers, nor does it present a specific hypothetical link between deficient "reward pathways" and "poly-drug abuse." It would seem the author thinks people who get less reward from drugs are more likely to abuse them.

Milkman and Sunderwirth's (1983) neurological model of addiction is not limited to drug abuse (as nothing in Dunwiddie's account would so limit it). These authors believe that addiction can result from any "self-induced changes in neurotransmission," where the more neurotransmitters that are involved "the faster the rate of firing," leading to the "elevated mood sought by cocaine users, for example" (p. 36). This account is actually a social-psychological one masquerading as neurological explanation, in which the writers introduce social and psychological factors such as peer influence and low self-esteem into their analysis by suggesting "that the enzyme produced by a given gene might influence hormones and neuro-transmitters in a way that contributes to the development of a personality potentially more susceptible to . . . peer group pressure" (p. 44). Both Dun-widdie's and Milkman and Sunderwirth's analyses cloak experiential events in neurological terminology without reference to any actual re-search that connects biological functioning to addictive behavior. These models represent almost ritualistic conceptions of scientific enterprise, and while their analyses are caricatures of contemporary scientific model build-ing, they come unfortunately close to mainstream assumptions about how the nature of addiction is to be interpreted.

Exposure Theories: Biological Models

The Inevitability of Narcotic Addiction

Alexander and Hadaway (1982) referred to the prevailing conception of nar-cotic addiction among both lay and scientific audiences—that it is the in-evitable consequence of regular narcotics use—as the exposure orientation. So entrenched is this viewpoint that Berridge and Edwards (1981)—while arguing that "Addiction is now defined as a disease because doctors have categorized it thus" (p. 150)—refer readers to an appendix in which Griffith Edwards declared "anyone who takes an opiate for a long enough period of time and in sufficient dose will become addicted" (p. 278). This view con-trasts with conventional beliefs about alcohol that would reject the same statement with the word "alcohol" substituted for "an opiate."

Underlying the exposure model is the assumption that the introduc-tion of a narcotic into the body causes metabolic adjustments that require continued and increasing dosages of the drug in order to avoid withdrawal. No alteration in cell metabolism has yet been linked with addiction, how-ever. The most prominent name in metabolic research and theory, Maurice Seevers, characterized efforts during the first sixty-five years of this century to create a model of addictive narcotic metabolism to be "exercises in se-mantics, or plain flights of imagination" (cited in Keller 1969: 5). Dole and

Nyswander (1967; cf. Dole 1980) are the modern champions of heroin addiction as a metabolic disease, although they have provided no explicit metabolic mechanism to account for it. Endorphin theorists have suggested that regular use of narcotics reduces the body's natural endorphin production, thus bringing about a reliance on the external chemical agent for ordinary pain relief (Goldstein 1976b; Snyder 1977).

This version of the relationship between endorphin production and addiction—like the one suggesting addicts inherit an endorphin deficiency (see above)—does not fit the data reviewed in chapter 1. Put baldly, exposure to narcotics does not lead to addiction, and addiction does not require the metabolic adjustments claimed for it. Those given the most reliable and purest supplies of narcotics, hospital patients, display—rather than an escalating need for the drug—a reduced desire for it. In an experimental trial of self-administration of morphine by hospitalized postoperative patients, subjects in the self-administration condition employed moderate, progressively declining doses of the drug (Bennett et al. 1982). That even infants and animals do not manifest an acquired hunger for opiates is the subject of chapter 4. On the other hand, compulsive street users of narcotics often do not show the expected hallmarks of addiction, such as withdrawal.

Endorphins and Nonnarcotic Addiction

Although unsubstantiated in the case of narcotic addiction, endorphin-related explanations have proved irresistible to those considering other addictive behavior. In particular, discoveries that food and alcohol—as well as narcotics—can affect endorphin levels have prompted speculation that these substances create self-perpetuating physical needs along the lines of those the narcotics supposedly produce. Weisz and Thompson (1983) summarized these theories while noting that "At this time there is not sufficient evidence to conclude that endogenous opioids mediate the addictive process of even one substance of abuse" (p. 314). Harold Kalant (1982), a distinguished neuroscientist, was more conclusive in his rejection of the idea that alcohol and narcotics could act according to the same neurological principles. "How do you explain . . . in pharmacological terms," he queried, that cross-tolerance occurs "between alcohol, which does not have specific receptors, and opiates, which do" (p. 12)?

To date, the most active speculation by clinicians about the role of endorphins has been in the area of compulsive running and exercising (cf. Sacks and Pargman 1984). If running stimulates endorphin production (Pargman and Baker 1980; Riggs 1981), then compulsive runners are presumed to undergo narcotic-like physical states to which they become addicted. Research on the relationship between endorphin levels, mood swings, and running motivation has failed to turn up regular relationships (Appenzeller et al. 1980; Colt et al. 1981; Hawley and Butterfield 1981). Markoff et al. (1982) and McMurray and his colleagues (1984) reported that exercising subjects treated with the narcotic-blocking agent naloxone reported no differences in perceived exertion and other physiological measures from those not treated. Addicted running—defined by inflexibility and insensitivity to internal and external conditions, running until the point of harming oneself, and being unable to quit without experiencing withdrawal—is no better explained by endorphin levels than is the self-destructiveness of the heroin addict (Peele 1981a).

Cigarette Addiction

Schachter (1977, 1978) has been the most vigorous proponent of the case that cigarette smokers are physically dependent on nicotine. They continue to smoke, in Schachter's view, in order to maintain habitual levels of cellular nicotine and to avoid withdrawal. Interestingly, Schachter (1971, 1977, 1978; Schachter and Rodin 1974) has proposed that different *types* of factors determine obesity and smoking: the former is due to an inbred predilection while the latter is due to an acquired constraint (avoidance of withdrawal). This is the same distinction drawn in traditional theories of alcohol and narcotic addiction. The distinction is necessary in order to defend biological causality in the case of excessiveness both in activities that are common to most people (eating and drinking alcohol) and activities that only some indulge in (smoking and narcotics use).

As with alcohol and narcotic use (see below), there is no prima facie reason why destructive eating and smoking habits need necessarily be dictated by separate classes of factors. Indeed, studies Schachter (1978) and his students conducted with cigarette smokers replicated results of Schachter and Rodin's (1974) work with the obese. For example, both smokers (while not smoking) and the obese were more distractible and more sensitive to negative stimuli like pain than were nonsmokers or normal-weight people. Both smokers and the obese apparently found their habits allayed anxieties and cushioned them against unpleasant stimulation (see Peele 1983e for further discussion). Furthermore, the apparent uniformity in the addictive use of cigarettes that Schachter's model suggests is illusory. Different smokers consume different amounts of tobacco and inhale different levels of nicotine; Best and Hakstian (1978) found such variations to reflect different motivations and settings for smoking and to suggest different circumstances under which smokers can quit.

Leventhal and Cleary (1980) have pointed out how inexact the regulation of nicotine intake is in Schachter's studies: Schachter (1977) found that a 77 percent reduction in nicotine level produced only a 17 to 25 percent increase in cigarette consumption. More tellingly, these authors reflected, "Schachter's model and studies ... assume a direct and automatic step from changes in plasma nicotine level to craving and [separately] smoking and say nothing about the mechanisms and experience that give rise to either" (p. 390). For example, Schachter (1978) himself noted that Orthodox Jews regularly withstood withdrawal to give up smoking during the sabbath. People's values do not cease to operate in the face of physiological forces. Later, in the same study in which he detected a high remission rate for obesity, Schachter (1982) discovered that over 60 percent of those in two communities who had tried to quit smoking had succeeded. They had ceased smoking on the average for 7.4 years. Heavier smokers—those consuming three or more packs of cigarettes a day—showed the same remission rate as lighter smokers. It would seem that Schachter's nicotine regulation model, which he designed primarily to explain why habitual smokers cannot quit, does not take the measure of the behavior in question. Whereas his formulation of nicotine addiction had emphasized the ineluctable, overwhelming nature of withdrawal from cigarettes, he now found the ability to overcome such withdrawal "to be relatively common" (p. 436). In other words, there needs to be some additional level of explanation for why people persist in smoking as well as for why they can give it up (Peele 1984a).

Alcohol Dependence

As narcotic addiction theorists have been forced by the recognition of individual variations in addiction to postulate innate neurochemical differences among people, alcoholism specialists have increasingly put forward the claim that alcohol problems are simply a function of excessive drinking. It might be said that conceptions of alcoholism and narcotic addiction not only are meeting on common ground but are passing each other going in opposite directions. The change in emphasis in alcoholism is in good part a result of the desire of psychologists and others to achieve rapprochement with disease theories (see chapter 2). It has led controlled-drinking clinicians to assert that a return to moderate drinking is impossible for the physically dependent alcoholic. Intriguingly, behaviorists have thus adopted Jellinek's (1960) formulation of the disease theory of alcoholism, in which he claimed that true (gamma) alcoholics could not control their drinking due to their physical dependence. (In his 1960 volume Jellinek was ambiguous about the extent to which this disability was inbred and irreversible, the traditional claims made by AA.)

The concept of alcohol dependence has been elaborated by a group of British researchers (Edwards and Gross 1976; Hodgson et al. 1978). In the same breath, it attempts to replace the disease theory (whose defects are more broadly agreed upon in Great Britain than in the United States) while rescuing important disease notions (see critique by Shaw 1979). The alcohol-dependence syndrome resembles the disease of alcoholism in conceiving of drinking problems as a condition that can be identified in isolation from the drinker's psychological state and situation and as one that endures beyond the alcoholic's active drinking. Severity of dependence is assessed purely in terms of how much people habitually drink and the physical consequences of this drinking (Hodgson et al. 1978), without regard for their reasons for drinking or cultural, social, and other environmental factors. Thus, those who are heavily dependent are thought to have a stable condition that makes their return to moderate drinking unlikely.

The alcohol-dependence syndrome suffers from the tension of acknowledging the complexity of alcoholic behavior. As its supporters note, "the control of drinking, like any other behavior, is a function of cues and consequences, of set and setting, of psychological and social variables; in short, control, or loss of it, is a function of the way in which the alcoholic construes his situation" (Hodgson et al. 1979: 380). Within this framework, Hodgson et al. regard withdrawal symptoms to be a strong cue for alcoholics to return to heavy drinking. However, the appearance of withdrawal in alcoholism is itself variable and subject to drinkers' subjective constructions. Moreover, such symptoms are regularly overcome by alcoholics in their drinking careers and in any case are limited in duration. Avoidance of withdrawal simply cannot account for continued drinking (see Mello and Mendelson 1977). There is a more basic objection yet to the alcohol dependence concept. In his critique of "the concept of drug dependence as a state of chronic exposure to a drug," Kalant (1982) remonstrated that dependence concepts have "ignored the most fundamental question—why a person having experienced the effect of a drug would want to go back again and again to reproduce that chronic state" (p. 12).

Whereas speculation about human drug dependence has been influenced greatly by generalizations from animal research (generalizations that are largely incorrect, see chapter 4), the alcohol-dependence syndrome has had to fly in the face of animal research. It is difficult to get rats to drink alcohol in the laboratory. In his seminal research, Falk (1981) was able to induce such drinking through the imposition of intermittent feeding schedules that the animals find highly uncomfortable. In this condition, the rats drink heavily but also indulge in excessive and self-destructive behavior of many kinds. All such behavior—including drinking—depends strictly on the continuation of this feeding schedule and disappears as soon as normal feeding opportunities are restored. Thus, for rats that had been alcohol-dependent, Tang et al. (1982) reported "a history of ethanol overindulgence was not a sufficient condition for the maintenance of overdrinking" (p. 155).

On the basis of animal research, at least, alcohol dependence seems to be strongly state-dependent rather than a persistent characteristic of the organism. Rather than being contradicted by human behavior, this phenomenon may be even more pronounced for humans. The supposed biological basis of drinking behavior in the alcohol dependence model is thus unable to deal with major aspects of alcoholism. As one of the authors (Gross 1977: 121) of the alcohol-dependence syndrome observed:

> The foundation is set for the progression of the alcohol dependence syndrome by virtue of its biologically intensifying itself. One would think that, once caught up in the process, the individual could not be extricated. However, and for reasons poorly understood, the reality is otherwise. Many, perhaps most, do free themselves.

Control of Alcohol Supply

Sociological theory and research has been the main counterpoint to disease theories of alcoholism (Room 1983) and has made decisive contributions in depicting alcoholism as a social construction, in discrediting the idea that drinking problems can be organized into medical entities, and in disproving empirical claims regarding such bedrock disease notions as inevitable loss of control and reliable stages in the progress of alcoholism (see chapter 2). Yet some sociologists have also been uncomfortable with the idea that social beliefs and cultural customs affect levels of drinking problems (Room 1976). In place of such sociocultural interpretations of alcoholism, sociology as a field has now largely adopted a supply-of-alcohol perspective based on findings that alcohol consumption in a society is distributed in a unimodal, lognormal curve (Room 1984).

Since a large proportion of the alcohol available is drunk by those at the extreme end of this skewed curve, increases or decreases in alcohol availability are believed to push many drinkers above or below what might be considered a heavy and dangerous drinking level. Alcohol supply policy recommendations thus include raising taxes on liquor to lower overall consumption. The alcohol supply model is most certainly not a biological theory and does not itself lead to theoretical derivations about alcohol metabolism. Yet as Room (1984: 304) has pointed out, it can be rationalized with the disease-theory view that those at the extreme of the curve have lost control of their drinking. In fact, the model fits best with the alcohol-dependence syndrome, where alcoholic behavior is conceived principally to be the result of excessive consumption.

At the same time, the alcohol-supply view violates a number of sociologically based findings. Beauchamp (1980), for example, propounded the alcohol-supply argument while reporting that Americans consumed from two to three or more times as much alcohol per capita in the late eighteenth century as they do today and yet had fewer alcohol problems in the colonial period. Nor does the supply model make good sense of discontinuities in consumption within a given region. Alcohol problems in France are centered in the nonwinegrowing regions that must import more expensive alcoholic beverages (Prial 1984). In the United States, fundamentalist Protestant sects consume less alcohol per capita because many of these groups abstain. However, these groups—and the relatively dry regions of the South and Midwest—also have higher alcoholism rates and incidences of binge drinking (Armor et al. 1978; Cahalan and Room 1974). How also do the Jews, located principally in the highest consumption areas in the country (urban and Eastern), maintain an alcoholism rate one-tenth or less than the nationwide rate (Glassner and Berg 1980)? On the policy side, Room (1984) noted that efforts to curtail supplies have often backfired and led to greater binges in consumption.

At a psychological level, the idea that people incur the costs of alcoholism simply because they have more alcohol available to them makes little sense. For example, what exactly is the impact on the alcoholic of making supplies harder to obtain? The result of limiting the ready medical supply of narcotics was to turn many men into alcoholics (O'Donnell 1969). Vaillant (1983) found that abstaining alcoholics were highly prone to abuse other substances or to form alternate compulsive involvements. Here the sociological level of analysis, like the metabolic, suffers from a lack of a grasp of the individual's overall addictive ecology. The popularity of alcohol-supply ideas within a community noted for its opposition to disease ideas may make one pessimistic about whether there still can remain any intellectual resistance to metabolic theories of alcoholism and addiction.

Exposure Theories: Conditioning Models

Conditioning theories hold that addiction is the cumulative result of the reinforcement of drug administration. The central tenet of conditioning theories is that (Donegan et al. 1983: 112):

> To say that a substance is used at a level considered to be excessive by the standards of the individual or society and that reducing the level of use is difficult is one way of saying that the substance has gained considerable control over the individual's behavior. In the language of behavior theory, the substance acts as a powerful reinforcer: behaviors instrumental in obtaining the substance become more frequent, vigorous, or persistent.

Conditioning theories offer the potential for considering all excessive activities along with drug abuse within a single framework, that of highly rewarding behavior. Originally developed to explain narcotic addiction (cf. Woods and Schuster 1971), reinforcement models have been applied to most popular psychoactive drugs and to nondrug addictions like gambling and overeating (Donegan et al. 1983). Solomon (1980), in a broadly influential approach he calls the opponent-process model of motivation, has extended conditioning principles to every pleasurable and compulsive activity. The complex processes that characterize learning also allow increased flexibility in describing addictive behavior. In classical conditioning, previously neutral stimuli become associated with reactions brought on in their presence by a primary reinforcer. Thus an addict who relapses can be conceived to have had his craving for the addiction reinstated by exposure to the settings in which he previously used drugs (Wikler 1973; S. Siegel 1979, 1983).

The Myth of the Universal Reinforcer: The Inherent Pleasurableness of Narcotics

Conditioning theories leave open one critical question: What is a reinforcing activity? The assumption in narcotic addiction is usually that the drug provides an inherent, biologic reward and/or that it has strong reinforcement value due to its prevention of withdrawal pain (Wikler 1973). This assumption is part of a wide range of theories of addiction (cf. Bejerot 1980; Dole 1972; Goldstein 1976a; McAuliffe and Gordon 1974; Wilker 1973). Indeed, the belief that narcotics are irresistible to any organism that, once having tried them, has free access to drugs is the epitome of the exposure model of addiction. The body of work thought best to demonstrate the truth of this belief is the observation that laboratory animals can readily be induced to ingest narcotics and other drugs. Chapter 4 shows this view to be unfounded: drug use is no more self-perpetuating for animals than it is for humans. No less a biological determinist than Dole (1980) has now declared that "most animals cannot be made into addicts. . . . Although the pharmacological effects of addictive substances injected into animals are quite similar to those seen in human beings, animals generally avoid such drugs when they are given a choice" (p. 142).

If the behavior of laboratory animals is not locked in by drug action, how is it possible for human beings to become addicted and lose the possibility of choice? One proposal to account for the feverish pursuit of drugs and other human involvements has been that these experiences bring inordinate pleasure, or euphoria. The idea that pleasure is the primary reinforcement in addiction is present in several theories (Bejerot 1980; Hatterer 1980; McAuliffe and Gordon 1974) and most especially has a central role in Solomon's (1980) opponent-process model. The ultimate source of this idea has been the supposedly intense euphoria that narcotics, particularly heroin, produce, a euphoria for which normal experience offers no near counterpart. In the popular image of heroin use and its effects, euphoria seems the only possible inducement for using a drug that is the ultimate symbol of self-destructiveness.

Some users describe euphoric experiences from taking heroin, and McAuliffe and Gordon's (1974) interviews with addicts revealed this to be a primary motivation for continuing to use the drug. Other research contests this notion vigorously. Zinberg and his colleagues have interviewed a large number of addicts and other heroin users over several decades and have found the McAuliffe and Gordon work to be extremely naive. "Our interviews have revealed that after prolonged heroin use the subjects experience a 'desirable' consciousness change induced by the drug. This change is characterized by increased emotional distance from external stimuli and internal response, but it is a long way from euphoria" (Zinberg et al. 1978: 19). In a survey of British Columbian addicts (cited in Brecher 1972: 12), seventy-one addicts asked to check their mood after taking heroin gave the following responses: Eight found the heroin experience to be "thrilling" and eleven found it "joyful" or "jolly," while sixty-five reported it "relaxed" them and fifty-three used it to "relieve worry"

Applying labels such as "pleasurable" or "euphoric" to addictive drugs like alcohol, barbiturates, and narcotics seems paradoxical, since as depressants they lessen intensity of sensation. For example, narcotics are antiaphrodisiacs whose use frequently leads to sexual dysfunction. When naive subjects are exposed to narcotics, usually in the hospital, they react with indifference or actually find the experience unpleasant (Beecher 1959; Jaffe and Martin 1980; Kolb 1962; Lasagna et al. 1955; Smith and Beecher 1962). Chein et al. (1964) noted the very special conditions under which addicts found narcotic effects to be pleasurable: "It is . . . not an enjoyment of anything positive at all, and that it should be thought of as a 'high' stands as mute testimony to the utter destitution of the life of the addict with respect to the achievement of positive pleasures and of its repletion with frustration and unresolvable tension" (in Shaffer and Burglass 1981: 99). Alcoholics' drinking does not conform any better to a pleasure model: "The traditional belief that alcoholism is maintained primarily as a function of its rewarding or euphorigenic consequences is not consistent with the clinical data" as "alcoholics become progressively more dysphoric, anxious, agitated and depressed during chronic intoxication" (Mendelson and Mello 1979b: 12–13).

The opposite picture—the rejection of positive drug rewards by those in a position to pursue more lasting satisfactions—is evident in a study of volunteer subjects' reactions to amphetamines (Johanson and Uhlenhuth 1981). The subjects originally reported the drug elevated their moods and preferred it to a placebo. After three successive administrations of the drug over several days, however, the subjects' preference for the amphetamine disappeared even though they noted the same mood changes from its use. "The positive mood effects, which are usually assumed to be the basis of the reinforcing effect of stimulants, . . . were not sufficient for the maintenance of drug taking, probably because during the period of drug action these subjects were continuing their normal, daily activities." The drug state interfered with the rewards they derived from these activities, and thus, "in their natural habitat these subjects showed by their preference changes that they were uninterested in continuing to savor the mood effects" (Falk 1983: 388).

Chein et al. (1964) noted that when ordinary subjects or patients find narcotics pleasurable they still do not become compulsive drug users and that a percentage of addicts find heroin to be extremely unpleasant at first but nonetheless persist in taking drugs until they became addicted. All these examples make clear that drugs are not inherently rewarding, that their effects depend on the individual's overall experience and setting, and that the choice of returning to a state—even one experienced as positive— depends on the individual's values and perceived alternatives. Reductionist models have no hope of accounting for these complexities in addiction, as illustrated by the most widely deployed of such models, Solomon's (1980) opponent-process view of conditioning.

Solomon's model draws an elaborate connection between the degree of pleasure a given state produces and its subsequent capacity to inspire withdrawal. The model proposes that any stimulus leading to a distinct mood state eventuates in an opposite reaction, or opponent process. This process is simply the homeostatic function of the nervous system, much the same way that presenting a visual stimulus leads to an after-image of a complementary color. The stronger and the greater the number of repetitions of the initial state, the more powerful the opponent reaction and the more rapid its onset after the first stimulus ceases. Eventually, the opponent reaction comes to dominate the process. With narcotics and other powerful mood-arousing involvements such as love, Solomon proposes, an initial positive mood is replaced as the individual's primary motivation for re-experiencing the stimulus by the desire to avoid the negative, or withdrawal state.

Solomon and Corbit (1973, 1974) constructed this model from experimental evidence with laboratory animals. As we have seen, neither the positive feelings it posits from narcotics use nor the traumatic withdrawal it imagines can account for human drug taking. Moreover, the model's mechanistic version of neurological sources of motivation creates a Platonic ideal of pleasure as existing independent of situation, personality, or cultural milieu. The model likewise holds that a person's response to this objective degree of pleasure (or else equally specifiable withdrawal pain) is a predetermined constant. People in fact display all sorts of differences in how ardently they pursue immediate pleasure or how willing they are to endure discomfort. For example, people vary in their willingness to delay gratification (Mischel 1974). Consider that most people find hot fudge sundaes and devil's food cake to be extremely enjoyable and yet only a very few people eat such foods without restraint. It simply isn't plausible that the main difference between compulsive and normal eaters is that the former enjoy the taste of food more or suffer greater withdrawal agony when not stuffing themselves.

Solomon uses the opponent-process model to explain why some lovers cannot tolerate the briefest of partings. Yet this separation anxiety seems less a measure of depth of feeling and length of attachment than of the desperation and insecurity of a relationship, which Peele and Brodsky (1975) called addictive love. For example, Shakespeare's Romeo and Juliet prefer to die rather than be parted. This state does not result from accumulated intimacies that were eventually replaced by negative sensations, as Solomon's model predicts. Shakespeare's lovers cannot bear to part from the start. At the time when they both commit suicide, they have met only a handful of times, with most of their meetings having been brief and without physical contact. The kinds of relationships that lead to the withdrawal extremes of murder and suicide when the relationship is threatened rarely coincide with notions of ideal love affairs. Such couplings usually involve lovers (or at least one lover) who have histories of excessive devotion and self-destructive affairs and whose feeling that life is otherwise bleak and unrewarding has preceded the addictive relationship (Peele and Brodsky 1975).

Associative Learning in Addiction

Classical conditioning principles suggest the possibilities that settings and stimuli associated with drug use either become reinforcing in themselves or can set off withdrawal and craving for the drug that lead to relapse. The first principle, secondary reinforcement, can explain the importance of ritual in addiction, since actions like self-injection acquire some of the reward value of the narcotics they have been used to administer. Conditioned craving leading to relapse would appear when the addict encountered settings or other stimuli that were previously connected with drug use or withdrawal (O'Brien 1975; S. Siegel 1979; Wikler 1973). For example, Siegel (1983) applied conditioning theory to explain why the Vietnam soldier addicts who most often relapsed after their return home were those who had abused drugs or narcotics before going to Asia (Robins et al. 1974). Only these men would be exposed to familiar drug-taking environments when they returned home that set off the withdrawal that in turn required them to self-administer a narcotic (cf. O'Brien et al. 1980; Wikler 1980).

These ingenious conditioning formulations of human drug use have been inspired by laboratory studies of animals and human addicts (O'Brien 1975; O'Brien et al. 1977; Siegel 1975; Wilker and Pescor 1967). For example, Teasdale (1973) demonstrated that addicts showed greater physical and emotional responses to opiate-related pictures than to neutral ones. However, the conditioned craving and withdrawal such studies uncover are by the evidence minor motivations in human relapse. In the laboratory, Solomon has been able to create negative opponent-process states that last for seconds, minutes, or at most days. O'Brien et al. (1977) and Siegel (1975) have found that responses associated with narcotic injections in humans and rats that can be conditioned to neutral stimuli are extinguished almost immediately when the stimuli are presented on unrewarded trials (that is, without a narcotic).

What is more important, these laboratory findings do not appear relevant to addicted street behavior. O'Brien (1975) reported a case of an addict just out of prison who became nauseated in a neighborhood where he frequently had experienced withdrawal symptoms—a reaction that led him to buy and inject some heroin. This case has been described so often that, in its repetition, it seems a typical occurrence (see Hodgson and Miller 1982: 15; Siegel 1983: 228). Yet it is actually a novelty. McAuliffe and Gordon (1974) reported that "We have interviewed 60 addicts concerning their many relapses, and we could find only one who had ever responded to conditioned withdrawal symptoms by relapsing" (p. 803). In their thorough study of the causes of relapse, Marlatt and Gordon (1980) found heroin addicts rarely reported postaddiction withdrawal to be the reason they relapsed. None of the cigarette smokers or alcoholics Marlatt and Gordon interviewed listed withdrawal symptoms as the cause of their relapse.

Conditioned responses are particularly unlikely to account for relapse, since most former addicts do not relapse to addiction after they use a drug again. Schachter (1982) found that former smokers would smoke at a party but not return to regular smoking. Vaillant (1983) noted that "relatively few men with long periods of abstinence had never taken another drink" (p. 184). Half of the addicted Vietnam soldiers used a narcotic at home, but only a minority became readdicted (Robins et al. 1975). Waldorf's (1983) investigation of heroin addicts who quit on their own found ex-addicts typically injected themselves with heroin after licking the habit to prove to themselves and others that they were no longer hooked. All these data point out that the unconditioned stimulus (actual drug use) is not sufficient provocation for a return to addiction. It is impossible that the weaker conditioned stimuli could provide sufficient motivation.

For Siegel and others who have analyzed the Vietnam remission data in conditioning terms, the crucial variable is simply situational change. All situational changes are equivalent in terms of this model as long as drugs have been taken in one environment and not the other, since then the new environment does not evoke conditioned withdrawal symptoms. This has prompted Siegel et al. to recommend a fresh setting as the best remedy for addiction. Yet it would certainly seem that other features of this new setting would be at least as important as familiarity for affecting addiction. Rats habituated to morphine in a diverse, social environment refused the drug in the same environment when offered a choice, while caged, isolated rats on the same presentation schedule continued to consume the morphine (Alexander et al. 1978). Zinberg and Robertson (1972) reported that addicts' withdrawal symptoms disappeared in a treatment environment where withdrawal was not accepted, while their withdrawal was exacerbated in other environments, such as prison, where it was expected and tolerated.

The Role of Cognition in Conditioning

Addicts and alcoholics—whether treated or untreated—who achieve remission often do experience important changes in their environments. These changes frequently result, however, from self-initiated attempts to escape the addiction and other life problems. There are also those who modify addictive habits without drastically rearranging their lives. This is especially true for those addicted to less socially disapproved substances like cigarettes but also holds for a distinct minority of former alcoholics and heroin addicts. Modification of the addict's environmental stimuli appears in these cases to be an entirely internal, or psychological process. Siegel (1979) recognized this role for cognitive stimuli when he explained why some Vietnam veterans relapsed without returning to old drug haunts. He speculated that these men had been "talking about drugs in group therapy," "seeing pictures of drugs and 'works,'" or just "imagining themselves injecting drugs in their customary setting" (p. 158).

The conditioned responses that occur with regard to subjective experience and as a result of environmental changes that addicts themselves bring about cast conditioning theories in a whole new light, where these responses seem an adjunct to individual self-control and motivation to change rather than the sources of such change. Moreover, conditioning theories in addiction are limited by their inability to convey the meaning the individual attaches to his or her behavior and environment. As a result, conditioning theories must be made so complex and ad hoc to explain the complexities of human drug taking that they lose the precision and predictive power that are their supposed scientific assets. They seem destined to suffer the same fate as did the U.S. intervention in Vietnam, the event that has prompted so much speculation about the role of conditioning in drug use. In both cases rationales become so cumbersome and counterproductive in the effort to respond to information from the field that they must collapse of their own weight.

Siegel's utilization of cognitive variables to account for conditioning anomalies observed in heroin use is part of a venerable tradition. The first explicitly cognitive conditioning model in addiction was Lindesmith's (1968, originally published in 1947), which contended that to be addicted the heroin user must be aware that the withdrawal pain he suffers is due to cessation of drug use and that readministering the drug will alleviate this pain. Thus so many nineteenth century narcotic users may have failed to become addicted because they simply didn't know that narcotics were addicting! Lindesmith elaborated how cognitions affect addiction in connection with hospital patients. Patients do realize they are taking a narcotic and understand the drug's effects, but they associate these effects with their illness. When they leave the hospital (or later when their prescription for painkillers runs out) they know any discomfort will be temporary and a necessary part of convalescence and thus they do not become addicted.

We may wonder why Lindesmith reserved the role of cognition in his model for this very limited number of ideas. For example, would not a hospital patient's belief that continued narcotic use was harmful or that other opportunities outweighed the option of giving in to the drug's effects be a part of the decision not to continue using narcotics? Such matters as self-conception, perceived alternatives, and values against drug intoxication and illicit activity would naturally seem to influence the individual's choices. It is not only the decision whether to continue using a drug that cognitions, values, and situational pressures and opportunities determine, however. They also determine how the drug's effects and withdrawal from these effects will be experienced. Contrary to Lindesmith's scheme, people who recover from illnesses almost never acknowledge craving narcotics outside the hospital (Zinberg 1974).

Adaptation Theories

Social Learning and Adaptation

Conventional conditioning models cannot make sense of drug behavior because they circumvent the psychological, environmental, and social nexus of which drug use is a part. One branch of conditioning theory, social-learning theory (Bandura 1977b), has opened itself to the subjective elements of reinforcement. For example, Bandura described how a psychotic who continued his delusional behavior in order to ward off invisible terrors was acting in line with a reinforcement schedule that was efficacious despite its existing solely in the individual's mind. The essential insight that reinforcers gain meaning only from a given human context enables us to understand (1) why different people react differently to the same drugs, (2) how people can modify these reactions through their own efforts, and (3) how people's relationships with their environments determine drug reactions rather than vice versa.

Social-learning theorists have been especially active in alcoholism, where they have analyzed how alcoholics' expectations and beliefs about what alcohol will do for them influence the rewards and behaviors associated with drinking (Marlatt 1978; Wilson 1981). Yet it has also been social-learning theorists who have launched the alcohol-dependence syndrome and who seem to feel subjective interpretation is far less important than the pharmacological effects of alcohol in causing drinking problems (Hodgson et al. 1978, 1979). This lacuna in their theorizing is most noticeable in the inability of modern social-learning theorists to make sense out of cultural variations in drinking styles and experiences (Shaw 1979). Whereas McClelland et al. (1972) offered an experiential bridge between individual and cultural conceptions about alcohol (see chapter 5), behaviorists have regularly rejected this kind of synthesis in favor of direct observations and objective measurements of alcoholic behavior (embodied by Mendelson and Mello 1979b).

In another area of social-learning theory, Leventhal and Cleary (1980) proposed "that the smoker is regulating emotional states and that nicotine levels are being regulated because certain emotional states have been conditioned to them in a variety of settings" (p. 391). In this way they hoped to "provide a mechanism for integrating and sustaining the combination of external stimulus cues, internal stimulus cues, and a variety of reactions including subjective emotional experience . . . with smoking" (p. 393). In other words, any number of levels of factors, from past experience to current setting to idiosyncratic thoughts, can influence the person's associations with smoking and subsequent behavior. In creating a conditioning model as complex as this one in order to account for behavior, however, the authors may have been putting the cart before the horse. Instead of conceiving of cognition and experience as components of conditioning, it seems easier to say that addiction involves cognitive and emotional regulation to which past conditioning contributes. In this view, addiction is an effort by an individual to adapt to internal and external needs, an effort in which a drug's effects (or some other experience) serve a desired function.

Social-Psychological Adaptation

Studies that have questioned users about their reasons for continued drug-taking or that have explored the situations of street users have revealed crucial, self-aware purposes for drug use and a reliance on drug effects as an effort to adapt to internal needs and external pressures. Theoretical developments based on these investigations have focused on the psychodynamics of drug reliance. Such theories describe drug use in terms of its ability to resolve ego deficiencies or other psychological deficits—brought on, for example, by lack of maternal love (Rado 1933). In recent years theorizing of this sort has become broader: less wedded to specific child-rearing deficits, more accepting of a range of psychological functions for drug use, and including other substances besides narcotics (cf. Greaves 1974; Kaplan and Wieder 1974; Khantzian 1975; Krystal and Raskin 1970; Wurmser 1978).

These approaches developed in response to the clearcut finding that very few of those exposed to a drug, even over extended periods, came to rely on it as a life-organizing principle. What they failed to explain adequately is the great variability of reliance on drugs and addiction in the same individuals over situations and life span. If a given personality structure led to the need for an specific kind of drug, why then did the same people wean themselves from the drug? Why did others with comparable personalities not become wedded to the same substances? What was obvious in the case of narcotic addiction was its strong association with certain social groups and lifestyles (Gay et al. 1973; Rubington 1967). Efforts to incorporate this level of social reality led to higher-order theories that went beyond purely psychological dynamics to combine social and psychological factors in drug use (Ausubel 1961; Chein et al. 1964; McClelland et al. 1972; Winick 1962; Zinberg 1981).

Such social-psychological theories addressed the function of drug use in adolescent and postadolescent life stages as a way of preserving childhood and avoiding adult conflicts (Chein et al. 1964; Winick 1962). They also dealt with the availability of drugs in certain cultures and the predisposing social pressures toward their use (Ausubel 1961; Gay et al. 1973). Finally, they presented the impact of social ritual on the meaning and style of use that a person in a given setting adopted (Becker 1963; Zinberg et al. 1977). What ultimately limited these theories was their lack of a formulation of the nature of addiction. While nearly all of them minimized the role of physiological adjustments in the craving and response to withdrawal that signify addiction (Ausubel 1961; Chein et al. 1964; Zinberg 1984), they provided little in the way of basic mechanisms to account for the dynamics of addiction.

As a result, the social-psychological literature exists in almost total isolation from the pharmacological and learning literature on addiction. Because they do not confront laboratory-based models directly, social-psychological theorists are forced to rely on biological concepts that their own data and ideas contradict (as illustrated by the discussion, in chapter 1, of Zinberg et al. 1978). This exaggerated deference to pharmacological constructs makes these theorists reluctant to incorporate a cultural dimension as a basic element in addiction or to explore the meaning of nonsubstance addictions—surprisingly so, given that their own emphasis on the socially and psychologically adaptive functions of drugs would seem to apply equally well to other involvements. What may curtail the social and psychological analysis of addiction most is the inappropriate meekness and limited scientific aspirations of those best suited to extend the boundaries of addiction theory in this direction. Such meekness certainly does not characterize modern conditioning and biological theorizing.

The Requirements of a Successful Theory of Addiction

A successful addiction model must synthesize pharmacological, experiential, cultural, situational, and personality components in a fluid and seamless description of addictive motivation. It must account for why a drug is more addictive in one society than another, addictive for one individual and not another, and addictive for the same individual at one time and not another (Peele 1980). The model must make sense out of the essentially similar behavior that takes place with all compulsive involvements. In addition, the model must adequately describe the cycle of increasing yet dysfunctional reliance on an involvement until the involvement overwhelms other reinforcements available to the individual.

Finally, in assaying these already formidable tasks, a satisfactory model must be faithful to lived human experience. Psychodynamic theories of addiction are strongest in their rich explorations of the internal, experiential space of their subject matter. Likewise, disease theories—while seriously misrepresenting the nature and constancy of addictive behavior and feelings—are based on actual human experiences that must be explained. This last requirement may seem the most difficult of all. One may wonder whether models built on social-psychological and experiential dynamics make any sense when confronted with the behavior of laboratory animals or newly born infants.

4
Adult, Infant, and Animal Addiction

Bruce K. Alexander
Stanton Peele
Patricia F. Hadaway
Stanley J. Morse
Archie Brodsky
and Barry L. Beyerstein

The idea that organisms lacking complex cognitions and social environments—namely, caged animals and human infants—become addicted when exposed to narcotics has been a primary argument for
the purely physiological genesis of addiction. The data on fetuses born to
mothers using narcotics and other drugs and on laboratory animals that are
administered such drugs are complicated and conflicting: primarily they
show that the appearance of addiction in these cases depends on a range of
psychological and situational variables. These facts tend to disprove a basic
irreducible concept of biological addiction. This chapter attempts both to
formulate a realistic model of the factors that play a role in addiction for
organisms other than adult human beings and to make clear just how pro-
found a phenomenon human addiction really is. There is no exact equivalent among animals or newborn babies to either the addiction, or the resistance to it, that appear in a fully developed human being.

The Effect on the Infant of Mother's Drug Use

Infant Narcotic Withdrawal

The idea of the addiction of the fetus to narcotics and the appearance of
postpartum withdrawal is an unquestioned fact for the public and most
addiction professionals and researchers. The appearance of infant withdrawal has been regularly observed since the 1970s under a very specific set
of research conditions. Only women known to be addicts (and who often
label themselves as such), whose drug use and lifestyle are clearly aberrant,
and who might themselves be undergoing withdrawal in the hospital alert
investigators to the possibility of addicted newborns. By definition, con-

trolled narcotics users would be excluded from this group. Once identified, high-risk subjects (mothers and children) are evaluated carefully for any signs of abnormality. Once observed, to what might these symptoms be attributed? Mothers' drug abuse tends to be global and indiscriminate, involving many licit and illicit substances. Moreover, addicts are less aware of and concerned about health maintenance in general. The women whose children are observed are thus likely to be only those whose overall lifestyle is degraded and marked by multiple drug abuse and a lack of regard for health.

Yet even under such conditions, withdrawal rarely constitutes a distinct pathological entity. The popular portrayal of infant addiction is invariably of a severe and life-threatening condition; Cummings (1979) in his presidential address to the American Psychological Association claimed, without citation, that 92 percent of the children born to heroin-addicted mothers manifested severe withdrawal. In fact, in 75 to 90 percent of cases withdrawal is nonexistent or difficult to detect with such mothers (Kron et al. 1975). Ostrea et al. (1975) did not find a single case of convulsions in 198 cases they studied. What is labeled as infant withdrawal is instead a variable syndrome defined as a "generalized disorder characterized by signs and symptoms of central nervous system excitation" (Desmond and Wilson 1975: 113). Typical indicators are undue crying and ineffective feedings followed cyclically by restless periods of sleep.

There is little or no direct evidence for attributing this distress to narcotic withdrawal. It does not vary in occurrence or severity with the heroin dosage intake reported by the mother (Zelson 1975) or the drug level measured in the infant's or mother's urine or in the cord blood (Ostrea et al. 1975). Rather than comprising a pronounced medical entity, "there are difficulties in diagnosing the narcotic withdrawal syndrome in the absence of prior knowledge of maternal addiction" (Kron et al. 1975: 258). Desmond and Wilson (1975) observed the severity of infant narcotic withdrawal to vary with other metabolic disturbances and particularly with low birth weight. Furthermore, the symptoms they found tended to persist or reappear, indicating more permanent damage rather than withdrawal. These investigators saw the problems of the newborn of heroin addicts to include damage from drug impurities and the cumulative effects of their mothers' lifestyles (many of the mothers of these infants were prostitutes, for whom infection is a danger along with polydrug use and other unhealthy habits).

Emotional factors have been shown to play a role in severity of neonatal withdrawal. Davis and Shanks (1975) found that—along with protein malnutrition, neglected health, and self-destructive behavior—addicted mothers' guilt and depression contributed to the problematic behavior of their infants. Mothers in this study were especially distressed by nonnutritive sucking, a major symptom of infant withdrawal. Yet ineffective feedings are frequently reported by nonaddicted mothers and the anxiety and personal problems manifested by the addicted women would be especially likely to produce this problem. Infants are also more likely to be separated from addicted mothers in the hospital. Maternal contact has been shown to have a reassuring and beneficial impact for the baby and to exacerbate behaviors that could be described as withdrawal (Klaus and Kennell 1981). A conventional research design involving blind observation of narcotics- and nonnarcotics-using mothers would thus not only allow most infants of using mothers to pass undetected (as in Kron et al. 1975) but would label as undergoing withdrawal at least some babies of nonnarcotics users (see below).

It is true, for a host of reasons that are difficult to separate, that both narcotics-using mothers and their offspring are likely to experience greater-than-average amounts of postpartum trauma. Coppolillo (1975) suggested an interactive model of what has been labeled withdrawal based on disturbances in addicted mothers' relationships with their newborn. Addicted mothers in this study were unusually likely to be upset by their children and to derive less than ordinary amounts of maternal gratification, creating a cycle of abnormal and nonnurturing behavior. Such a complex model of withdrawn neonate functioning is a far cry from the specific biological addiction syndrome claimed to exist independent of infant (or adult) social and psychological setting. We may even recall that infants were commonly dosed with paregoric and other opium preparations in the nineteenth century in the United States and England (Berridge and Edwards 1981; Courtwright 1982) without parents' being aware of the phenomenon of infant withdrawal. Nonetheless, all public accounts of infant withdrawal depict it in the most monochromatic, lurid light possible, as if to recognize its frequent mildness or its complexity would encourage more pregnant women to take illicit narcotics (see, for a recent account, "Addicted Mothers and Babies" 1984).

Fetal Alcohol Syndrome

Desmond and Wilson's (1975) analysis of neonate withdrawal as a misidentification of more basic damage to the fetus from a variety of causes has proved prescient for later developments in the field. In the mid 1970s and increasingly into the 1980s there was a shift in concern from neonatal narcotic withdrawal to the effects of alcohol on the fetus. The term "fetal alcohol syndrome" (FAS) was applied to abnormalities in offspring of alcoholic women, most of whom had serious alcohol-related health problems (Hanson et al. 1976; Jones and Smith 1973). FAS incorporates a large number of observed deficits in such infants, including increased mortality, birth defects, and smaller size to "failure to thrive, hyperirritability and motor dysfunction" (Cushner 1981: 202). The syndrome has been conceived from the beginning as involving long-term organic damage, even though reported symptoms are often similar to those attributed to heroin withdrawal. Also from the onset of this research, complications have been noted in separating the factors contributing to the appearance of FAS, particularly because heavy drinking and heavy smoking are strongly correlated (Ouellette et al. 1977).

Research on FAS has advanced to include a more general, multivariate framework where other factors—such as time during the woman's pregnancy when drinking occurred—are taken into account. In addition, earlier dramatic reports about FAS have been replaced by more modulated accounts of the nature of the syndrome. Chernick et al. (1983) called the current definition of FAS inadequate because among heavy drinking mothers (who were typically also heavy smokers), the extreme morphology that had been reported for FAS was infrequent. Wright et al. (1983) found *no* cases of FAS among 903 women even though some were very heavy drinkers, causing the chief investigator to remark that FAS "is a rare disease . . . associated with pathologically heavy drinking" ("Drink/Smoke Combo . . ." 1983). The only difference due to drinking found by these investigators was in birthweight, with moderate drinking (50 to 100 grams of alcohol weekly) being associated with a slightly higher risk of delivering a lightweight baby (Chernick et al. 1983 did not note moderate drinking to be a risk). Greater drinking and smoking increased this likelihood, with mothers who were heavy drinkers and smokers being about four times as likely as moderate drinkers to produce lightweight offspring.

Perhaps the most comprehensive study of fetal alcohol syndrome to date was conducted at Boston City Hospital, employing 1,690 mothers and their infants. Hingson et al. (1982) approached the question by reviewing a range of studies that both have reported the appearance of FAS and have failed to find it. Their own data revealed "neither level of drinking prior to pregnancy nor during pregnancy was significantly related to infant growth measures, congenital abnormality, or features compatible with the fetal alcohol syndrome" (p. 544), although the number of seriously alcoholic mothers in the study was limited. What did predict infant size at birth and other features representing FAS were lower maternal weight gain, maternal illnesses, cigarette smoking, and marijuana use. "The results underline the difficulty in isolating and proclaiming single factors as the cause of abnormal fetal development. . . . In this study the quantitative impact of each behavior was relatively minor, whereas the impact of a lifestyle that combines smoking, drinking, marijuana use, etc., is more marked" (p. 545).

At this point, a fair summary might be that introducing any of a (large) variety of foreign substances during pregnancy is potentially risky, the more so when this reflects an overall lack of concern for health, heavy alcohol or licit or illicit drug use, and other problematic maternal behavior. To connect serious and clear-cut abnormalities, either short-lived or more enduring, to use of specific substances by mothers has not been possible. Once again, in the case of fetal alcohol syndrome as with infant narcotic withdrawal, the focus and magnitude of attention directed at a cause of fetal distress or defect has been determined more by external social forces than by the evidence at hand. In the early 1970s, when infant withdrawal was discovered, concern was focused on narcotics epidemics (see chapter 6), while in the late 1970s and the 1980s, coinciding with FAS publicity, we have had a concerted campaign against drinking (see chapter 2). Predictably, in the current climate toward alcohol use, early discoveries of dangers from drinking by pregnant women were built into the recommendation from the U.S. Surgeon General that prospective mothers abstain entirely, a claim from which investigators whose study prompted the recommendation have dissented (Kolata 1981).

The Addicted Animal

The fact that laboratory animals, under the right conditions, will persistently ingest opiates and other drugs has been generalized by many drug commentators to a belief that human beings, along with other mammals, find such drugs inherently rewarding and their use self-perpetuating. This generalization has led to the proposal of metabolic and conditioning theories that support the concept of an inexorable, pharmacological addiction process (see chapter 3). As with other data on drug use and addiction, experimentation with animals yields far more complex results than has been recognized. In particular, research indicates that animals consume opiates only under very limited circumstances. Moreover, research that takes the *setting* of the animal's drug use into account strongly suggests that many of the same environmental and even psychological mechanisms that play a role in human drug use in fact also do so for animals.

Opiates have generally been at the forefront of the attention of animal researchers in the United States. Studies of animal narcotic self-administration were pioneered by Seevers (1936), who showed that morphine-habituated monkeys willingly submitted to continued injections. Subsequently, Nichols et al. (1956) demonstrated that rats could be made to drink morphine solutions in preference to water. In the 1960s, investigators at the University of Michigan developed a technique whereby restrained animals were able to inject themselves with drug infusions through a permanently implanted catheter (see Weeks and Collins 1968, 1979; Woods and Schuster 1971). This led to a profusion of studies of the self-administration of such substances as cocaine, amphetamines, and other CNS stimulants; heroin, morphine, methadone, and other narcotics; and alcohol, tobacco, and hallucinogenic drugs. Overall, the quantity and regularity of self-dosing were highest for the stimulants but were also high for the narcotics. Tobacco, alcohol, and hallucinogenics were taken less consistently, although this may result from difficulties in administering these substances (Kumar and Stolerman 1977).

Aided by the self-administration apparatus, researchers investigated such pharmacological areas as the effects of physiological states on self-administration rates and different schedules of drug reinforcement. However, the most prominent result from this work has been the idea that drugs (particularly narcotics) are powerfully reinforcing—even irresistible—to the organism with free access to them. This conclusion has regularly been put forward (see Bejerot 1980; Dole 1972; Goldstein 1972, 1976a; Jaffe 1980; McAuliffe and Gordon 1980; Wikler and Pescor 1967), one version of which is as follows (Goldstein 1972: 291–92):

> Extensive studies on self-injection of opiates by monkeys show that any animal, having discovered that pressing a lever injects a narcotic intravenously, will inject itself repeatedly, raise the frequency to maintain drug effects . . . and develop full-blown addiction. It seems, therefore, that becoming addicted requires nothing more than availability of the drug, opportunity for its use, and (in man) willingness to use it.

Such conclusions have provided the major scientific support for popular conceptions about heroin addiction in the United States, including the belief that there is a biological and neurological underpinning for addictive behavior (Peele 1977). The nature of this putative mechanism in addiction—whether a metabolic process, cellular adjustment, or chemical change in the brain—has never been established, as Seevers (1963) made clear. Currently, the endorphins and opiate receptors in the brain are being investigated to find the key to addiction. Pharmacologists express caution and appropriate scientific modesty about this search (Goldstein 1976b), a restraint not apparent in writing by popularizers of work in the neurosciences (Restak 1979).

Biological and neurological theory have had notable difficulty in explaining basic data from animal psychopharmacology studies: for example, the large range of dissimilar chemicals that animals have been found to self-administer chronically. No single physiological mechanism seems likely to be triggered by such a diverse array of substances, each with its individual molecular structure. Moreover, animal researchers and pharmacologists have been forced to create elaborate, abstract conceptions to fit laboratory results. When Wikler and Pescor (1967) found some rats relapsed to morphine use months after having been withdrawn, they hypothesized that withdrawal symptoms had been conditioned to appear in response to cues associated with the animals' previous drug use (see chapter 3). Keller (1969) described these researchers' hypothesis to be an "arbitrary pronouncement—remembering that they had not demonstrated any biochemical changes in the delayed withdrawal symptoms of their post-addicted rats, but only a behaviorial syndrome." Keller suggested "that these investigators are addicted to the physicalist-pharmacological explanation of anything that involves drugs" (p. 13).

A potentially more important issue for evaluating theories about drug use derived from the observation of laboratory animals is that the animals that are studied are deprived of normal social life, environmental richness, and mobility. The investigation of drug self-injection by animals has taken place for the most part with animals who are encaged and harnessed to an implanted catheter, conditions that may well be painful and that certainly prohibit the normal activity of a healthy animal. Animal researchers like Yanagita (1970) have declared strong reservations about generalizing from behavior under these conditions—in which social inhibitions are absent, drugs are constantly available and require next to no effort to obtain, and the organism is deprived of stimulation and is under constant stress—to the behavior of human beings.

Furthermore, the behavior of these laboratory animals may not generalize *to animals in natural environments*. Animals, even in laboratory environments, do not readily self-administer hallucinogenic drugs (Griffiths et al. 1979). The study of hallucinogen behavior has been extended to animals in the field, where similarly most herbivores do not self-administer the drugs, except episodically (R. Siegel 1979). Yet when placed in sensory isolation chambers for several days, rhesus monkeys were found continually to self-administer the hallucinogen DMT (Siegel and Jarvik 1980). This study indicates that the restrictiveness of the animal's environment is a crucial determinant of its drug-taking behavior. To what extent is this also true of the use of narcotics by animals in the laboratory, a phenomenon on which pharmacologists have built the notion of the inherent addictiveness of narcotics?

Animal Narcotics Use in Rat Park

An ongoing body of research at the Simon Fraser University Drug Addiction Research Laboratory (conducted by Patricia Hadaway, Robert Coambs, Barry Beyerstein, and Bruce Alexander) has addressed the question of how physical and social environment affects opiate use among rats. Rats—along with mice, monkeys, and apes—are the usual subjects in drug experiments. The Simon Fraser experiments utilized Wistar strain albino rats, which are easy to obtain and are extremely gregarious, curious, and active. Their progenitors, wild Norway rats, are intensely social animals (Lore and Flannelly 1977) whose social responses remain largely intact even after hundreds of generations of laboratory breeding (Grant 1963). The opiate used in the experiments was morphine hydrochloride (MHCI) a salt of morphine manufactured by ICN Canada and used in morphine tonics for oral consumption. Both popular and clinical experience indicate that morphine and heroin are readily interchangeable (Zentner 1979), and Lasagna (1981) has made a clear case that there are no important differences in the relative analgesic efficacy of the two drugs for humans.

The purpose of the Simon Fraser studies was to determine whether and how laboratory housing conditions influenced the animals' consumption of the morphine solution. The hypothesis was that animals in isolated, constrained housing—that typical for the University of Michigan and other laboratories in which animal research has been conducted—would ingest more morphine than animals in more nearly natural surroundings. To test this initial, basic idea, a housing environment was constructed that differed radically from the typical cage and that mimicked the rats' natural environment as much as possible. This laboratory environment was dubbed Rat Park. It was more spacious than a standard cage (about 200 times as large in square footage), was more stimulating (with painted walls and objects rats seem to enjoy such as tin cans strewn about), and contained a rat colony (groups of sixteen to twenty rats of both sexes).

Measuring each rat's consumption of morphine solution is a straightforward matter in a cage. In these experiments, a drinking bottle of the solution was fastened next to the animal's regular water bottle on the side of the cage. Weighing both bottles daily provided a measure of drug solution and of water (or other inert substance) that was consumed. The rats in Rat Park required a more elaborate mechanism to measure individual consumption. Accordingly, a short tunnel was built which allowed one rat at a time access to two drop dispensers. One dispenser contained the drug solution and the other the inert control substance; a device automatically recorded how many times each rat activated each drop dispenser, while a photoelectrically activated camera recorded an identifying dye mark on the back of the animal (see Coambs et al. 1980 for a full description). Raw consumption data were converted into three measures of each rat's daily morphine consumption: grams of morphine solution, mg morphine/kg body weight, and proportion of morphine solution to total fluid consumption.

Morphine solutions are unpleasantly bitter to human taste and also, apparently, to rats, since they reject it with the same signs of distaste as they show towards extremely bitter nonnarcotic solutions. Offered a simple choice between water and morphine solution, rats take only a drop or two of the drug solution and ignore it thereafter. Khavari et al. (1975) found concentrations of morphine and sucrose that were sweet enough that rats would drink them in preference to water in quantities great enough to produce signs of withdrawal when the solution was removed.

An early Rat Park experiment was designed to measure differences in the consumption of sweetened morphine solution between eighteen individually caged rats (nine of each sex) and eighteen rats (also nine of each sex) living in a Rat Park colony (see Hadaway et al. 1979). In order to discover any differences that the two housing environments produced in attraction to the taste of sugar, an initial phase in the experiment offered the rats a choice between tap water and sugar solution without morphine. The second phase offered rats a choice between water and morphine (no sugar) solution. In five subsequent phases of the experiment, the solution contained both sugar and morphine. The morphine was made increasingly palatable to the rats in each successive phase by either raising the concentration of sugar or lowering the concentration of morphine compound. In a final phase, sugar solution alone was again presented.

The results show clearly that the caged rats ingested more morphine than the animals in Rat Park (see Figure 4–1). There was no housing effect on preference for the plain sugar water in the initial phase, and the Rat Park animals actually drank more of the sugar solution in the last phase. In the first couple of phases in which morphine–sugar solution was used, few of the rats in either environment drank any morphine solution. As the flavor improved, caged rats increased their consumption of morphine dramatically, while those in Rat Park increased theirs by only a small amount. The differences in morphine consumption were large and highly significant in the last three morphine–sugar solution phases. Alexander et al. (1981) replicated this experiment with a second pretest in addition to the one offering rats a choice between water and a sugar solution. This additional phase presented rats with water and a bittersweet quinine–sugar solution that was, to the human palate, almost indistinguishable from one of the morphine–sugar solutions. The purpose of this pretest was to rule out the possibility that the differences in morphine consumption were due to an aversion to the bitterness of the morphine solution. There were no significant housing effects on either pretest in the replication, and the differences in the subsequent morphine phases were about as large as those in the first Rat Park experiment.

Habituating the Animals in Rat Park

Rats in Rat Park were less likely to be lured into drinking a sweetened morphine solution than were caged rats. Would this same difference in susceptibility to narcotic effects also hold for animals that had first been habituated to the drug? In other words, would Rat Park animals ingest less

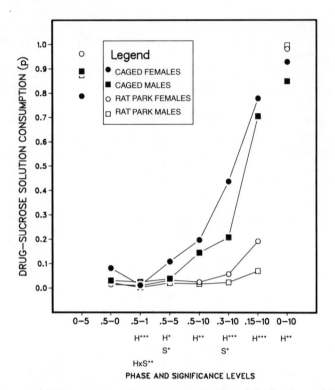

Morphine–sucrose solution consumption as proportion of total fluid consumed. Numbers identifying phases are mg MHCl per ml followed by percentage of sucrose in solution. Significance levels from analyses of variance for each phase use following symbols: H = housing effect, S = sex effect, H × S = housing by sex interaction; * = p < .05, ** = p < .01, *** = p < .001.

Figure 4–1. First Rat Park Experiment

narcotic than caged animals when both groups were being withdrawn from narcotics use?

To test the housing effect under these conditions, Alexander et al. (1978) habituated caged and Rat Park rats to narcotics by making morphine solution (0.5 mg morphine hydrochloride/ml water) their only source of fluid for fifty-three days. A number of prior experiments indicated that the amount of narcotic these animals ingested was more than enough to cause withdrawal symptoms (e.g., Fuentes et al. 1978). Interspersed in this forced consumption phase were four choice days during which the rats in both environments were given access both to water and to morphine solution. At the end of this fifty-seven-day period, in the second phase of the experiment, the rats were put on a training regimen developed by Nichols et al.

(1956) to teach rats that drinking morphine solution would relieve their withdrawal symptoms. The Nichols phase of the experiment consisted of repeated three-day cycles comprising one day of no fluids, one of only morphine solution, and one of only water. This cycle was repeated eight times interspersed with four morphine–water choice days. In the final, abstinence phase of the experiment, all morphine was withdrawn except for two morphine–water choice days, one each at two weeks and five weeks after the Nichols cycle phase.

Again results were highly significant. In all these phases of the experiment, caged rats consumed more morphine; during the Nichols phase, caged rats consumed about eight times as much morphine solution during the four choice days as did Rat Park rats (see figure 4–2). Figure 4–3 examines the changes in morphine consumption that took place during the Nichols cycle. The training regimen apparently achieved the purpose of

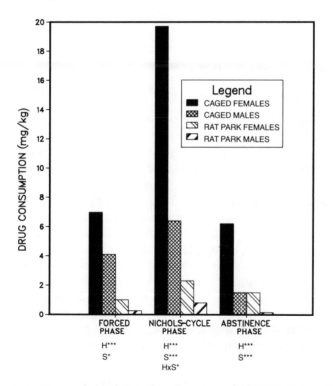

Morphine consumption on choice days in three phases as mg MHCl/kg body weight. Significance levels indicated as in figure 4–1.

Figure 4–2. Second Rat Park (Forced Consumption) Experiment

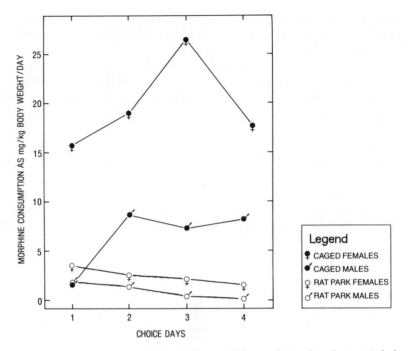

Morphine consumption as mg MHCl/kg body weight/day on choice days during Nichols-cycle phase.

Figure 4–3. Nichols-Cycle Phase of Second Rat Park Experiment

teaching the caged rats to take the drug in response to withdrawal, and they increased their morphine consumption over the four choice days. The Rat Park animals, on the other hand, decreased their consumption slightly over the same period, as if learning about the drug's effects *reduced* their willingness to ingest it. The results of this second Rat Park experiment call into question conventional notions of withdrawal as the impetus to opiate consumption. Just as with human beings, an animal's response to being withdrawn from a narcotic is influenced by situational factors. Withdrawal from even a regularly administered narcotic is not so overwhelming as to eliminate the creature's concern with other drives and attractions. When given reasonable alternatives, animals in this experiment did *not* act as though the motivation to avoid withdrawal discomfort were an all-purpose reinforcer with which ordinary motivations could not compete.

What Factor(s) Cause the Rat Park Housing Effect?

The Rat Park data that have been reviewed so far had an essentially negative purpose: to disprove an ill-founded generalization from previous re-

search on caged animals. The data clearly show that the readiness to consume opiates displayed by caged animals does not hold for rats living in an
environment that resembles the animals' natural setting, even after the rats
have been habituated to drug use. While these data show that differences in
housing conditions can produce a considerable difference in the amount of
morphine rats consume, the many distinctions between Rat Park and a
standard cage make it impossible to pinpoint the specific factors that affect
the animals' morphine intake. This section reports studies that explored
these factors in an attempt to cast light on the reasons for continued morphine consumption in animals and in human drug addiction.

Social interaction, which is known to be a powerful factor in animal
and human behavior, was the first environmental feature tested for its effect on morphine consumption. A group-size experiment was devised that
placed one, two, and four rats in single cages about two-and-a-half times
the size of a standard cage. Some of the duos and quads were all female,
some all male, and some mixed. The animals were then exposed to the
same sequence of solutions used in the first Rat Park experiment and their
consumption of morphine measured by weighing the bottles in their cages.
The results of this experiment clearly supported the null hypothesis—that
group size per se did not affect morphine consumption. Groups of four rats
(whatever the sexual composition) ingested about four times as much morphine as one rat and twice as much as two.

Space was taken as the next most obvious environmental feature to be
explored. Twelve pens, each five-feet square (making them one-third the
size of Rat Park but still more than sixty-five times as large as standard
cages), were constructed. Four of the pens contained single males, four single females, and four male-female pairs. A comparison group of twelve rats
(six male and six female) were housed in individual cages. Both a quinine
solution pretest and posttest were employed along with the presentation of
three increasingly sweet morphine solutions. No significant differences
were found between the caged and the penned singles in the pretest or posttest or in any of the morphine-intake phases. However, as figure 4–4 shows,
the *penned pairs* drank *less* morphine than both the penned and the caged
singles. The housing difference for the .3–10 phase was significant for the
proportion data.

The last result suggested that it is neither space nor the presence of
other rats taken alone but rather the *combination* of space and companionship that brings about the housing effect noted in Rat Park. To test this
possibility directly, rats in an experiment with four housing conditions—
caged singles (six male and six female caged single rats), caged duos (six
caged male–female pairs), penned singles (five male and five female penned
single rats), and penned duos (five penned male–female pairs)—were exposed to morphine according to the standard design. The results of this

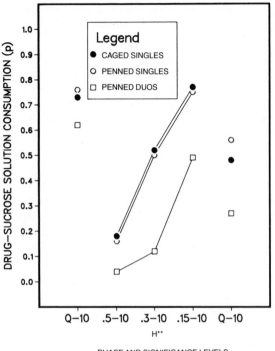

Morphine consumption as proportion of total fluid consumed. All abbreviations same as for figure 4–1, with the addition of Q-10 to represent 0.06 mg quinine sulfate/ml water + 10 percent sucrose.

Figure 4–4. Morphine Consumption by Individual Rats in Cages and Individual and Paired Rats in Pens

study corroborated the important finding in the earlier study: rats that have both space and a companion ingested significantly less morphine in the .3–10 phase than those lacking either or both of these assets (see figure 4–5). In this experiment space alone did seem to make a difference, with both penned singles and duos consuming less morphine than rats in either of the two caged conditions. No such effect was found for the social condition alone. In fact, the caged duos ingested more morphine than the penned *or* caged singles.

Unfortunately, in this case alone among the experiments reported here, there was a significant quinine phase pretest difference in the same direction as the difference in morphine consumption. It is thus possible that differences in morphine consumption among the groups could have resulted from an aversion to bittersweet solutions somehow produced by the differ-

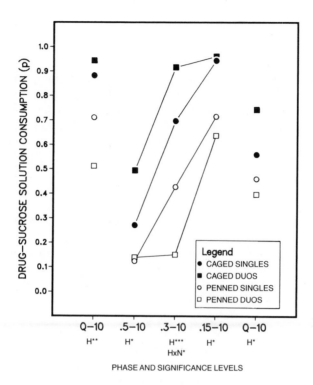

Morphine consumption as proportion of total fluid consumed. H represents housing factor (cage vs. pen) and H × N is interaction between housing and number of rats (one or two).

Figure 4–5. Morphine Consumption by Individual and Paired Rats in Cages and Pens

ent housing conditions. Still, the differences in the .3–10 phase were larger than the quinine pretest differences, even though the bittersweet taste of the quinine– and morphine–sucrose solutions were matched for these phases. An analysis of covariance yielded a significant housing effect for this phase when the initial taste preference was partialled out. Because it is not possible to test all the assumptions about these data required for analysis of covariance (see Ferguson 1981: 370–73), these results can only indicate trends in the data rather than establishing a firm level of significance.

Complications in Rat Park

In order to resolve the possibility of taste preference differences suggested by the experiment combining the housing and social factors, the Simon Fraser Drug Addiction Research Laboratory investigators ran an experiment employing a tasteless narcotic, etonitazene. At the same time, they utilized new computer equipment for measuring fluid consumption in Rat Park. The Rat Park housing effect was *not* confirmed under these conditions, nor with two subsequent experiments utilizing morphine in the original Rat Park experimental designs (Alexander et al. 1978; Hadaway et al. 1979). Subsequently, an alcohol researcher employing Wistar rats announced that a new line of the Wistar strain, which had also been introduced into the Rat Part colony, failed to replicate basic alcohol consumption data achieved with the previous line (Boland 1983). Lastly, the laboratory investigators replicated the results of the earliest experiment (Alexander et al. 1978) with a completely new strain of rats: Sprague Dawleys.

The Rat Park housing effect cannot be taken to be as robust as it originally appeared to be. Separating out the influences of type of narcotic, measurement system, and type of rat from that of environment in producing this effect may be a long process or even an impossible one. At the same time, housing differences in narcotic consumption were also found at the Drug Addiction Research Laboratory for rats housed in pens and cages. The Rat Park and related studies have demonstrated, under specific conditions, that environmental factors will affect narcotic consumption, as Siegel and Jarvik (1980) have found to occur with hallucinogens. Environmental effects in Rat Park and related studies, all with their limitations, must be analyzed with reference to corroborating data from both the Drug Addiction Research Laboratory and other investigators. More important than the specific housing effect in these data may be some overriding results concerning the likelihood of rats consuming narcotics under all conditions.

What Causes Animals to Accept Narcosis?

Not only the rats in Rat Park but the comparison animals in cages failed to consume opiates with the avidity that Goldstein (1972) described or that seems typical for animals studied at the University of Michigan and elsewhere. In the current studies, rats only took a drug when it was presented in a highly sweetened solution and then only irregularly—with high day-to-day variation in consumption. These results suggest a need to reevaluate the extant hypotheses for why caged animals seek narcotic effects.

Relief of stress and pain. The Rat Park and similar data on the impact of isolation and being caged could be explained by the stress that constrained housing causes the animals and that narcotics relieve. Working against this interpretation is the surprising absence of independent evidence that stress or pain induces opiate consumption in rats. In several experiments, Chipkin (1976) found that intermittent electric shocks spread over periods as long as fourteen days failed to increase methadone consumption in caged rats. In the Drug Addiction Research Laboratory at Simon Fraser, Brunke et al. (1980) found no increase in the oral self-administration of morphine for caged rats that underwent surgical implantation of venous catheters.

Constitutional differences. Panksepp (1980) has presented evidence that brief isolation makes young rats more sensitive to pain. Such sensitivity could be caused by an inability to maintain normal endorphin levels or by other physiological deficits that enhance the utility of the pain relief provided by narcotics. Some support for this idea comes from reports that long-term isolation can increase the effectiveness of morphine for relieving pain (DeFeudis et al. 1976; Kostowski et al. 1977). However, some of the same studies have also shown that long-term isolation does *not* make animals more sensitive to pain (Adler et al. 1975; DeFeudis et al. 1976) and that isolation makes animals *less* sensitive to the analgesic effects of morphine (Katz and Steinberg 1970; Kostowski et al. 1977). The latter data suggest an alternative physiological hypothesis that partially contradicts the first. If morphine has less of an analgesic effect on rats in isolation, then it could be that isolated rats need to consume more morphine than those living with other rats to achieve the same level of pain relief.

Both of these arguments bear an obvious affinity to those that trace human addiction to inherited or acquired endorphin deficiencies (cf. Goldstein 1976b). Both also fit with animal research showing that quality of the early postweaning environment for rats has major effects on the anatomy and physiology of the developing nervous system (cf. Greenough 1975; Horn et al. 1979; Rosensweig 1971), some of which have been related to later drug use (Prescott 1980). To the extent that isolation has its effect through permanent or long-term changes in the animal's nervous system, isolation early in life should be more influential than later isolation in the consumption of morphine. This possibility was explored at the Simon Fraser Laboratory. Thirty-two rats (sixteen of each sex) were divided between individual cages and Rat Park at weaning (age 21 days). At age 65 days, half the rats in each setting were moved to the other, creating four housing conditions: C-C, or caging both early and late; C-RP, or caging early and Rat Park late; RP-C, Rat Park early and caging late; and RP-RP, Rat Park both early and late. At age 80 days the rats began a sequence of choice tests, starting with a sucrose and a quinine–sucrose pretest, proceeding through the usual sequence of morphine–sucrose solutions, and ending with a sucrose posttest.

Figure 4–6 depicts results of this experiment for male rats (data on female rats indicate the same effects, although not with the same degree of statistical significance; see Alexander et al. 1981). No significant pretest or posttest difference appeared. Significant results were found for late housing, with rats housed in cages consuming much more morphine than did rats

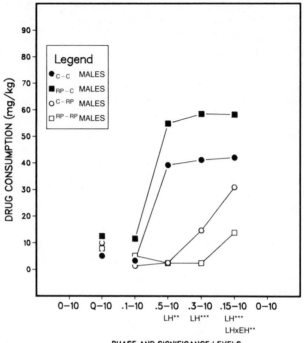

Morphine consumption as mg morphine/kg body weight/day. Additional abbreviations for housing conditions are C for caged and RP for Rat Park and for analysis of variance significance levels are EH for early housing and LH for late housing.

Figure 4–6. Morphine Consumption for Rats Housed Early/Late in Cages and Rat Park

living in Rat Park. Early experience had no consistent effect on the rats in this experiment, although there was a slight tendency for the C-RP rats to consume more morphine than RP-RP rats over all the measures reported in Alexander et al. (1981). These data showed clearly that the Rat Park housing effect is more the result of the environment of the animal at the time it is tested than of its early postweaning experiences and is less attributable to constitutional differences than to situational factors.

Interference with normal activity. The importance of contemporaneous environment for morphine consumption supports the results of the study of penned and caged rats. Both indicate that it is the inhibition of current opportunities for activity that favors the animals' consumption of morphine. The comparison of caged and penned rats alone and together showed that neither space nor companionship taken separately suppressed rats'

morphine consumption as much as both together did. Perhaps this is because rats housed in a spacious environment with others of their species
perform many complex social activities that are inherently rewarding and
with which the drug's effects interfere. Rat sexual behavior, for example,
occurs on the run with the female starting and stopping over several square
meters while the male keeps up as best he can. Perhaps the caged duos
consumed more morphine than caged singles because putting two rats in a
cage restricted their individual activities while not providing enough space
for interactive ones. For rats—a colonial species and not a pair-bonding one
(Lore and Flannelly 1977)—larger, more populated housing conditions
would most closely resemble their natural habitats and might be most effective for inhibiting drug use.

There are other indications that rats learn to avoid morphine because
it interferes with complex rodent activity. Even small doses of narcotics
significantly reduce sexual behavior (Mumford and Kumar 1979; McIntosh
et al. 1980) and social cohesion among rats (Panksepp et al. 1979). Alexander et al. (1978) noted a marked reduction in activity of all sorts among
animals forced to drink morphine solution. The case that species-typical
behavior is in and of itself reinforcing has been forcefully argued by Glickman and Schiff (1967). Garcia et al. (1974) have meanwhile shown that rats
learn to avoid foods or solutions that produce sickness even hours after
consumption. Taken together, this information suggests that rats could
learn to avoid narcosis when it prevents them from experiencing the rewards brought on by normal activity.

What comes through most strongly in the Rat Park and related studies
is how much experimental pressure is required—including heavy sweeten-
ing of morphine solutions and forced habituation in addition to depriva-
tional housing—to cause rats regularly to self-administer a narcotic. The
fact that rats reject morphine when offered a choice between unsweetened
drug solution and water is usually attributed to the bitter taste of the opiate
solution. This notion has not born up under testing, however. Huidobro
(1964) reported that caged rats whose sense of taste was destroyed (through
sectioning their lingual and glossopharyngeal nerves) rejected morphine solutions. Wikler and Pescor (1967) found that naive rats rejected the opiate
drug etonitazine even though it was essentially tasteless in the concentration used.

The alternate possibility—that the effects of narcotics themselves are
what prevent animals from drinking a morphine solution—was tested in
two studies at the Drug Addiction Research Laboratory. In the first of these
experiments, rats in cages and in Rat Park were given twenty-four-hour-a-
day access to two bittersweet solutions. The bitter taste in one solution
came from quinine sulphate and in the other from morphine hydrochloride.
The two tasted almost identical to human taste. In this arrangement, rats

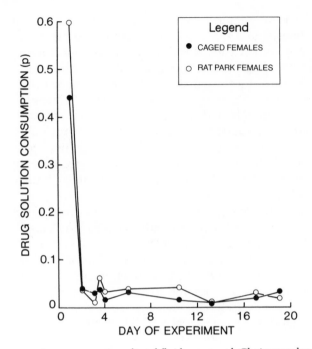

Morphine consumption as proportion of total fluid consumed. Choice was between morphine–sucrose (.5–5) solution and quinine–sulfate solution (.1–5) that were equally bitter to taste. The decline in morphine consumption after the first eight-hour test period was significant at p < .001, while differences between housing groups were not significant.

Figure 4–7. Morphine Consumption by Females in Rat Park and in Cages Given Choice of Quinine and Morphine Solutions

did not have to sacrifice palatability in order to obtain a drug effect. The results in figure 4–7 for female rats confirm that the solutions were equally tasty to the animals, with both caged and Rat Park animals drinking about half their total fluid intake as morphine for the first eight hours of the experiment. Then both sets of rats drank very little morphine for the remaining nineteen days (Coambs 1977). Caged males did drink significantly more morphine than Rat Park males for the last ten days of the experiment. In the absence of such a difference between Rat Park and caged females, however, the best overall summary of these results is that rats under both housing conditions will not ingest appreciable amounts of morphine when there is an equally palatable and inert alternative.

In a follow-up experiment, Coambs (1980) gave a choice between sweetened quinine and morphine solutions to caged rats. The quinine concentration was increased with the intention of forcing the animal to drink morphine. The initial effect of what appeared to be an unpleasant choice for the animals was that they did not drink at all for the first few days. In a result that did not occur with any other experimental procedure, the rats eventually split into two distinct groups: Roughly half the rats drank mostly the morphine solution, while the other half drank mostly the quinine. On day 15, naltrexone was introduced into both solutions with the effect of neutralizing the action of the morphine solution. Figure 4–8 shows that there was a dramatic jump in morphine consumption at this point. While the rats that had initially preferred the morphine continued to do so, the rats that had preferred the more bitter quinine solution quickly shifted to the morphine *once its psychoactivity had been removed.* The results of this study unambiguously indicated that even caged rats find the psychotropic effects of morphine to be aversive.

The evidence from both these studies seemingly contradicts a body of research that shows laboratory animals will inject themselves with opiates

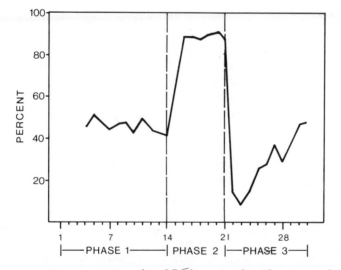

Morphine consumption as proportion of total fluid consumed. In Phase 1, rats chose between .5 mg morphine hydrochloride/ml water + 8 percent sucrose and .2 mg quinine sulfate/ml water + 8 percent sucrose (first three days omitted because very low intake made calculation of proportions unreliable). In Phase 2, 0.1 naltrexone hydrochloride added to both solutions. In Phase 3, the choice was the above morphine and naltrexone solution and a solution of 0.1 mg naltrexone/ml water + 8 percent sucrose.

Figure 4–8. Morphine Consumption by Caged Rats Given Choice of Quinine and Sweetened Morphine Solutions and Quinine and Morphine–Naltrexone Solutions

continuously without added inducements. The differential performance of animals in the morphine solution and the self-injection experiments may highlight the abnormality of the latter setting (Peele 1977; Yanagita 1970). For caged animals implanted with catheters, normal gratifications are curtailed at the same time that animals are able to produce—almost effortlessly—an immediate, reliable infusion of a drug. Yet research has shown that modifying these forces even slightly, as by increasing the amount of bar pressing required to produce an injection of drug, will reduce the doses that animals self-administer (Kumar and Stolerman 1977).

Self-injection research has been built on optimum situations for inducing an organism to ingest narcotics. Rats in experiments employing narcotic solutions, on the other hand, must drink an appreciable volume of fluid to gain a somewhat delayed effect in an environment that permits them a wider range of alternative activities. Under these conditions, which better correspond to those naturally obtaining for the animals, most animals seem to react with the same distaste for narcotics that most humans express in ordinary circumstances (see chapter 3). The same holds for alcohol, which laboratory animals regularly reject in preference to water. Falk (1981) was able to induce rats to consume alcohol and other drugs (such as barbiturates) in large quantities by creating an intermittent feeding schedule that the animals found highly disturbing. As Falk (1983) summarized over a decade's research: "Schedule-induced drug overindulgence remains strictly a function of current induction conditions. Even with a long history of schedule-induced drinking, with the development of physical dependence, termination of the scheduled aspect of feeding produces an immediate fall in alcohol intake to a control level" (p. 389).

The Implications of Infant and Animal Research for Conceptions of Addiction

The most important conclusion to emerge from an examination of animal and infant addiction is that addictive behavior is not rigidly determined by the properties of drugs. Falk (1983) noted the results of schedule-induced alcohol consumption studies: "Once again we have a picture of a reputedly enticing molecule failing to take over behavior in spite of chronic binging" (p. 389). Infants and animals continue to respond to such environmental factors as nurturance and a stimulating environment in the face of narcotic withdrawal pangs. The richness of the organism's repertoire of responses with regard to narcotics and other drugs may enhance our awareness of the complexity of the determinants of the behavior of all mammals and of human beings of all ages, including cognitive, emotional, and experiential complexity that has often gone unnoticed. In particular, the research on animals and infants is reminiscent of findings about narcotics use by adults (such as the Vietnam War data)—namely, that full-fledged craving for narcotics and abhorrence of withdrawal appear mainly under abnormal conditions. Animals and infants apparently share with the adult human being an urge to experience life normally that outweighs the allure of narcosis.

At the same time, we must be careful to avoid the error of overgeneralization that has bedeviled animal self-injection research. Addiction as we know it is a purely human phenomenon (Peele 1977). This is because addiction entails behavior that gains its meaning only in human social and psychological context (see chapter 1). For example, we decide a person is addicted—as opposed to being a controlled user of a substance—when he or she disregards health, personal well-being, and social propriety in order to continue a behavior. There are no real parallels for this among animals and infants. Another distinction between adult human beings and other organisms is the greater cognitive and situational resources the adult human may counterpoise against addiction: Only an adult would quit an addiction like narcotics or cigarettes or overeating because it violates other values, such as a desire for self-control (see chapter 5). The animal or infant must face withdrawal without the benefit of any such salutary resolve.

On the other hand, adult human experience provides unusual opportunities for addiction to take hold. While Robins et al. (1974) found that most soldier narcotics users and addicts gave up their habits when returning home, a small percentage continued to be addicted. These veterans were more likely to have abused drugs before entering the service. What we see in these men is an enduring disposition—one that transcends situation—to seek narcosis or some other addiction. Peele and Brodsky (1975: 63) attempted to analyze this phenomenon in terms of animal and infant research:

> When we think of the conditions under which animals and infants become addicted, we can better appreciate the situation of the addict. Aside from their relatively simple motivations, monkeys kept in a small cage with an injection apparatus strapped to their backs are deprived of the variety of stimulation their natural environment provides. All they can do is push the lever. Obviously, an infant is also not capable of sampling life's full complexity. Yet these physically or biologically limiting factors are not unlike the psychological constraints the addict lives with.

While a concept of addictive personality that disregards the individual's opportunities, life stage, and personal desires is a limited analytic tool, the *absence* of a conception of personal disposition is also limiting in the analysis of addiction. Animal research can illuminate such a personality construct only indirectly. Falk's (1983) insightful analysis of animal and human excess discerned that drug abuse "depends upon what behavior opportunities are available in life's situations, and *whether the individual is prepared to exploit these opportunities*" (p. 390, italics added). The reliance on addiction is, in other words, as much an indication of how people experience and react to their environment as it is a result of the particular addicting properties of a substance or of the environment's objective qualities, barring the most abject environmental impoverishment.

While situations predispose people to addiction, individuals also show greater or lesser susceptibility to it. At one extreme, people who cannot generate productive or rewarding experiences are at a disadvantage in avoiding addiction. Lower achievement values (or greater fear of failure), fewer interests, an inability to structure one's time, less concern for health or other moderating values, and an unfamiliarity with functional coping techniques are elements in the addictive equation. Animal research reminds us that the sources of addiction lie in the ways human beings are denied—or deny themselves—the opportunities for rewarding experiences that characterize life for our species. As Peele and Brodsky (1975) evoked this idea, "The difference between not being addicted and being addicted is the difference between seeing the world as your arena and seeing the world as your prison" (p. 64)—or is it cage? It is striking that animal research in laboratories, even that conducted with a reductionist bent of mind, affirms this complex truth about addiction.

5
Addiction to an Experience

P eople become addicted to experiences. The addictive experience is the totality of effect produced by an involvement; it stems from pharmacological and physiological sources but takes its ultimate form from cultural and individual constructions of experience. The most recognizable form of addiction is an extreme, dysfunctional attachment to an experience that is acutely harmful to a person, but that is an essential part of the person's ecology and that the person cannot relinquish. This state is the result of a dynamic social-learning process in which the person finds an experience rewarding because it ameliorates urgently felt needs, while in the long run it damages the person's capacity to cope and ability to generate stable sources of environmental gratification.

Because addiction is finally a human phenomenon, it engages every aspect of a person's functioning, starting with the rewards (as interpreted by the individual) that an involvement provides and the individual's need for these rewards. The motivation to pursue the involvement, as compared with other alternatives, is a function of an additional layer of social, situational, and personality variables. All of these elements are in flux as the individual grows up, changes environments, develops more mature coping mechanisms, loses and gains new opportunities for satisfaction, and is supported or undermined in forming new outlooks and self-conceptions. There are indeterminate elements—for example, those activated by the person's value commitments—affecting whether the person will continue to return to an experience that is progressively more damaging to the rest of the person's life. Even after the person has developed an addictive attachment, he or she can suddenly (as well as gradually) rearrange the values that maintain the addiction. This process is the remarkable one of maturing out, or natural remission in addiction.

Elements of the Addictive Experience

Addictive experiences are not random; people become addicted to experiences that have clear-cut and specifiable elements. First and foremost, addictive experiences are potent modifiers of mood and sensation, in part because of their direct pharmacological action or physical impact and in part because of their learned and symbolic significance. In the United States, for example, both heroin and one-to-one love relationships have extreme cultural weight placed upon what are inherently affecting experiences (Peele and Brodsky 1975). The centrality of experiential effects in addiction makes clear why and how nondrug involvements become addictive; experiential definitions of addiction encompass all those powerful involvements noted as addictive. Falk et al. (1983) described the commonalities among the objects of excessive involvement: "Drugs, foods, gambling, and aggressive episodes all have *prompt effects on the person or upon their immediate environment.* The preferred drugs of abuse are typically those with a rapid onset of effect. Gamblers prefer fast 'action,' that is, a high rate of play with an immediacy of consequence for each wager" (p. 92; italics in original).

In addition to explaining the prevalence of nondrug addictions, the notion that addiction takes place with regard to an experience does away once and for all with such thoroughly debunked misconceptions as that addiction is maintained by the desire for pleasure or the avoidance of withdrawal (see chapter 3). Rather, an addictive experience is rewarding because it provides gratifications that the addict acknowledges are inferior to genuinely pleasurable and satisfying involvements; withdrawal is, in this context, better described as the absence of either such primary gratification or the ameliorative, substitute gratification sought from the addictive involvement. Consider Robbins and Joseph's (1982, cited in Sachs and Pargman 1984: 235) description of the kind of withdrawal observed in runners:

> Among runners for whom the activity serves to modify dysphoric mood states of psychophysiological distress, return of distress once the effects of the run have decreased may be misunderstood as symptoms of physiological withdrawal. In this instance, withdrawal may not be the pain associated with the body adjusting to the physiological changes of nonrunning, but a reexperience of the pain felt *before* the physiological changes of running.

If theorists could resist reducing self-destructive running or other, similar behavior to neurological terms or contrasting it with mythical visions of drug addiction, such compulsive involvements would shed essential light on the nature of addiction. Both the analysis of such involvements and what they highlight in the effects of drug involvements focus attention on the crucial matter of addiction: namely, what about drug and other potent experiences is attractive to people predisposed by personality and situation to addiction, and what additional elements besides their power characterize addictive experiences?

The Diminution of Pain, Tension, and Awareness

Although addiction has parallels to everyday, ordinary experiences, a model of addiction must explain the clinical extremities of the behavior of those who devote their lives—and sometimes destroy themselves—in the pursuit of an addiction. These people experience the addiction as being necessary for their continued existence. The most powerful descriptions of this outlook come from interviews with narcotics addicts. Zinberg et al. (1978) revealed that their subjects underwent a change in consciousness that was "characterized by increased emotional distance from external stimuli and internal response, but it is a long way from euphoria." The desire for this consciousness change "had little to do with warding off withdrawal sickness" and did not "stem from a wish to feel normal." For these addicts, "the ordinary, rational, self-aware state was an uncomfortable one" (p. 19). In Peele and Brodsky's (1975) formulation, "opiates are desired because they bring welcome relief from other sensations and feelings which the addict finds unpleasant," including a "distasteful consciousness of . . . life" (pp. 51, 61).

The erasure of sensation and of awareness that mark the heroin experience are a result of that drug's depressant action on the central nervous system—a characteristic of all drugs used for analgesic, or pain-relief, purposes. This recalls a peculiar anomaly in twentieth-century pharmacologia: the search for a nonaddictive analgesic (Eddy and May 1973; Peele 1977, 1978, 1979). Beginning with the introduction of heroin in 1898, new pharmacological discoveries have regularly been promoted as offering potent pain relief that will not create addiction. A substance with these combined qualities has yet to be identified, however. The history of sedatives is also typified by initial optimism about a new drug's usefulness, followed by increasing reports of abuse and eventual classification of the drug as being addictive or incurring physical dependence (Kales et al. 1974; Solomon et al. 1979). Having pain, anxiety, or other negative emotional states relieved through a loss of consciousness or a heightened threshold of sensation is a primary component of addictive experience; for this reason, all effective pain relievers will inevitably be addicting for some people.

That pain and tension reduction are essential functions of addictive chemical experiences is challenged by the appearance of addiction to stimulant drugs such as cocaine, amphetamines, nicotine, and caffeine. Research with smoking has been instructive in this regard. Nesbitt (1972), Gilbert (1979), and others have noted a paradoxical tranquilizing component to tobacco use. That is, while nicotine is a stimulant, habitual smokers report that the drug relaxes them and relieves tension. Apparently, the increased activity in the nervous and circulatory systems of smokers lessens their sensitivity to outside stimuli. In this way habitual drug stimulation inures them to events that they otherwise find anxiety-producing; as a result, smokers smoke more when tense (Leventhal and Cleary 1980). The same kind of paradoxical tension relief is apparent in the excitatory atmosphere surrounding gambling (Boyd 1976).

Findings about the relief of tension through drinking alcohol have been complex. Alcohol is a depressant drug; all levels of drinkers cite alcohol's relaxing quality as a motivation for drinking. McClelland et al. (1972) found only heavy alcohol consumption actually reduced tension. Selzen and his colleagues (1977) found alcoholics—compared with both drunken drivers and ordinary populations—were the most likely to drink for tension relief. Several major experimental studies, on the other hand, have failed to detect any tension reduction from heavy drinking (Cappell and Herman 1972; Marlatt 1976). What research has consistently shown is that alcoholics drink in the *expectation* of reducing tensions, even though—as their drinking proceeds—they do not experience this effect and instead become even more tense (Mello and Mendelson 1978; Stockwell et al. 1982). This paradoxical component to addictive drinking—that it intensifies negative sensations that drinking is sought to relieve—is a crucial component in addiction (see the section of *The Addiction Cycle* below).

Bruch (1973) proposed that eating was a tranquilizer for the obese, who had learned to rely on food as a form of emotional reassurance due to childhood feeding patterns. The systematic research spawned by the internal–external model of obesity originally rejected the idea that overeating was a response to negative emotions (Schachter 1968). However, Schachter and Rodin (1974) discovered the obese were hyperresponsive to emotional stimuli and ate more when afraid or uncomfortable. Herman and Polivy (1975) found overweight people ate more when depressed or anxious because, these researchers felt, the obese are usually trying to diet and emotional distress overcomes their eating restraint. Slochower (1983) has found this to be an incomplete explanation of overeating by the obese. She showed in several laboratory studies that obese subjects ate in response to anxiety (although only when they could not affect the source of their anxiety directly) and that eating *did* reduce their anxiety, at least temporarily.

Social-learning models propose that addicts learn from past experience and social conditioning to anticipate that alcohol and other drugs solve specific dilemmas about which they are concerned. In other words, highly charged emotional states or settings evoke the addictive behavior in response. In Tokar et al. (1973), alcoholics reported that they went to bars or drank when they were depressed, anxious, or angry but that they pursued other activities when feeling comfortable. Leventhal and Cleary (1980) suggested that smokers learn to rely on nicotine's pharmacological effects as a way of coping with negative feelings. Zinberg (1984) noted that addicts were distinguished from controlled users of heroin in that addicts used the drug to escape depression and intolerable conditions, while controlled users took the drug for diversion and entertainment. Similarly, Russell and Bond (1980) found that alcoholic subjects more often believed drinking would compensate for unpleasant feelings, while most normal college students believed that alcohol magnified existing feelings. Beckman (1978) reported that alcoholics of both sexes drank more when tense or depressed or when feeling powerless, inadequate, or out of control.

An Enhanced Sense of Control, Power, and Self-Esteem

An overall rubric for the variety of functions drug experiences serve in addiction is that they offer addicts control over areas of behavior or emotions that they otherwise feel unable to cope with. Power and control are frequent images offered by cocaine users to describe the effects of the drug (Stone et al. 1984). Power and aggressiveness have been strongly implicated in the nexus of emotions, expectations, and pharmacological effects surrounding drinking by men. Lang et al. (1975) found that the belief by men that they had drunk alcohol—whether or not they had—led to increased aggressiveness. McClelland and his co-workers (1972) explored the inner experiences connected with drinking among college students and blue-collar drinkers. For the college students, McClelland et al. found that men with a high need for power but little opportunity to exercise power developed extravagant fantasies of personal domination when intoxicated. Heavy drinkers among the blue-collar sample expressed similar images when drinking, which the researchers termed fantasies of personalized power. Brown et al. (1980) discovered that the heavier drinkers in their study expected greater enhancement of their aggressiveness and their sexual responsiveness than did lighter drinkers.

There was a gender distinction in Brown et al.'s (1980) findings for those at all levels of drinking: Women were motivated by expectations of generally positive social experiences from drinking, while men's drinking expectations centered around sexual arousal and potential aggressive behavior. Differences have consistently been uncovered between male and female drinking. Unlike the McClelland et al. model of male drinking, Wilsnak (1976) found that women drank to allay their anxieties about their femininity rather than to induce feelings of power. While males who believe they have drunk alcohol become more sexually aroused regardless of having actually consumed alcohol (particularly if they are guilty about and repress sexual feelings, Lang et al. 1980), women's sexual responses are diminished by actual alcohol consumption. Yet women also associate sexual arousal with the effects of alcohol (Wilson and Lawson 1978). It seems that men and women act out reciprocal sex roles when drinking, where men become more desirous and sexually aggressive while women, although less sexually motivated, become more accommodating sexually (Wilson 1981). Burnett (1979) maintained, based on clinical experience, that alcoholic women use the drug to assist them in fulfilling a hyperfeminine role just as males rely on alcohol to produce stereotypical feelings of machismo.

A theme that unifies the drinking experiences of men and women is that alcohol enables both sexes to feel more adequate to their sex roles. That is, while gender-typical behavior varies between men and women, both sexes rely on alcohol to enhance self-esteem by making them feel closer to an ideal sex type. McGuire et al. (1966: 25) summarized the effects male alcoholics expected from drinking and how these related to subjects' self-esteem:

> The chronic alcoholic subjects expected transformations in their relationships and feelings when they became intoxicated. They believed they would become "masculine," "admired by women," more sociable, and better able to carry out tasks, and that they would have a better estimate of themselves, feel less "anxious," and become more "integrated" as individuals. No similar expectations or beliefs were noted in the nonalcoholic subjects.

Cocaine addicts frequently report sexual mastery to be a primary motivation for drug use (Stone et al. 1984), and heroin addicts have been noted to use the drug to remedy feelings of personal inadequacy (Krystal and Raskin 1970; Wurmser 1978) and specific sexual dysfunctions, such as premature ejaculation (Khantzian et al. 1974).

When asked to describe their normal, ideal, and drugged selves on an adjective checklist, heroin addicts rated their drugged selves closer to their ideal than they rated their normal selves, particularly on a dominance dimension (Teasdale 1972). Chemicals may be particularly suited for fulfilling an ego-boosting function through their success in supressing the negative self-attributions with which addicts are ordinarily weighed down. Hull and Young (1983) have proposed such a model for the effects of alcohol. These researchers found that alcohol reduced self-awareness for all drinkers and that alcoholics and those predisposed to alcoholism were particularly sensitive to this result of drinking. Alcoholics were more likely to return to drinking following treatment if they encountered situations that damaged their self-esteem. In a very different area, Robbins and Joseph (1982) found that running addicts—unlike other frequent runners—believed the activity was a sign of their mastery and used running as a "regular experience that acts to reinforce one's perception of competence and self-worth" (cited in Sachs and Pargman, 1984: 235). Slochower (1983) found overeating by the obese to be related to periods of self-doubt and low self-esteem.

Simplification, Predictability, and Immediacy of Experience

That alcoholics anticipate they will be better at handling life when drinking (McGuire et al. 1966) suggests the alcohol experience is valued for making the world appear to be a more manageable place. Zismer and Holloway (1984) validated a measure of alcohol reinforcement that identified five factors distinguishing between treated alcohol abusers and a general population of drinkers. Along with the familiar dimensions of self-confidence, social adequacy, and sociability, the instrument labeled factors of cognitive control (sample item: "alcohol makes thoughts flow better") and reduction of complexity ("life is easier to figure out after a few drinks" and "people are honest only when they drink"). This cognitive focusing and simplification is independent of any other psychological goals addicts seek to achieve and stands as a separate dimension of addictive experience.

The importance of ritual in addiction—for example, heroin addicts' rejection of noninjectable substitutes for heroin or other departures from their addictive routines (Solomon 1977) and their acceptance of nonnarcotic injections in place of heroin (Light and Torrance 1929)—also reflects the value addicts place on the simplification of experience. The repetition of a highly focused activity is rewarding for addicts in itself. Beyond the specific effects powerful psychoactive substances and other mood-altering involvements offer, they attract people because of their immediacy and predictability, or what Falk et al. (1983) termed their "ritualized saliency" (p. 92). They enable addicts to bypass the ordinary efforts required to bring about a desired state, thus eliminating the anxiety such taxing and uncertain real-world activities cause addicts.

The Range of Addictive Objects and Its Consequences

That addiction takes place with a range of objects, including quite common activities, drives home that no involvement or object is inherently addictive. Rather, people become addicted to a given involvement due to a combination of social and cultural, situational, personality, and developmental factors; these factors identify the topics of the following sections. Addiction can be understood only as a multifactorial phenomenon: It takes place along a continuum, in degrees, and is not limited to a single object. Unless we measure the range of addictive possibilities in a person's life, we cannot evaluate the degree to which the person is addicted (Peele 1983c). Switching from heroin to alcohol or methadone or from alcohol to compulsive eating or running or from any of these things to compulsive group involvements may mark an improvement in a person's life (or it may not). However, focusing on any one such involvement will not tell us to what extent the person is addicted.

The criteria that establish if an individual is addicted must be independent of type of involvement and must instead focus on the involvement's harmfulness to the individual, its limiting of other sources of gratification, the perception by the individual that the involvement is essential to his or her functioning, and the upset to the person's overall social, psychological, and physical system from deprivation of the involvement (see Peele 1981a; Peele and Brodsky 1975). The combination of these criteria eliminates from consideration both trivial activities, such as hair brushing, and activities that are functionally necessary to existence but that do not normally interfere with life, such as breathing and drinking water. Rejecting the idea that we can look to one activity, object, or set of involvements to discover addictions raises two questions: What causes a given individual to become addicted, and to which involvement or object will the person become addicted? The following sections address these fundamental issues in addiction.

Susceptibility to Addiction and the Choice of Addictive Object: Social and Cultural Factors

Social Class

Social class has little relationship to *initiation* of drug or alcohol use (Jessor and Jessor 1977; Kandel et al. 1978). However, social class is strongly related to problem drinking (Cahalan and Room 1974), to overweight (Garn, Bailey, and Higgins 1980), and to health behaviors in general (Becker 1974). Some of the social-class differences that have been uncovered are massive; in Stunkard et al. (1972) lower-class girls were obese nine times as often as girls from upper-class homes. What complicates relationships between socioeconomic status (SES) and drug behavior is that lower-SES groups are more likely both to be abstinent (in the case of alcohol) and to show high levels of treated alcoholism (Armor et al. 1978). While lower-SES groups may insist on avoiding drugs and alcohol altogether, they inspire less commitment to health as a general positive value (Becker 1974). For example, the value placed on weight control is primarily an upper-middle-class one, and immigrant groups show reduced weight levels as they adopt middle-class value orientations (Goldblatt et al. 1965). Alcohol intoxication also conflicts with the more stringent middle-class emphasis on sobriety.

It has become fashionable to deny that lower-SES groups differ from higher-SES groups in anything but money and what it can buy. Investigators who focus on social and political forces maintain that greater incidences of self-destructive or unhealthy behavior are simply the results of poverty, enforced repression, and perhaps resulting self-hate (cf. Lewontin et al. 1984;

Pelton 1981). From the other direction, disease and biological determinists like Vaillant (1983) deny that alcoholism can be socially caused, despite Vaillant's finding that his lower-class subjects were more than three times as likely to be alcoholic as those in his middle-class college sample. Social-class differences in addiction nonetheless appear to be persistent and substantial and to be based in differences in attitudes as well as behavior. Whether these differences mean that some groups are less susceptible to addiction overall remains cloudy, however. The broadening of an awareness of the forms of addiction may indicate that higher-SES addictions simply occur in different guises. For example, Yates et al. (1983) found anorexics (who were all women in this study) and compulsive runners (who were usually men) came from uniformly middle-class backgrounds. Subjects were preoccupied with their appearance and health, which in these extreme cases led to behavior that contributed to the physical deterioration subjects dreaded.

Peer and Parental Influence

Cahalan and Room (1974) found that social drinking context was more important than demographic factors in predicting drinking problems. That is, who one drinks with determines drinking problems more than one's social background. The study of adolescent drug and alcohol use has identified important strands of both peer and parental influence on the initiation of marijuana, alcohol, and other illicit drug use (Jessor and Jessor 1977; Kandel et al. 1978), as well as smoking (Williams 1971). Different constellations were apparent for each type of drug use: Peer influence was most important for initiation of marijuana use, somewhat less important for drinking, and least important for other illicit drug use, where parent–child closeness was the major determining factor (Kandel et al. 1978). Parents' influence was felt both through their modeling of alcohol (and cigarette) use and other values they conveyed. The connection between peer group influence and drug taking combined equally the shaping of attitudes and behaviors by the peer group with the seeking out by adolescents of peers who shared already existing attitudes (Kandel 1978).

Cahalan and Room's findings indicated that more than the initiation of drinking, actual *patterns* of drinking were determined by the social context. Such social drinking influences have been studied over a range of contexts (Harford and Gaines 1982). Peer social influence has an even larger role to play in the case of illicit substances, where parents and other social figures do not ordinarily provide models of behavior. Becker's (1953) work is a landmark in the description of social learning and drug effects. In his study of marijuana use, Becker found novices were instructed by experienced users not only how to notice and interpret the drug's effects, but why these effects were positive ones. Jacobson and Zinberg (1975) found that groups that fostered controlled use of narcotics were typified by values encouraging moderate use; the maintenance of outside professional, scholastic, and social interests and connections; and rules limiting drug use to certain occasions and specific settings.

Culture and Ethnicity

Cultural outlooks on the appropriate use and the corrupting influence of a substance affect its addictive potential. In cultures where use of a substance is comfortable, familiar, and socially regulated both as to style of use and appropriate time and place for such use, addiction is less likely and may be practically unknown. Addiction is prevalent, however, when a substance is seen culturewide as both an effective mood modifier and as dangerous and difficult to control. These societal variables act on the inner experience produced by a substance and the individual's sense of his ability to control this experience. Chapter 2 described the historical evolution of views of alcohol in this country and the implications these have had for approaches to and conceptions of alcoholism, as opposed to the ideas about narcotic addiction that have grown up in this country and the Western world generally (see chapter 1). Historically, within the United States, narcotics and alcohol have exchanged places more than once as embodiments of chemical enslavement.

Within these larger cultural patterns dwell substantial group differences, particularly in attitudes toward alcohol. Ethnic patterns of drinking are robust, even for groups that have been otherwise assimilated into mainstream American values (Greeley et al. 1980). This suggests that the stylistic aspects of socialization into drinking practices—such as the introduction of children to mild spirits in ritual and family contexts (as discussed in chapter 2)—may not be as important as more basic views that are communicated to the child about what alcohol does to the individual. The kinds of mood-modifying and spiritual efficacy that are a part of addictive alcohol experiences can underlie cultural and parental socialization of drinking practices (Christiansen and Goldman 1983; Zucker 1976). Moderate versus excessive drinking practices may then be more the result than the cause of attitudes toward alcohol. Attitudes about alcohol can also be part of a larger perspective toward experience. For example, some have connected Irish intemperance to an Irish ethos that is at once mystical and tragic (cf. Bales 1946), while Jewish sobriety is seen to stem from Jews' traditional dedication to rationality and self-control (Glazer 1952; Keller 1970). The opposite poles of Eskimo and Indian drinking, on the one hand, and Chinese and Japanese drinking, on the other, exist within larger value contexts. The

Chinese and Japanese in the United States have embraced achievement—a value with which alcohol intoxication is incompatible—while Eskimos and Indians do not measure high in achievement. Observers have noted instead that Eskimos simply place a different value on the sobriety and moderation that limit alcohol intoxication for other groups (cf. Klausner et al. 1980).

MacAndrew and Edgerton (1969) painstakingly analyzed historical data to show that American Indians were *not* intrinsically debauched drinkers but that white traders encouraged the development of rampant alcoholism among Indian groups. Mangin (1957) found universal drinking but few signs of drinking pathology among the Andean Indians, who had strong ceremonial drinking customs. Mohatt's (1972) fascinating analysis of the role of alcohol in the Teton Sioux culture traced alcoholism in this tribe to the destruction by whites of the traditional means Indians had used to achieve adulthood and a sense of masculine competence. Before the advent of whites, the brave became an adult through displays of courage and underwent a mystical transformation brought on by fasting and prayer in an isolated setting. As the opportunities for exercising personal competence and undergoing psychic journeys were reduced and denigrated by the intrusion of whites, alcohol—which produced similar kinds of experiences—became a debilitating replacement source of fantasy and male sense of self. McClelland et al. (1972) analyzed this as a typical instance of cultural sources of heavy drinking. They found in societies that valued the demonstration of male power, but that made the achievement of such power difficult, drinking was heavier and was associated with antisocial aggression.

Bales (1946) provided a general analysis of the relation between problem drinking and cultural dilemmas such as the one McClelland et al. described in the case of male power. Bales saw three general cultural factors leading to alcoholism: (1) "the degree to which the culture operates to bring about acute needs for adjustment, or inner tensions, in its members"—whether connected to sex, guilt, aggression, and so on; (2) whether cultural attitudes toward alcohol suggest drinking "as a means of relieving . . . inner tensions"; and (3) "the degree to which the culture provides suitable substitute means of satisfaction" (p. 482). MacAndrew and Edgerton (1969), in their classic work *Drunken Comportment,* have provided the most detailed survey of the behaviors and feelings that result from imbibing alcohol. Cultures vary tremendously in the extent to which alcohol leads to aggressive and other socially disruptive behavior. MacAndrew and Edgerton further noted that the cultures in which such drinking appears see drinking as a time out from ordinary societal standards and as offering an excuse for antisocial behavior that otherwise is not tolerated. This is in sharp distinction to the moderate drinking of Jews, Italians, Chinese, et al., who disapprove strongly of drinking that leads to antisocial behavior.

These moderate-drinking cultures do not seem to have a category for loss of control of drinking. Paradoxically, those cultures and groups most fearful that substance use will become uncontrolled are those that display the highest incidence of abuse of the substance. It was among Irish subjects—those who expressed the most pronounced views of alcohol's good and evil qualities—that Vaillant (1983) discovered by far the largest amount of alcohol dependence. Compared with other ethnic groups, it was also Irish subjects in the study who were most likely to respond to drinking problems by abstaining entirely, while other ethnics were more likely simply to cut back their drinking. This perspective on alcohol's effects is similar to cultural views of other potent drugs of abuse, like the opiates. All such substances have been "deemed capable of tempting, possessing, corrupting, and destroying persons without regard to the prior conduct or condition of those persons" (Blum 1969: 327).

Such views are not inherent to a drug or fixed in a given culture, as Blum made clear in tracing the development of opium as anathema in China in the eighteenth century, despite the drug's long historical presence as an indigenous substance in Asia. Berridge and Edwards (1981) described a similar evolution of views of opiates in nineteenth-century Britain, one that led to the modern definition of addiction as an uncontrollable physical urge for a drug. Levine's (1978) analysis carefully detailed how, in a relatively short time, large parts of American society came to conceive of alcoholism as an uncontrollable disease commonly induced by regular drinking. Nineteenth-century temperance adherents were unable to discover (despite assiduous efforts) historical first-person accounts of loss of control of drinking by colonial Americans. By the 1830s, however, loss of control had become a stereotyped feature of the public confessions of drunkards who took up the temperance pledge.

These cultural perceptions of drugs and their effects are fundamental to the entire debate in the United States about the nature, incidence, and cure of addiction (see chapters 1 and 2). The notions of uncontrollable alcoholism and narcotic addiction are the results of complex social processes in this country. These processes include population shifts, urbanization, and the breakdown of stable community structures (Clausen 1961; Rothman 1971; Zinberg and Fraser 1979); nativistic sentiments, the assertion of Puritanical values, and social stereotyping of drug or alcohol use with foreign or outcast elements in the society (Clausen 1961; Goode 1972; Gusfield 1963); the medicalization of psychic maladies and deviant behavior and the assertiveness of key organizations such as the Federal Bureau of Narcotics, the American Medical Association, and the National Council on Alcoholism (Foucault 1973; King 1972; Wiener 1981). In pivotal eras, as groups of people lost both real and perceived control of their lives and as excess characterized major areas of social behavior, concepts of addiction were presented that embodied and explained prevalent feelings (cf. Peele and Brodsky 1975).

Although these social developments cannot be reduced to psychological terms, their impact on individual psychology is monumental. Paradoxically, those people most ready to acknowledge their addictions are those most susceptible to cultural stereotypes about these addictions, despite their own often contrary experiences. Consider that Robins et al. (1980) discovered that heroin users among Vietnam veterans were no more likely to become regular users than were amphetamine and barbiturate users; nor did regular heroin users suffer more adverse consequences in their lives than did regular users of the other drugs. Yet heroin users in the study *claimed* that heroin was more dependence-producing and more dangerous. Confessed alcoholics typically trumpet the uncontrollable nature of their disease, while their own behavior bespeaks a range of motivations and variations in drinking; those mired in heroin addiction most vividly describe the withdrawal and craving that they themselves have often overcome. Thus the cultural stereotype of a drug infiltrates the kinds of relationships people believe they have with a substance. Addiction becomes a label and an explanation those who behave addictively apply to themselves.

The cultural analysis suggesting that drug addiction occurs to the extent that a drug experience serves crucial emotional functions and is viewed as having power over the individual applies to other experiences as well. This view helps to answer the question of whether cultures or groups with high rates of alcoholism or drug addiction suffer more psychopathology than other cultural groups. While this idea may hold for certain severely stressed groups like Indians, Eskimos, and blacks, it makes less sense as a description of comparably assimilated and well-off ethnic groups. For example, it does not seem possible that Irish Americans in Vaillant's inner-city group are seven times more often the victims of psychopathology than inner-city Italians and Jews, as their alcoholism rates alone would indicate.

What rather seems to be the case is that groups with lower drug or alcohol addiction rates express their distress and potential for addiction in other ways. Glassner and Berg (1980) noted that Jews referred to overeating as the Jewish version of alcoholism. "What this quasi-joking reference meant is that Jews who have emotional and coping problems that lead to substance use that is harmful and degrading would be more likely to eat than to drink excessively" (Peele 1983c: 964). Indeed, Jewish and some other ethnic groups with low rates of alcoholism do show greater overweight and obesity problems (Patai 1977: 447–53; Stunkard 1967), perhaps because it is more common for such groups to invest eating and food with emotional significance as signs of love and caring (cf. Bruch 1973). In our contemporary youth culture, the preoccupation is with thinness as a signal of a person's worth and ability to inspire love, an ethos of which compulsive exercise and bulimia are symptomatic (Boskind-White and White 1983; Polivy and Herman 1983). Accompanying this development is the tendency for runners to describe themselves as addicts and to refer, however vaguely, to endorphins as the source of their addiction. Peele and Brodsky (1975) meanwhile found interpersonal addictions to be more prevalent for the middle class. Peele (1977) described the social setting in which relationships are more often addictive as being one "where social values hold out the possibility of falling in love as a life solution, where love is seen as a transcendent experience and as a rite of passage into adulthood, and where social life is organized almost entirely around being with the one you love" (p. 121).

Susceptibility to and Choice of Addiction: Situational Factors

The Vietnam War experience offered something as close to an experimental study of the effect of environment on human susceptibility to narcotic addiction as we are ever likely to have. That is, drug abusers (or others rated high in susceptibility to drug abuse) and those not previously involved with drugs (or likely to become so) were exposed to a setting where narcotics were readily available and drug use was accepted. Follow-up investigations assessed how many of these men became addicted in Vietnam and evaluated how many of those addicted remained addicted in the States and how many achieved permanent remission here. Within the broad outcomes of using narcotics or not after returning to the United States, it was possible to compare those who became readdicted with those who did not. Although data were collected on groups of men comparable to those who served in Vietnam but who did not enter military service, these data were analyzed mainly for initiation to drug use and not addiction to drugs (Robins 1978), so that comparisons with nonsoldier addicts are implicit rather than direct.

The analysis of these data under the direction of Lee Robins, a sociologist, has overwhelmingly pointed to situational determination of drug addiction. Around 50 percent of the men in Vietnam used a narcotic, and about 20 percent became addicted there, figures far greater than occur for even highly susceptible populations in the United States (Robins 1978; Robins et al. 1975). What is more, addiction largely disappeared on returning to the United States, even for those who used narcotics at home (Robins et al. 1975; Robins et al. 1980). The most obvious feature of the Vietnam environment from the standpoint of narcotic addiction was the ready availability of drugs. However, this does not clearly or entirely explain the addiction of Vietnam soldiers and veterans. Soldiers in other parts of Asia who had easy access to drugs showed nothing like Vietnam addiction levels (Zinberg 1974). Among those veterans who used narcotics at home, 84 percent quickly found a supplier in the United States, yet most still did not become addicted (Robins et al. 1975). Thus, the elements in the Vietnam or U.S. environment that caused people to respond addictively to narcotics or other drugs went beyond simple availability.

The variables Robins and her co-workers found to predict drug use in Vietnam and post-Vietnam addiction were prior abuse of drugs and other deviant behavior (Robins et al. 1980). Those who came from settings where drug use was likely, such as inner-city ghettos, were most likely to use drugs in Vietnam even if they had not previously used drugs (Robins 1978). Robins et al.'s data do not point to personality traits but rather to aspects of the soldiers' pre-Vietnam environment as factors predisposing to addiction. The complex interaction between home and neighborhood environment and the personal disposition to be addicted is perhaps best described in Chein et al.'s (1964) classic work, *The Road to H.* These investigators also found it hard to separate personality from situation. The kind of bleak inner-city existences that typified most of their addict subjects were reflected in a personal outlook that welcomed narcosis just as much as the outlook engendered by serving in an Asian war zone.

Stress and Control of Stress

Stress is often proposed as a likely candidate for causing and maintaining addiction. Smokers smoke more when stressed and find it easier to cut back or quit when not stressed (Caplan et al. 1975; Leventhal and Cleary 1980). Relapse in all types of addiction, including smoking, drinking, gambling, overeating, and narcotics, is most frequently prompted by situational stressors and negative emotional reactions to them (Marlatt 1982). However, it was not stress alone that caused overeating by obese subjects in Slochower (1983), but rather the presence of stress that subjects could not affect directly. Lazarus (1966), Leventhal and Nerenz (1983), and Sarason and Sarason (1981) have proposed inclusive models of stress reactions that combine people's subjective interpretation of stressful events, their resources—both psychological and situational—for dealing with stress, and their belief in their ability to cope with it along with the beliefs and support of those around them. Both the Vietnam and ghetto settings were ones where sources of stressful feelings were not readily addressed and where deeply engrained pessimism about the possibility of ameliorating the situation reigned.

Uncontrollable stress at a microsituational level seems to parallel the larger societal conditions that encourage addiction. That is, groups whose values and social structure are disturbed (e.g., by foreign invasion or eco-nomic underclass status) and who then show pathological extremes in be-havior, including addiction, can be thought of as undergoing stress they cannot realistically hope to modify. Do cultures in general show historical shifts in addiction that correspond to the greater stressfulness of life? A more complex, interactive model suggests that it is the socially available means to handle what might be stressful situations that is at issue. In Bales's (1946) and McClelland et al.'s (1972) analyses, the question is how readily culture members can find concrete ways to deal with central, ten-sion-producing demands made on them by the society rather than accept society's offer of magical, chemical, or other nonrealistic means for re-sponding to these demands.

Social Support and Intimacy

Allen (1984) proposed a model for health behavior change and maintenance that focuses on the strength of the social group's support for such change. On the other hand, the Vietnam and inner-city ghetto situations are ones where social supports have often encouraged narcotic addiction. These ad-dictive support groups are composed of young male peers, the same kind of peer groups Cahalan and Room (1974) connected with the highest rates of problem drinking. What was lacking for the soldiers in Vietnam was the presence of people to whom they could turn for emotional support that did not involve taking drugs. This deficiency was part of the general absence of opportunity for the kinds of intimacy provided by family, older people, and women. Chein et al. (1964) noted that ghetto adolescent addicts did not view family, friends, and sexual relationships as offering intimacy so much as holding out contacts and money for obtaining drugs. Schur's (1962) de-scription of British addicts who were maintained on heroin also empha-sized their lack of intimate social networks, even though the British ad-dicts as a group were more often from the middle class and came from less socially disturbed environments than U.S. addicts.

Opportunity for Enterprise and Positive Rewards

Along with the absence of a range of emotional supports, the soldier in Vietnam was deprived of rewarding, productive activity. While many peo-ple find the work of war—combined with its lethargy and boredom—diffi-cult to tolerate under any circumstances, the Vietnam soldier had in addi-tion to withstand intense moral questioning of his purpose and effort. The street heroin addict Chein and his co-workers studied was likewise de-prived of the opportunity for positive enterprise. "Unlike others, ... he could not find a vocation, a career, a meaningful, sustained activity around which he could . . . wrap his life." Instead, he relied on the addiction to provide "a vocation around which . . . [he could] build a reasonably full life" and establish an identity, albeit a negative one (Chein 1969: 23–24). More fundamentally, the ghetto addict saw the entire world as a dreary and dangerous place, one it was just as well to avoid. As chapter 4 demonstrated, it is not possible to separate the appeal of a drug from the environment in which it is administered and especially the richness of the environment, or at least the drug user's perception of its richness.

The ghetto addict interviewed by Chein and his colleagues (1964) demonstrated that "the likelihood . . . [a person] will become an addictive user of opiate drugs is most significantly affected by his experiences with drug use in the context of his current situation *as this has been structured by his entire experience*" (in Shaffer and Burglass 1981: 95, italics added). Chein et al.'s exploration of the heroin addict's world revealed this experience to be similar to that brought on for many young men by the Vietnam War, only the domestic addict's outlook was not so easily remedied by a change in external circumstances. For Chein et al., the New York City addict's very craving during addiction was "an expression of the preferred modes of gratification adopted by the individual and, as such, is dependent on the individual's attitudes toward objects and sources of satisfaction independently of and preceding experience with opiate drugs" (in Shaffer and Burglass 1981: 106). In other words, this addict showed a residual—or personality—effect from his deprived surroundings, one that is not likely to be exclusively a property of ghetto inhabitants.

Susceptibility to and Choice of Addiction: Individual Factors

Only a small minority of users of the most powerful psychoactive agents become addicted, even in the most barren of urban environments (Lukoff and Brook 1974). At the same time, there are notable individuals who consistently create addictions out of all their involvements (Peele 1982b). That either the resistance most people show to addiction or the panaddictive tendencies displayed by others is due to physiological make-up cannot be maintained; nor is it possible that people become addicted solely as a result of the cumulative, excessive use of a substance (see chapter 3). On the other hand, since the 1970s, the tide has run strongly against the belief in personality determinants of addiction. A survey of assessments of alcoholics by Miller (1976) found that they did not have significantly abnormal personality traits. Vaillant (1983) likewise found no reliable indication of personality-based sources for alcoholism. Research with narcotics addicts has yielded similar results (Platt and Labate 1976; Robins et al. 1980), and Lang

(1983), examining studies of both alcohol and drug abuse, found few indications of universal personality patterns.

The complex relationships between personality and behavior extend beyond addiction. Because personality traits do not reliably predict people's actions in all situations, interactive, personality-situation models now dominate psychological thinking (Magnuson 1981; Mischel 1984). The template-matching procedure is a variety of this approach in which a situation is specified and the different types of behavior possible within it are delineated (Bem and Funder 1978). An ideal type of person is then described who would be most likely to behave one way or the other. Actual individuals are evaluated in terms of how close to an ideal type they are, and their likelihood of performing the various behaviors is thereby gauged. For example, Bem and Lord (1979) hypothesized that an intensely competitive and undermining person would be most likely to undercut a potential partner in a mixed-motive game. Subjects who fit this description most closely (measured by their roommates' descriptions of them) did most often choose the competitive strategy.

A completed model of addiction requires that a template be constructed of the person most likely to be addicted. The analysis of addictive experiences and of the situational and social pressures most likely to encourage addiction creates a complementary mold of a person to whom addictive experiences are appealing and who is susceptible to addictive pressures. The mold is a composite construction and includes individual value orientations along with personality traits that have been discovered to be relevant to addiction. What guide this analysis of the addicted person are the linkages among behavior, setting, and individual characteristics and the need for a model to make sense out of these complex relationships.

*Interpreting the Meaning of the Individual's Choice of
Addictive Object*

Some people will become addicted to one object and show no interest, even after frequent exposure, in another. Addicts—even after having demonstrated panaddictive tendencies—will express a preference for one object of addiction. There is some evidence relating personality type to choice of addictive drug. Spotts and Shontz (1982) related the life histories and psychological profiles of abusers of different classes of drugs to psychoanalytic, developmental crises; the investigators later (Spotts and Shontz 1983) found some basis for these differences in MMPI and other quantitative personality measures. Kern (1984) found that preference for stimulant versus depressant drugs was a function of the user's need for augmentation versus suppression of incoming stimuli. Milkman and Sunderwirth (1983) suggested that drug users and others were responsive to three classes of stimulation: arousal, depression, and fantasy experiences.

While indicating an appropriate emphasis on the addict's relationship to an experience, these perspectives on personality leave out central elements in the addictive formula and, at their worst, mirror useless reductionist assumptions about addiction. Preference for a type of stimulus is not equivalent to addiction and, indeed, does not address the essential question of when, how, and why a person becomes addicted to any class or source of stimulation. Moreover, addicts do not seem to be responding exclusively, or even largely, to a physiological dimension of the drug experience. For example, the hospital patients who almost never report a desire to continue drug use (generally of narcotics) after leaving the hospital may be addicted to cigarettes or other drugs or involvements. In particular, some will be alcohol abusers. Yet their abhorrence of the narcotic addict role prevents them from experiencing narcotic drug effects as an appealing, everyday involvement.

In an almost total reversal of this kind of rejection of the pursuit of illicit drug experiences are the outsiders Becker (1963) identified who preferred these experiences. Such differences in attitudes toward licit and illicit drugs are sometimes mirrored by particular ethnic groups. In his autobiography, *Mine Enemy Grows Older,* Alexander King (1958) claimed never to have known a Jewish alcoholic, although many of the heroin addicts he encountered in treatment were Jewish (among whom he himself was numbered). The Jews as a group epitomize the way ethnic attitudes influence the desire for drug experiences. Eddie Fisher (1981), in his autobiography *Eddie: My Life, My Loves,* described himself as a lifelong—if irreligious—Jew. He began getting amphetamine injections early in his career and depended on the drug to perform. Later, Fisher injected the drugs himself, became addicted both to amphetamines and cocaine, and also became strongly dependent on sedatives (Fisher reported experiencing withdrawal from all these substances).

Yet despite being part of a heavy-drinking world and periodically becoming intoxicated, Fisher never developed an urge to drink. Similarly, when forced to inhale cigarettes for over a year for a television sponsor (and being married to at least one smoker), he detested the experience and never took up smoking on his own. Fisher is an example of how ethnic, social, and parental socialization colors experience so as to permit addiction to take place to some varieties of drugs in a given pharmacological class but not others. The legality of a substance is one salient dimension of the preference for drug experiences: It explains why narcotics addicts will often readily turn to alcohol (O'Donnell 1969), but why the reverse shift rarely occurs. There are other attitudinal dimensions to the preference for a given drug or addictive involvement. For example, a person can inherit attitudes that make cigarette smoking an acceptable habit but that rule out over-weight at any cost.

Lack of Values Toward Moderation, Self-Restraint, and Health

While addicts may find special or idiosyncratic rewards in the addictive ex-perience, it is also possible they seek the same rewards as nonaddicts do from these involvements, only they seek them without restraint. For ex-ample, findings on social assertiveness and drinking indicate that normal drinkers (as opposed to alcoholics) use alcohol to facilitate social interac-tions (Beckman 1978) *and* that men use alcohol to feel dominant and sex-ually aggressive (Brown et al. 1980). The difference in alcohol-related social experiences here may not be so much one of type as degree. Similarly, Rob-bins and Joseph (1982) distinguished nonaddicted runners from addicted runners on the grounds that the former used running as an escape, while the latter used it as an essential means of coping with stress. Both may find that running relaxes tensions, but the addict seems to crave this effect in an extravagant way.

That the same people abuse all kinds of substances has been a regular and notable finding in the addiction field (cf. Kandel 1984; Robins et al. 1980). In his formulation of "Drug Abuse as Excessive Behavior," Gilbert (1981) analyzed drug abuse as a tendency some people have toward excess in general. For example, Gilbert noted in reviewing a study by Marlatt et al. (1973)—which demonstrated that alcoholics drank more when they thought a drink contained alcohol whether it actually did or not—that al-coholics drank more than nonalcoholics in *all* experimental conditions. "One might conclude from these data that alcoholics drink a lot of alcohol because they drink a lot of all fluids" (p. 233). Recently, Istvan and Mataraz-zo (1984) summarized a large number of studies that have examined the correlations among consumption of alcohol, tobacco, and caffeine. Rela-tionships were generally positive and in many cases quite strong—particu-larly at the highest levels of consumption. For example, most studies have found that over 90 percent of alcoholics smoke. Dielman (1979) found heavy gamblers drank heavily.

People who behave excessively are characterized by their failure to de-lay gratification. Mischel (1979) has analyzed the "development of self-con-trol competencies" among children and their awareness of "effective delay rules" (p. 750). Combined with this ability to moderate consumption is the *value* people place on avoiding excess or postponing gratification. No mat-ter how much some people enjoy eating banana splits, they restrain them-selves in line with other values they have. One such value is a generalized desire to be healthy; valuing health may be an important component in the attitudes that are communicated from parent to child (Peele 1983b) and within social groups (Becker 1974) that influence the likelihood of drug, alcohol, and other harmful excess. Those who use substances dangerously have regularly been found to take risks with their health generally (Istvan and Matarazzo 1984); for example, Kalant and Kalant (1976) showed that users of psychoactive substances—both licit and illicit—engaged in a variety of behaviors that led to illness, injury, and death. In addition, people may value sobriety sufficiently so that even if they find drinking or sedatives to bring welcome tension relief, they refuse regularly to resort to emotional palliatives that would cloud their awareness.

Antisocial Attitudes and Aggression, Alienation, and
Lack of Achievement

After a time when the emphasis has been exclusively on addiction as a behavioral, physical, or psychological—and not a moral—problem, Jessor and Jessor (1977), Kandel (1984), Peele (1981a), and others have reemphasized the relationship between values and drug and alcohol use. Drug and alcohol abuse among the young is connected to antisocial acting out (Jessor et al. 1980; Wingard et al. 1979) and to independence, nonconformity, and autonomy (Jessor and Jessor 1977). Unfortunately, this literature generally does not distinguish degree of harmfulness of drug use, so that relationships between measures of drug use and of independence and autonomy confuse destructive alienation and the desire for exploration and new experience (cf. Jessor and Jessor 1977; Kandel et al. 1978). Several studies of marijuana users have found them to be more spontaneous, open, and inquisitive than their nondrug-using peers (Goldstein and Sappington 1977; Kay et al. 1978; Segal 1977), although heavier users show poorer psychological adjustment (Kilpatrick et al. 1976). Prison inmates who used only marijuana were significantly less likely to become alcoholic than those who used *no* illicit drugs (Lewis et al. 1983).

Problem drinking, narcotics use and addiction, and smoking have been repeatedly related to deviance-proneness, rebelliousness, disturbed family backgrounds, and antisocial behavior generally (Cahalan and Room 1974; Newman 1970; Robins et al. 1980). Robins et al. (1980) found that social deviance was related to all kinds of illicit drug use, but more so to heroin use. "That we find higher levels of social disability among heroin users . . . is probably attributable to the kinds of people who use heroin. Men disposed to social problems are likely to use drugs, and those with the very greatest predisposition . . . are the ones likely to use heroin" (p. 229). An important component in the constellation of heavy drug and alcohol use for men is aggressive and violent behavior. MacAndrew (1965) noted that personality inventory items indicating pathological aggression distinguished alcoholics from nonalcoholic psychiatric outpatients; the same test items also identified drug abusers and addicts in later studies (Burke and Marcus 1977; MacAndrew 1981). A similar MMPI profile characterized compulsive gamblers (Roston 1961). McClelland et al. (1972) focused on an individual's desire for dominance or personalized power as being at the core of heavy drinking. Lewis et al. (1983) found in a prison population that alcoholism and drug abuse were more common for men with antisocial personalities.

Vaillant (1983) strenuously argued that rather than drinking in line with their antisocial and aggressive tendencies, alcoholics have these tendencies instigated by their drinking regardless of their values and personalities. He cited the case of the subject "James O'Neill," who was a model of socialized behavior when sober but who became totally irresponsible and a reckless philanderer when drunk. In Vaillant's (1977) previous work with the same subject population, he identified alcoholism as a form of psychological adaptation. There he discussed the case of "Robert Hood" (pp. 177–80)—who was a juvenile delinquent who became an early smoker and heavy drinker (and an eventual alcoholic) and who was sexually promiscuous and beat his child—in the context of the "less adaptive aspects of acting out." Promiscuity and child abuse cannot be explained exclusively as the result of drinking too much; for example, Hood never saw his child after he stopped drinking. Vaillant's change of heart on this issue from his 1977 perspective to the one he adopted in 1983 was due to his conversion to the view that alcoholism is a so-called primary disease and not the result of psychological dysfunction.

Vaillant's two views of alcoholics do serve to illustrate, however, the difficulties in determining the nature of addictive behavior as a cause or as a consequence of the characteristics of addicts. Robins et al. (1980) found that regular or addicted users of heroin, amphetamines, and barbiturates showed more social disturbance than did nonusers or casual users. This was due *both* to their predispositions before initiating drug use and to the consequences of their involvement with drugs. Jessor (1979) has established prospectively that a lack of achievement and of other positive social values causes drug use. This lack of positive values in turn makes achievement and constructive involvements less likely (Jones and Berglas 1978). Kandel (1984) found that greater use of marijuana (combined with other drug use) was associated with increasing disaffection and alienation from social institutions.

Fear of Failure, Intolerance of Uncertainty, and the Belief in Magical Solutions

The lack of positive motivation that Jessor (1979) uncovered in young drug users was part of a larger negative outlook in which these users doubt the possibility of gaining satisfaction from the world. Jessor's portrait is very close to that of the adolescent addicts Chein et al. (1964) depicted, who pursue a life centered around drugs as part of an alternative value system that offers them "a sense of a personal identity, a place in society, a commitment, personal associations based on a seemingly common purpose, a feeling of belonging to an in-group, a vocation and an avocation, and a means of filling the void in an otherwise empty life" (in Shaffer and Burglass 1981: 106). Chein and his co-workers found that addiction served as a life- and consciousness-organizing principle for those who were overwhelmed by fear and pessimism at the same time that the addiction confirmed these addicts' world view.

Achievement-oriented behavior is positively motivated by one stable personality disposition—the need to achieve—and negatively motivated by another—the desire to avoid failure. Fear of failure is the disposition to regard challenging situations solely for their potential to bring about failure and embarrassment. Atkinson and Feather (1966: 369) provided the classic description of the person whose behavior is dominated by the fear of failure. Such a person

> resists activities in which his competence might be evaluated against a standard or the competence of others. Were he not surrounded by social constraints . . . he would never voluntarily undertake an activity requiring skill when there is any uncertainty about the outcome. . . . [Thus] constrained, . . . he will defend himself by undertaking activities in which success is virtually assured or activities which offer so little real chance of success that the appearance of trying to do a very difficult thing . . . more than compensates for repeated and minimally embarrassing failures. Given an opportunity to quit an activity that entails evaluation of his performance for some other kind of activity, he is quick to take it . . . [while displaying] dogged determination in the pursuit of the highly improbable goal. . . . [His] general resistance to achievement-oriented activity opposes any and all sources of positive motivation to undertake the customary competitive activities of life . . . [and] his long history of relative failure means he will view his chances in new ventures more pessimistically.

What is most telling in the description of the person high in fear of failure is how he tolerates the assured failure from self-defeating activity better than he does the middling probability of success in ordinary involvements. There are many harkenings here to the behavior of addicts and drug abusers: a lack of feeling for positive opportunity, ritualized behavior as a replacement for fear-inspiring challenge, and the self-handicapping strategy by which the person's previous failures (brought on by involvement in ill-fated activities highly unlikely to bear fruit) are used as excuses for continued failure (Jones and Berglas 1978). Indeed, Birney et al. (1969) have analyzed the rise in drug abuse through the 1960s as the result of the increase in learned fear of failure. The addict too prefers highly ritualized behaviors in place of engaging in uncertain and challenging enterprise where he will be evaluated by dominant cultural standards. More generally, addicts show great "difficulty in tolerating ambiguity and ambivalence" (Zinberg et al. 1978: 19). Focusing attention on a drug and its effects eliminates the anxiety created by unstructured activities and their uncertain results.

Chein et al. (1964, in Shaffer and Burglass 1981: 111–112) noted this characteristic in addicts' search for "kicks":

> Normally, the search for new experience leads to the broadening of one's intellectual and sensory horizons and to the pleasures of working at challenging and difficult situations and tasks which, despite anxiety and strain, are capped with some degree of mastery or even with nondisgraceful failure. . . . In other instances, the outcome is not so fortunate. At one extreme, there is the total blunting of this complex drive; these are people who lead a life of stultifying routine. . . . The search for kicks is, on the surface, at the other pole. . . . [However, it actually represents a comparable experience to stultifying routine] as though the experience of novelty per se were substituted for the confrontation and mastery of ever-new and challenging situations. . . . The kicks they seek are inseparably linked with trouble from the onset. Their kicks are usually highly mannered, group-oriented, and stereotyped. . . . [and] are limited to new ways of being intoxicated and . . . mannerisms of dress, hair style, speech and gesture.

Because of a lack of persistence in goal-oriented activity, the person high in fear of failure prefers easy and quick solutions over ferreting out the roots of a problem. Drugs provide a means of modifying troubling feelings and sensations without influencing their actual causes. Those who rely on drug-induced moods want simply to modify their feelings, since they don't genuinely believe they can influence the situations that cause these feelings through real activity. Peele (1982a) labeled this method of coping as one involving "magical solutions." Such solutions include drug addiction and involvements like binge shopping, compulsive gambling, destructive love relationships, and even murder said to be the result of insanity. In all these cases, people are drawn to a conclusive resolution for their existential problems that has no chance for actual success and that paradoxically provides its own excuse for failure: that is, perpetrators are claimed to be addicted, insane, in love, or otherwise under the control of inexorable urges.

Low Self-Esteem, Lack of Self-Efficacy, and External Locus of Control

The connections between the measures in this section and addiction are marked by the intuitive sense they make, the important theories and some findings that favor them, and the lack of definitive support for them. Addicts have repeatedly been described as having low self-esteem, based primarily on clinical impressions. There have been findings of low self-esteem in surveys of drug abusers (cf. Lang 1983; Lindblad 1977). As Benson and Wilsnack (1983: 66) found, for example, "the composite picture . . . on female alcoholics is that of a woman who is uncertain or conflicted about her womanliness, who has little self-esteem, [and] who has no clear sense of identity." Yet consistent differences in self-esteem have not been uncovered between alcoholics, addicts, or drug users and other groups, perhaps because many people who have low self-esteem still do not end up taking drugs or becoming addicts (Lang 1983; Miller 1976). Discussions of addicts' self-concepts include that of Peele and Brodsky (1975), who saw addicts of all kinds—including those involved in addictive interpersonal relationships—as lacking a sense of self in the absence of which the addiction becomes the core of their identity. Chein (1969) described how addicts acquire "a socially validated human identity, [albeit] a despised identity" through their addiction to heroin (p. 23). That is, the very self-esteem function that the addiction is required to serve itself contributes to the maintenance of addicts' negative self-images.

For Chein (1969), the addict's need for self-esteem is a result of his life history: "From his earliest days, the addict has been systematically educated and trained into incompetence" (p. 23). This incompetence refers both to an inability to arrive at a life vocation and also to a general inability to achieve desired results from life. Competence here suggests efficacy, or the ability to bring about desired aims for oneself. Bandura (1977a) has made the concept of self-efficacy a central one in psychology by asserting that therapeutic interventions achieve success by enhancing a person's sense of self-efficacy. At the same time, a general rubric for the problems that require therapy is the lack of self-efficacy. While competence describes objective coping abilities, self-efficacy connotes a person's subjective sense of his or her ability to control relevant aspects of the environment.

Since loss of control is a defining trait of alcoholism and other addictions, the belief in one's ability—and the actual ability—to harness drinking or other drug use has seemed to be a major factor in addiction. Laboratory investigations of alcoholics' drinking have made clear that no internal, biological mechanism leads to loss of control (see chapter 2). In lieu of such a mechanism, psychologists have investigated the internal–external locus of control of addicts—that is, their belief that they control the forces that regulate their lives (internal control) or else that their lives are controlled by forces outside themselves (external control). Different authors have provided divergent summaries of the results of such research in the case of alcoholism. Lang (1983) maintained that "In sum it appears that the popularity of I-E and related measures in personality and addictive behavior research is not supported by any decisive results they have produced" (p. 200).

Rohsenow (1983), on the other hand, claimed that "In summary, virtually all the studies that use adequate control groups have found that alcoholics and problem drinkers are more external in locus of control than nonproblem drinkers are" (p. 40).

Investigations have focused on alcoholics' beliefs about their ability to control their alcohol intake and their behavior while drinking and about the etiology of their drinking problems (cf. Stafford 1980: the Locus of Drinking Control Scale). For example, Heather et al. (1982) showed that alcoholics who believed that one drink inevitably led to relapse were more likely than other alcoholics to be drinking alcoholically six months after treatment and that alcoholics who viewed the nature of both their drinking problems and alcohol problems in general in uncontrollable, disease terms were more likely to drink destructively if they did drink (Heather et al. 1983). These studies are reminiscent of how heroin addicts' expectations about drugs affect their ability to withstand withdrawal and relapse pressures. Zinberg et al. (1978) remarked that addicts often "are well aware of their excessive fear of withdrawal" (p. 19). Peele and Brodsky (1975) reflected that the addict's sense of his impotence "has made him feel helpless not only against the rest of the world, but against the addictive object as well, so that he . . . believes he can neither live without it nor free himself from its grasp" (p. 62). Finally, Winick (1962) contrasted those addicts who matured out of addiction with those who remained lifelong addicts, "who decide that they are 'hooked,' make no effort to abandon addiction, and give in to what they regard as inevitable" (p. 6).

Susceptibility to and Choice of Addiction: Developmental Factors

> I am very grateful to old age because it has increased my desire for conversation and lessened my desire for food and drink.
> Cicero, *De Senectute*

The Incidence and Age of Remission in Addiction

Consistent findings indicate that alcohol, heroin, and other drug abuse are characteristic of young people, males in particular. Cahalan and Room (1974) described alcohol abuse as almost a rite of passage among certain groups of working-class males in their early twenties. Annual surveys of high school seniors throughout the 1970s and 1980s have shown that ritualized, weekend binge drinking has spread to a wider group, with approximately 50 percent of all high school senior males (and 30 percent of females) reporting having five or more drinks at one sitting in the previous two weeks (Johnston et al. 1981). In his pioneering study of maturing out of narcotic addiction, Winick (1962) estimated from examining the rolls of known narcotic addicts that two-thirds outgrew their reliance on heroin. Community and national surveys have regularly found a lessening of heroin use among males through their twenties (Brunswick 1979; O'Donnell et al. 1976; Robins and Murphy 1967). Similarly, Johnston et al. (1978) found that—during the height of the American college drug culture—the percentage of regular users of marijuana and other popular illicit drugs declined after the ages 19 to 22.

Quitting cigarettes and alcohol do not typically occur at the same peak periods for cessation of illicit drug use. People begin smoking and drinking in the same late adolescent and early adulthood period when illicit drug use begins, and they do show some slight trends toward quitting these legal drugs in their late twenties (Fishburne et al. 1980). Men have far fewer drinking problems as they proceed through their twenties, but this is rarely accomplished through abstinence, and most continue to drink moderately (Cahalan 1970; Roizen et al. 1978). The continuation of cigarette use later in life does not bespeak the same kind of moderation that takes place with drinking: Most middle-age smokers are probably addicted. One type of drug use that begins and peaks later in life is that involving medically prescribed substances such as tranquilizers and sedatives (Kandel 1980).

Disease theorists argue that the kind of alcohol abuse that moderates with age cannot be genuine alcohol addiction (Keller 1975). While propounding this case, Vaillant (1983) reported more than half his sample of alcohol abusers—who had generally more severe and longer-lived drinking problems than those studied by Cahalan and his colleagues—achieved remission, most without any kind of therapy. Remission in this study and others occurs *throughout* the life span. Twenty percent of the former problem drinkers in Vaillant's study became moderate drinkers, while even among the rest (whom Vaillant termed abstainers) total abstinence was unusual. Along with Vaillant, Tuchfeld (1981)—in the case of alcoholism—and Waldorf and Biernacki (1981) and Maddux and Desmond (1981)—in the case of narcotics—have chronicled remission from addiction at later stages in life. Indeed, Cahalan et al. (1969) identified later age spans as representing the greatest drop-offs in heavy drinking: While 24 percent of men age 60 to 64 were heavy drinkers, only 7 percent of those over age 65 were thus classified; 10 percent of the women age 45 to 49 were heavy drinkers, after which ages the percentage of heavy drinkers never rose above 2 percent.

Because they do not disturb normal life patterns in the same way that illicit drug use does, licit addictions such as smoking and overeating are more readily maintained into adulthood and beyond. While such eating disorders as anorexia and bulimia reach their greatest proportions in young age groups (Boskind-White and White 1983; Bruch 1973), the long-term excessive consumption that often leads to obesity is more of a middle-age phenomenon. The very range of ages over which overweight appears might be thought to argue against its essential addictive nature, at the same time that popular theories of overweight—particularly the set-point model (Bennett and Gurin 1982; Nisbett 1972; Polivy and Herman 1983)—present a physiologically deterministic basis for obesity. In fact, the gradualness, variety, and discontinuity of the behaviors leading to overweight are a sound paradigm for addictions of every type. Substantial remission in cigarette addiction and obesity may provide the best illustration of the essential—if inexact—self-regulating nature of much of human behavior including addiction.

Schachter (1982) countermanded his own and his co-workers' theories of obesity and smoking by discovering remission rates in the 50 to 60 percent range for both addictions (see chapter 3). Longitudinal and retrospective community surveys provide general support for his findings. Garn, Bailey, and Cole (1980) found in a longitudinal study that two-thirds of men (though only about 20 percent of women) lost their overweight within a ten-year period. Twenty-nine million Americans quit smoking between 1965 and 1975 (*Adult Use of Tobacco* 1975). A survey by the Public Health Service (1979) found three-quarters of those who had ever smoked had tried to quit and over half of this group had succeeded. In other words, even for addictive behaviors that are not illegal and that do not call into play the same level of social sanction as heroin addiction (or alcoholism), people are generally capable of eliminating self-destructive involvements to which they have become wedded.

The Meaning and the Means of Remission in Addiction

Schachter (1982) noted that the remission rates he uncovered were far superior to the typical 10 to 25 percent cure rates reported by therapy programs for smoking and obesity. These differences are not due to the severity of treated patients' smoking or obesity problems: Schachter found no differences in remission rates between heavy and light smokers or severely and mildly obese subjects. Conclusions about the efficacy of self-cure versus therapeutic cure are hard to draw from Schachter's and similar studies, however, because untreated and treated subjects are self-selected and because community studies like Schachter's examine outcomes over people's lifetimes, while therapy programs often report the success of a single therapeutic effort. On the other hand, Vaillant (1983) did not find differences in outcomes for his alcoholic hospital patients and comparable groups of untreated alcoholics at standardized two- and eight-year follow-up periods, while programs for alcoholics and narcotics addicts rarely show as much as 10 percent remission rates for follow-up periods from one to several years (Califano 1983; Emrick and Hansen 1983; Gordis et al. 1981).

Studies that uncover mild but distinct treatment effects for alcoholism have emphasized that what improvement does occur is traceable to developments in patients' lives outside the therapeutic milieu (Baekeland et al. 1975; Costello 1975; Orford and Edwards 1977), leading some theorists to maintain that a model linking cure solely to treatment inputs is inadequate and inaccurate (Moos and Finney 1982). That is, even when remission occurs following treatment, it is the result of improvements in a person's external involvements. Waldorf (1983) identified the same processes as accompanying cures both for heroin addicts who achieved remission on their own and for those who succeeded via treatment. The factors identified with cure in all these studies represent the basic building blocks in human functioning: improvement in intimate relationships (like marriage), changes in social networks, increased work opportunities and other professional considerations, health concerns, and more global factors such as maturation and a sense of who the addict is or wishes to be. These factors alternately stand for gratifications that will replace those from the addiction or that will be lost to people if they persist in the addictive behavior.

Divergent approaches to assessing natural remission in addiction disclose two different views of the phenomenon. Interviews with ex-addicts—particularly those who put themselves forward as having quit an addiction—emphasize subjective epiphanies or moments when people recognized their problems clearly and once and for all cast their addictions off (cf. Peele 1983d; Tuchfeld 1981; Waldorf and Biernacki 1981). Studies that on the other hand trace populations of people over their lifespans point toward natural progressions in habits dictated by age and other demographic factors (cf. Cahalan et al. 1969; Cahalan and Room 1974; Winick 1962). The former perspective depicts a sudden realignment of people's values and self-image that propels them to change; the latter describes a gradual process whereby people develop the emotional strength and environmental supports to find a new lifestyle.

Peele (1983d) found that the sudden insights that led to remission for all addictions involve people's juxtaposing an irrefutable image of their behavior against their self-image; they find they can no longer justify their behavior in terms of basic values they hold about themselves as parents, people in control of themselves, or people who would not consciously harm themselves. Greaves (1980) likewise saw the quitting of addiction to represent an existential realization and resolve, one that withstood nearly all pressures toward relapse. The opposite perspective—that of a gradual ripening into remission—is provided by the maturing out process. Winick (1962) and others have described adolescent addiction as an evasion of the responsibilities of adulthood. As addicts develop the emotional and practical resources to meet these demands, they find adulthood less frightening and its rewards more desirable and attainable. Consider the enigmatic love relationships that teenagers and young adults often pursue compulsively while finding only fleeting (or nonexistent) satisfaction from these connections (Peele and Brodsky 1975). As most young people become more confident with age, they make commitments to relationships that entail more realistic personal and practical satisfactions.

Shifting life pressures and subjective rewards continue to characterize remission through the life span. Caplan et al. (1975) detected that middle-age blue-collar workers who quit smoking had become more comfortable with the requirements of their jobs. Gomberg (1980) speculated that a principal cause of the drop in heavy drinking among retired men was relief from the pressures of the daily work grind, in combination with a loss of income for buying liquor and physiological changes that made heavy drinking more unpleasant. Nowhere is addicts' awareness of the continuing costs of an addiction more pronounced than among seasoned heroin users who decide to get free of their drug habits. Repeatedly such people indicate they were no longer willing to incur the damage to their lives from every aspect of the addiction (cf. McAuliffe and Gordon 1980; Waldorf and Biernacki 1981). Explanations by former overeaters and smokers who changed compulsive habits also often reflected a sound evaluation of health and other practical considerations (cf. Gerin 1982).

In a larger sense, there may be no contradiction between the perspective that people change their behavior as a result of sudden insight and the view that they become able to change over time as they mature. Vaillant (1966, 1983) reported that both recovered heroin addicts and former alcoholics usually identified a specific moment when they decided to quit drinking or drugs. Yet Vaillant doubted the decisiveness of these individual events, preferring to see instead the ripening of forces that had been incubating for months or years. It is true, for example, that former addicts both to cigarettes and heroin have often experienced previous revelations or made similar resolves to quit that did not produce lasting results (Marlatt and Gordon 1980; Jorquez 1983). Whatever means addicts do use to eliminate their addictions, they very often restructure their lives to facilitate a nonaddicted lifestyle. In the one view, they intentionally make such changes in line with their resolve to go straight; in the other view, the changes already had to be in progress in order for them to eschew their addictions (cf. Wille 1983).

In leaving behind one addiction, the person may simply adopt another one, or may retain a simultaneous addiction. Robins et al. (1975) reported that although addicted narcotic use fell off for the large majority of returned Vietnam veterans, a sizeable minority replaced narcotic addiction with unhealthy drinking or dependency on non-narcotic drugs. Eighty-three percent of Zinberg's (1984) sample of controlled narcotics users—many of whom had been addicted to narcotics previously—still smoked cigarettes daily. The correlations Istvan and Matarazzo (1984) noted among different forms of substance use remained, even for those who had been (but no longer were) addicted to one of the substances. For example, former smokers drank more coffee than those who had never smoked. Vaillant (1983) found that many abstinent alcohol abusers (although not those who had moderated their drinking) created substitute dependencies. The range of these correlations between both former and current substance abuse and other compulsive attachments affirms that a general tendency toward addiction is an often persistent part of a person's style of dealing with the world.

For Vaillant (1983), addicts' substitute dependencies included religious commitments and AA membership and often constituted a positive step for the addict. Other studies of reformed addicts have highlighted the changes addicts make in their social networks, such as joining religious groups or other organizations that, while not explicitly therapeutic, do rule out drug use (cf. Tuchfeld et al. 1983; Waldorf 1983; Wille 1983). At the same time, some addicts retain old lifestyles and acquaintances while changing addicted behavior, seemingly performing nothing more than an intrapsychic reappraisal of who they want to be (Jorquez 1983; Peele 1983d; Waldorf and Biernacki 1981). This latter approach is typical of reformed smokers and overeaters, who are unlikely to reject spouses, friends, and jobs when they shift behavior. Most subjects in Schachter's (1982) study of remission in smoking and obesity reported employing conscious policies for modifying their habits while making few external changes in their lives (cf. Gerin 1982). Again, the dichotomy may be more apparent than real. Group support is an indisputably central factor in people's ability to select and maintain a course of action (cf. Allen 1984), yet subjective factors such as identity, personal values, and the degree of satisfaction obtained from an activity play key roles in addiction.

Lastly, personality dispositions are part and parcel of the escape from addiction as well as its formation. These dispositions influence both the success of efforts at cure and the methods attempted for such cures. Condiotte and Lichtenstein (1981) found that smokers' feelings of self-efficacy predicted the success of outcomes of a smoking cessation program. On the other hand, high self-efficacy may be the best description of those who refuse therapeutic help and attempt self-cures (Peele 1983d). Tuchfeld's (1981) presentation of self-reports by those who quit or cut back drinking revealed an almost willful independence and a rejection of outside support: One man reported he would rather die than seek help from a therapist. Whereas disease theorists see such attitudes as proof of a defensive inability to change, these dispositions may actually hold out the most positive prognosis. Schachter (1982) found remission rates to be higher for those who never sought treatment than for those who had, no matter how severe the person's overweight or reliance on nicotine. Wille (1983) noted that heroin addicts who found it most difficult to kick the habit were those who believed they needed institutional support the most and who had the greatest trouble making social changes and developing a new identity on their own.

The Nature of Addiction: The Addiction Cycle

Substantial life-span variations in addiction—along with the findings that addictive behavior is situationally, socially, and culturally determined—vitiates disease views of addiction. Responding to these findings, sociologists, clinical psychologists, and social psychiatrists often lose sight of the reality of addiction as a recognizable syndrome, and of people's personal dispositions to be addicted. Paradoxically, when confronted with the extremities of addictive behavior or with the degree of substitution of addictions, these social scientists suspect the operation of the same inbred and/or biological mechanisms that disease theorists posit for addiction. The interpretation of addiction among opposing theorists simply becomes a matter of degree, whereby all concede that the most severe instances of addiction or addictiveness represent the same biological imperatives. The authorities agree that if addiction is real and persistent, it *must* be biological. The same limitations in imagination cause scientists—as well as addicts themselves—to reify into concrete entities what are, in fact, relativistic personal impulses. Loss of control is real to the person; the effort of conceiving that it is also a culturally and subjectively induced sensation is insurmountable. Human thought is not well-equipped for understanding that intense motivations are not inevitably biological at their source and do not necessarily hold true for all humans, at all times, in all places.

That the addiction syndrome can appear with any type of involvement has led to the same conceptual difficulties, in the form of the denial or trivialization of nondrug addictions or of the claim that they are biological syndromes like those that alcoholism and opiate addiction supposedly represent. Compulsive gambling, running, overeating, etc., actually offer clear insights into the nature of addiction as an experience. Runners such as those interviewed by Robbins and Joseph (1982), who experienced cessation of running as traumatic because it removed what had become a shield against previously overwhelming pressures, reveal the fundamental nature of aversive withdrawal. Recognizing such truths means we no longer have to separate addiction from other human experiences and that we can bring to bear on the syndrome all the knowledge we have about human social and psychological functioning.

The addiction-experience model incorporates cultural processes with individual and situational vectors and includes all the experiences people find to be addictive (Peele 1980). A society—and all the subsocieties to which people belong—creates a need for an addictive experience by setting forth key values that are not realizable. The society simultaneously presents alternative experiences as having the power and quality to fulfill these needs in other than realistic ways. As summarized in this chapter, people are susceptible to these addictive experiences to the extent that they occupy unsatisfying and stressful postions in the society, to the extent that they feel concrete consensual social rewards are unobtainable or not worthwhile, and to the extent that they relate to the world through dependencies and believe in the efficacy of external forces. (See figure 5–1.)

Becoming involved in substitute experiences offered by the social milieu as a resolution for crucial but unsatisfied needs limits people's abilities to fulfill these needs naturalistically, through functional effort and acknowledged accomplishment. People experience a consequent drop in their self-efficacy and social worth, and the ritualized addictive involvement becomes more firmly ensconced as an admittedly inferior—but nonetheless essential—source of gratification. Addicts seek an addictive experience to achieve a desired feeling—a state of being—that is not otherwise available to them. The experience is powerful and gratifying and ultimately becomes both necessary and distressing. Through habit and inclination, those who are addicted participate immoderately in these involvements, while perceiving this excess to signal a lack of control that defines addiction for themselves and others.

This is an exacerbating cycle of experience where the results of exposure to the involvement ensure continued involvement, and the life of the involvement perpetuates its own existence. Not an abnormal dimension of human experience, the process achieves the extremes of addiction when people—in turning to the experience to modify feelings—abandon all functional coping efforts. At this point, the addictive experience becomes the sole means for asserting control over addicts' emotional lives and becomes the core of their self-concepts (Peele and Brodsky 1975). No additional constructs are necessary to account for the fervor of pursuit of an addictive object (craving) and the anguish resulting from its abandonment (withdrawal). Shorn of the reassurance of the addictive involvement, addicts reemerge into worlds from which they have "grown increasingly alienated" (p. 62) and face physical readjustments that they understand as a sickness and feel inadequate to cope with.

With drugs, the reliance on pharmacological effects to create a desired state of being makes the achievement of this state through other means more difficult. McClelland et al. (1972) noted the inherent futility in alcohol intoxication as a fulfillment of power needs, since drunkenness *detracts* from the recognition and influence that the drinker is seeking. Such paradoxical temporary or illusory gratifications are a regular part of addic-

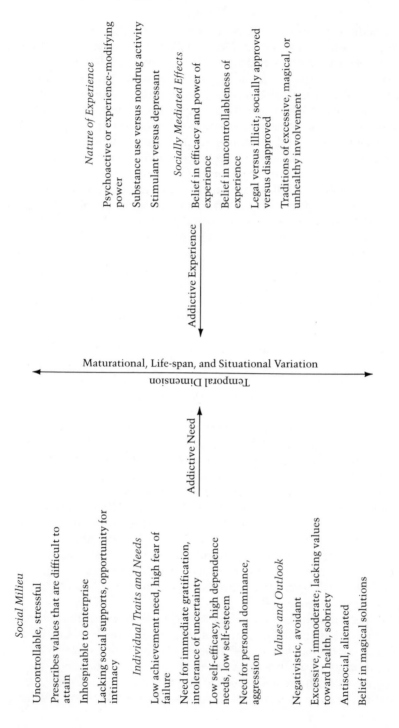

Figure 5–1. The Addiction Formula

tion. Nathan and his colleagues (1970) found short-term reduction of anxiety from drinking for alcoholics but long-term augmentation of anxiety. This is very similar to the paradoxical effects noted from smoking for nicotine addicts (Gilbert 1979; Nesbitt 1972). Aneshensel and Huba (1983) detected the same sequencing of improved mood followed by greater depression with drinking. Overall, while alcoholics *anticipate* positive affects from drinking, they in fact become more dysphoric, agitated, and depressed during drunken episodes (Mello and Mendelson 1978).

The failure of addicts either to find sufficient satisfaction in an act to resort to it only when appropriate, or else to quit because of continuing dissatisfaction, is the core paradox of addiction. Gray (1978) analyzed the use of tranquilizers to allay anxiety as having an inherently dysfunctional character. If anxiety is a signal of some inadequacy in coping, then blocking this signal makes appropriate responses less likely—because drug users become less aware of the sources of their anxiety—and the need for the drug greater. Illicit drug use and other activities carry with them feelings of shame or guilt that then add to the motivation to return to the drug or other experience. Thus drinkers who seek a sense of power from alcohol are aware that this is not a socially approved means of asserting oneself. They feel more debased by this guilty realization and experience simultaneously an increased need for intoxication as an illusory way of fulfilling power needs.

Addictive eating offers a commonsensical illustration of this central addictive process. The binge eater undergoes a similar cycle of emotions to those experienced by drug addicts and alcoholics, whereby the guilt and bad feelings that result from immoderation prompt greater excess (cf. Bruch 1973). Bulimics in one study were asked to report in to investigators whenever they were beeped on an electrical device they carried. Subjects revealed that they ate to escape anxiety, loneliness, and self-doubt: the very feelings that were exacerbated by their eating (Johnson and Larson 1982). In the reaction-formation characteristic of addiction, bulimic subjects then induced vomiting to regain a sense of control and self-worth. Television viewers studied by the same research group (Csikszentmihalyi and Kubey 1981) also indicated that they felt depressed while watching TV and, although they chose to continue doing so, the longer they watched the more depressed they became! A frequent element in this addictive cycle is that a single violation by binge eaters (or other addicts) of their intermittent resolutions to curtail their behavior often leads to a binge episode (Herman and Polivy 1980; Marlatt 1978; Peele and Brodsky 1975; Rollnick and Heather 1982). The addicts see any such slips as proof of their lack of control and as an indication that relapse is inevitable.

Over time, the mix of addictive and functional coping can shift. When stress lessens and situations improve or when successful experiences buoy addicts' sense of efficacy, the addictive involvement becomes less necessary and appealing. Addicts finally break out of the small world of addiction through combinations of changes in their external situations (such as removal from war zones or ghettos), changes in self-efficacy that enable them to achieve personal goals, and shifts in the reward value addicts attach to the addictive experience relative to their other values. The escape from the addiction becomes permanent as they invest themselves more heavily in the involvements that drug use interferes with or detracts from—involvements that provide rewards that are stronger and more valued than those from the addiction. The final stage of remission is one in which these rewards are so firmly established that some people no longer imagine the possibility of returning to the addictive involvement or that it ever held any appeal. Former addicts may, at this final stage, revise entirely their self-estimates so as no longer to conceive of themselves as addicts or potential addicts; indeed, this is customary for youthful addicts when they mature into their adult lives. Strangely, it is the primary aim of our current policies toward drug and alcohol addiction to deny that this possibility exists and thereby to eliminate it.

6

The Impaired Society

A model of addiction must be judged on its ability to ameliorate a society's addictive problems. The dominant disease and exposure models of addiction have been widely marketed with the promise of reducing drug and alcohol abuse. The models propose that the behavior we are concerned to rectify cannot be stopped without external therapeutic intervention and that controlled use of some substances is never possible (at least for certain people who are congenital addicts). They attribute virtually all the motivation in addictive behavior to factors over which the individual has no control once initial contact is made with a substance. These views of addiction, as I have shown, do not fit the facts. The model of addiction I put forward in this book calls into question all the treatment programs and public policies that rely on such models of addiction for their support.

The dangers in misperceiving the nature of the problem are more than that a futile effort will be mounted that will then die of its own inconsistency, vagueness, and failure. Disease notions of addiction undermine actual successes, as when they deny that alcoholics can incur fewer drinking problems without abstaining entirely or that people can quit addictions themselves (one television advertisement likened a person trying to cure his own alcoholism to someone trying to operate on himself). More strikingly, disease notions of addiction have an uncanny ability to redefine their own failures as successes. A close look at the correlations between drug (most notably heroin) and alcohol abuse and the monies and effort spent on them reveal a relationship that is not random, as would occur if contemporary approaches were simply harmless. Indeed, the relationship is a positive one: The more effort and money spent on drug and alcohol problems, the greater their magnitude.

There are two possible explanations for this phenomenon. One is that current approaches represent futile attempts to catch up with addiction: We are always chasing, but never get a grip on, its causes. The other possibility is more insidious—that our very efforts contribute to and worsen addiction. This has been a characteristic of the attention the United States has focused on heroin since the beginning of the century and now extends to its exporting concerns and policies about drugs to the rest of the world. In large part, what have been exported are U.S. drug-policing efforts, efforts that originated early in this century and that have grown exponentially in the last two decades. Early opponents of the law enforcement approach to narcotic addiction problems frequently endorsed a medical, or treatment, model as a superior alternative. In the United States today, enforcement and treatment approaches have been combined; their convergence is based on *essential commonalities in assumptions about the nature of addiction.* Both assume that addiction is primarily a function of exposure to substances and that prohibiting drug use or drinking by specified individuals and groups can eliminate addiction. Doctors, legislators, and the police increasingly agree that Americans need to be protected against themselves and their own desires.

Medical conceptions of alcoholism and addiction grew in the United States during the nineteenth and twentieth centuries as part of the idea that mental and emotional disorder was an illness. Yet the number of people that could be affected by conceptions of mental illness was limited. Not so the case with alcohol abuse and drug use, since they describe a range of behaviors and apply to a large portion of the population at one point or another in their lives. The application of disease notions to alcohol- and drug-related problems has accelerated in recent decades, at the same time that health professionals have found the disease model to describe eating disorders, destructive sexual relationships, compulsive gambling, child and wife abuse, and even such disparate maladies as phobias, anxiety, and depression. Disease conceptions of substance abuse may be a paradigm for self and cultural conceptions in our era.

None of these approaches has had much success in treating or preventing the disorders that are being addressed. The focus on physiological mechanisms in substance abuse has been completely wrongheaded, with any benefits that appear from it stemming from artifacts connected with natural remission or simply paying some attention to the addicted individual; yet research on inherited sources of addiction is now the primary focus of the funding for explorations of substance abuse. Nor has labeling compulsive gamblers or self-destructive lovers as diseased produced any additional benefits for such people beyond those resulting from religious conversions, growing up, or the act of getting hold of oneself. The dominant approaches to these and other psychic and social disorders are nonetheless hailed as successful because they conform to cultural stereotypes of individual treatment and cure, medical infallibility, and a kind of scientific mysticism that has grown up around the neurosciences in the 1970s and 1980s.

People do improve, from addiction and other maladies, and there are ways in which individual therapy can help this process. Treatment must be mediated, however, by the crucial awareness that a functioning individual's relationships to other people, to work, and to the environment are essential to keeping any healthy behaviors in place and any behavioral dysfunctions at bay. The failure to acknowledge these connections has hindered behavioral psychologists as much as it has medical therapists and disease counselors. An even more difficult connection for those concerned about drug abuse to make has been that between the social order and addiction. In order to deal with addiction on a scale that will make a difference in the United States, we need to understand what about our society encourages addiction, often in forms besides the abuse of the particular substances that attract our attention in any given era.

The Narcotic Connection—Supply and Demand

Interdicting narcotics and other imported drug supply lines has been a major preoccupation in U.S. addiction policy since the beginning of the century. This approach is notable for its failure. It has not limited addiction. It has had little impact on the availability of the drugs concerned, and where it has demonstrated momentary success in curtailing a drug's availability it has still had negative consequences. The entire legal apparatus for arresting drug dealers and users has produced a major enforcement industry that is self-perpetuating without ameliorating drug problems; in fact, even when failure is widely acknowledged (as in the 1982 "War on Cocaine"), the response has been to redouble the efforts that have led to the consequent failure.

The story of the legal proscription, demonization, and rise of narcotic addiction in the United States has by now been thoroughly, even conclusively told (Brecher 1972; Clausen 1961; King 1972; Musto 1973; Peele and Brodsky 1975; Trebach 1982). Abundantly present in nineteenth-century America, narcotics use had decreased considerably by the turn of the century and at the same time shifted in nature from use of opium and morphine to heroin and from the middle to the lower class. After the passage of the Harrison Act of 1914, the extent and the damaging nature of addiction were dramatically portrayed by medical organizations and Harry Anslinger's Federal Bureau of Narcotics, leading to the eventual elimination of legal heroin prescription in the United States. At the time of the Harrison Act and the vigorous propaganda campaign that followed it, there were perhaps 100,000 American heroin addicts (or, more likely, users of any sort), yet the public believed the number to be in the millions. When narcotic clinics were set up in major U.S. cities to replace maintenance of opiate addicts by private physicians, no more than 15,000 addicts showed up for treatment (Trebach 1982).

Thus began an extended period when a hard core of heroin users and addicts maintained their habits illegally in numbers that probably increased gradually (until numbering 500,000 daily users by the 1970s) and that were certainly higher than for any other advanced country and probably any nation in the world but were minuscule compared with the number of active alcoholics. The 1960s saw the development of methadone maintenance programs, in which addicts were given the substitute narcotic while (ideally) being treated for their drug dependence. The 1960s, when drug use of various kinds became highly visible, marked a period of increased awareness of and alarm about narcotics use. It is still not clear to what extent this concern was justified by an actual rise in the supply and use of narcotics and to what extent it was caused by moral and political issues that determined social reactions to what usage existed (Lidz and Walker 1980).

The concern about heroin peaked in the late 1960s and early 1970s under the Nixon administration and was accompanied by an unprecedented international police and public relations effort directed against heroin suppliers and heroin use. In his exhaustive study of this period, Epstein (1977) has made clear exactly how this campaign was orchestrated exclusively according to political considerations. Throughout the 1970s—during and following this campaign—heroin use and addiction *increased* dramatically worldwide (Ball et al. 1977), including a tenfold increase in Western Europe (Trebach 1982). The U.S. information program about the dangers of narcotics actually fueled heroin problems. For example, Epstein described how U.S.-inspired television commercials about the drug propelled heroin addiction from a nonexistent concern in France to a position as the country's number one health problem. Despite these developments, President Richard Nixon announced in 1973 that the corner had been turned in dealing with heroin around the world.

Nixon made his announcement after enlisting the active support of the Turkish government in eradicating its poppy fields—then the major source for American markets. By 1974, Mexico had assumed this position, auguring a new epidemic and eventual headlines that "Mexico Making Progress in War on . . . Opium Poppies" (1980). The articles about the Mexican war on poppy growers revealed that new sources for heroin were appearing in Asia's Golden Triangle region, leading to subsequent announcements—one year later—of "Heroin Trade Rising Despite U.S. Efforts" (1981) and of "Heroin in West a 'Widening Crisis'" (1981). This led President Reagan to announce his own War on Drugs in 1982, although this time the focus was on a new drug scourge: cocaine. Two years later, in 1984, the suppliers of street cocaine had increased, prices had actually fallen, and estimates of both the number of users and compulsive users had jumped ("U.S. Is Seen as Losing War on Cocaine Smuggling . . ." 1984). The response: an intensification of efforts to intercept drug supplies and drug dealers and to frighten Americans and supplier nations about the dangers of cocaine.

The New York region is a bellwether for drug use trends. It was in 1973 that Governor Nelson Rockefeller authored the most draconian drug measure ever, providing for mandatory life sentences for people convicted of selling or *possessing* heroin or cocaine. By 1979, Governor Hugh Carey—noting the ineffectuality of this legislation—oversaw major revisions in the law. In 1980, Carey announced a new "state of emergency because of the heroin epidemic" and pledged a war "against terrorists of the drug trade, both here and abroad" (cited in Peele 1982c). This concern for the epidemic proportions of drug abuse in New York carried over to Governor Mario Cuomo's regime. Coordinated city, state, and federal task forces raided drug dealers on New York City streets in 1984. This too proved largely ineffectual—except for moving the drug markets around the city—and New York Mayor Edward Koch was moved to up the ante from the Rockefeller laws by suggesting that pushers convicted repeatedly be executed.

Public policy toward illicit drug use has assumed a pattern—alarm and rising concern about the extent of the problem, strict laws and increased police activity, visible arrests and incidental drops in drug supplies, re-emergence of the problem (often at a higher level)—that appears as ineluctable as it is doomed. What drives this approach to preventing addiction, given its futility? From a political standpoint, there is no cost and considerable benefit to embracing tougher laws and enforcement, even if several years later the same politician is forced to report a new wave of drug abuse (and in fact it is often not the same political figure who confronts the fruits of previous policies). Apparently there is something inherently rewarding to politician and public alike about tough drug policies. Adherents of the get-tough approach are not challenged if abuse levels set new records: They instead point to these data as signaling how appropriate and necessary their efforts were in the first place (cf. Peele 1982c).

These policies do not work because they focus on supply and not demand. Given the number of potential producers of heroin and other drugs among third-world nations, there will always be another region ready to take on the role of supplying the United States and other consumer nations. Within the United States, the profits to be made from the drug trade likewise guarantee a steady stream of drug dealers. This very fecundity of drug-trade labor makes the laws against individuals futile. As it is, the dealers rounded up by police in New York City are nearly all released immediately because they are too numerous to be retained by the justice system ("For Drug Prosecutor, A Sense of Frustration" 1984). The punitiveness of the Rockefeller legislation (and Koch's suggested amplification of this approach) cannot work because it is patently unjust—as well as useless—to penalize so severely the small minority of those apprehended from among the overwhelming numbers of people engaged in similar activities.

What would be the result if somehow, magically, it were possible to shut off the supply of drugs from outside the country? All indications are that committed drug users—the group toward which these efforts are targeted—would simply switch to available alternatives (which they often do of their own choice already). In the case of heroin, these substitutes include barbiturates and other sedatives, alcohol, and synthetic narcotics such as Demerol, Talwin, and methadone itself. Yet nearly everyone is persuaded by prima facie logic that the simple abundance of a drug like cocaine affects the extent of its abuse. For this and other reasons, even commentators like Zinberg (1984) will not endorse legalizing such illicit substances as heroin and cocaine. Berridge and Edwards (1981), while noting that the gradual and arbitrary entrenchment of increasingly negative public attitudes and laws toward narcotics has not improved—and often seems to have exacerbated—narcotic abuse, maintain that legalizing heroin would not reverse the social trends that cause addiction and thus legalization would result only in more drug abuse.

There is surprisingly little evidence to indicate that shorter supplies of drugs like heroin, cocaine, and marijuana translate into fewer drug abusers or addicts. What evidence there is for such a supply-side view comes mainly from epidemiological studies of alcoholism suggesting that individual drinkers consume a relatively fixed proportion of the total supply of alcohol, so that those who drink the most are pushed toward excessive consumption when more alcohol is consumed society-wide (Beauchamp 1980; Room 1984). Yet projected public policies making use of this finding involve such relatively minor steps (compared with prohibition) as raising taxes on alcoholic beverages. That is, the drug will still be readily available but somewhat more costly to procure. Considering that more or less the same can be said of marijuana (Johnston et al. 1981, reported 85 percent of high school seniors could obtain marijuana) or cocaine (at least among certain groups of affluent professionals), controlled legalization would hardly change the availability picture for these drugs.

Discussing drug policy rationally is, unfortunately, an anomalous activity. The proscription of cocaine, heroin, and marijuana is no more nor less than an expression of cultural prejudice. Although banning substances is a prerogative of any society—and one in which all societies indulge—we deny this arbitrariness by justifying prohibition on scientific grounds. The ordinary explanation offered is the harmfulness of these substances. Yet smoking tobacco is inherently harmful—but legal—while heavy drinking is more toxic than the heavy administration (if antiseptic) of a narcotic. Defenders of the public good point out that many of the known users of illicit substances use them compulsively, as though this were the natural order of things. This impression is created by studiously ignoring all indications of controlled use of these substances. Zinberg (1979) argued that our policy seems best geared to making sure that as high a percentage as possible of those who use illicit drugs will not find out how to do so moderately. (The editors of the volume in which Zinberg's article appeared felt it necessary—while acknowledging the value of his research—to disown his treatment policy recommendations.)

The very discrepant perspectives that evolve from realistic versus moralistic stances is evident in an article in the *New York Times* about high school cocaine use ("Prep Schools in a Struggle to Curb Spread of Cocaine" 1984). One student claimed, "It used to be such a big thing to have it, . . . now everyone's so blasé," and another said, "I never met anybody who was really messed up by cocaine." The students' statements were contradicted by the former NIDA director Robert Dupont, who asserted that "Cocaine is the most powerfully reinforcing [i.e., addictive] of all drugs. . . . These kids don't have a clue of what they're fooling around with."

Why should we disregard the beliefs of these users in favor of the experiences of cocaine addicts who seek treatment? In addition, a systematic research program found regular cocaine users could not distinguish the drug's effects from standard pharmaceutical applications of amphetamines (Van Dyke and Byck 1982). These researchers questioned "whether the potential for the abuse of cocaine justifies the intensity" of current international policing efforts. They noted that "in Andean Indian societies blood-plasma levels comparable to those encountered among intranasal cocaine users are common, yet there is little evidence of physical harm" and Indian ceremonial "use of cocaine cannot be termed drug abuse." Nonetheless, they correctly concluded, "cocaine policy and regulations take little account of these conclusions" and "the final decisions about cocaine will be political and economic, not scientific" (p. 141).

Oddly, the traditional battlelines have been realigned on this issue. Heroin iconoclast Norman Zinberg has publicly agreed that cocaine use is unusually likely to become compulsive and that we should focus on limiting the drug's availability ("U.S. Social Tolerance of Drugs Found on Rise" 1983), apparently as a result of his active involvement in a cocaine hotline network that has turned up large numbers of cocaine addicts. Thus Zinberg contributes to the hysteria surrounding the glamor drug of the 1980s (cf. Peele 1984b), despite having fought irrationality about heroin in previous decades. Meanwhile, disease theory proponent David Smith, director of the Haight-Ashbury Free Medical Clinic, has correctly noted that equivalent percentages of cocaine, Valium, and alcohol users—involving often the same individuals—become addicted (while incorrectly deducing from this the existence of some genetic malady). As a result, Smith has come under attack from the conservative groups one thinks of as forming the constituency for disease views, which claim Smith is endorsing drug use for those who don't have a tendency to be addicted ("The Collision of Prevention and Treatment" 1984).

The Negative Effects of the Belief in Chemical Dependence

In the period extending from the outlawing of the private prescription of heroin and the brief lifespan of public clinics for heroin users to the emergence of methadone maintenance as the preferred mode of treatment for heroin addicts, nearly all acknowledged narcotics users were sent to federal hospitals for treatment, most notably the Public Health Service Hospital in Lexington, Kentucky. Although research conducted at Lexington has provided important glimpses of the lives and habits of addicts, it appears no one actually was cured there. That is, when the heroin-user net apprehended successful physicians due to their suspicious prescription records, the hospital was provided with patients who naturally could return to work after treatment without difficulty (Winick 1961). Street addicts, however, presented a different picture (Brecher 1972: 71):

> At any given time after being "cured" at Lexington, from 10 to 25 percent of graduates may appear to be abstinent, nonalcoholic, employed and law abiding. But only a handful at most can maintain this level of functioning throughout the ten-year period after "cure." Almost all become readdicted and reimprisoned early in the decade, and for most the process is repeated over and over again.

Brecher estimated that relapse to addiction among such patients was closer to 100 percent than to 90 percent.

Prior to his 1973 life imprisonment law, Rockefeller had directed passage of the 1966 Narcotics Addiction Control Act providing for the civil commitment and treatment of heroin addicts in New York state. By 1972, $224 million had been spent on this program. According to one source, "Of 5,172 individuals treated and released under the . . . compulsory treatment program, only 141 managed to stay drug-free at the end of a year and a half, which meant each cure [this is assuming that those drug-free at a year and a half remained so for the rest of the decade] had cost New Yorkers about $1.6 million" (Collier and Horowitz 1976: 473). At the end of this period, Rockefeller announced the existence of the heroin "epidemic" that prompted his life imprisonment plan.

By the mid-1970s, the developers of methadone maintenance, Drs. Dole and Nyswander (1976), were forced to concede that the benefits of the program had been "small at best" (p. 2118). This admission does not tell the full story, however. Epstein (1977) revealed that addicts often used other drugs in conjunction with their methadone and that there was an active black market in the drug. In the midst of Governor Carey's war on drugs, a consultant's report he commissioned claimed that no more than 10 percent of those in treatment in the state got off heroin permanently, while those taking methadone were *at least* as likely to be using other illicit drugs as were street heroin addicts (Califano 1983; Peele 1982c).

From its inception, some have questioned the rationale behind methadone maintenance (Lennard et al. 1972; Peele and Brodsky 1975). On what basis was the replacement of one narcotic drug with another considered to contribute to the cure of addiction? For psychopharmacologists like Dole (1980), Goldstein (1976b), and Snyder (1977), addiction is a metabolic process from which the addict is to be weaned. This can be accomplished through gradually replacing the effects of heroin with another drug (for Dole, 1980, this means permanent maintenance with methadone) or through blocking heroin's effects with antagonistic drugs such as naltrexone (Goldstein 1976a). There are exactly comparable procedures for nicotine weaning, by replacing cigarette-induced nicotine levels with gradually reduced levels of chemically pure nicotine. Based on nicotine dependence models that conceive of addicted smokers as striving to maintain habitual nicotine levels (cf. Krasnegor 1979), conferences on nicotine addiction are now sponsored by drug companies promising eventual drug remedies for the problem ("Tobacco Use as an Addiction" 1982). In fact, chemically supported nicotine withdrawal has shown no better results than has medical supervision of heroin withdrawal. There may be marginally greater success at cigarette withdrawal when nicotine is administered, although research has indicated little effect over that produced by administering a placebo (Best and Bloch 1979). Nonetheless, withdrawal is incidental to the actual problem of living a nonaddicted life, and the large majority of withdrawn cigarette addicts—like narcotics addicts—ultimately relapse. Yet metabolic theorists assert the primary nature of chemical reactions in the addiction syndrome, along with the centrality of managing the withdrawal syndrome for escaping addiction.

As a result, popular therapeutic programs for cigarette and illicit drug addiction advertise their ability to alleviate withdrawal distress. One noteworthy example of this approach was the highly publicized treatment of former rock star John Phillips under the supervision of Dr. Mark Gold at the Fair Oaks Hospital in Summit, New Jersey. Phillips—who had been taking enormous amounts of heroin, cocaine, and other drugs—was carefully guided through withdrawal through the use of clonidine to suppress withdrawal symptoms and then naltrexone to eliminate craving. In media interviews and magazine articles about the case, Phillips reported having gone through detoxification many times. Why should this last drug-aided withdrawal have led to any greater success than his prior efforts to quit drugs after detoxification? What Phillips's experience actually indicates is the secondary importance of withdrawal to the outcome of treatment, suggesting that the entire focus on withdrawal is wrongheaded.

Withdrawal from alcohol—as represented by delirium tremens—became a major topic for medical research in the United States in the 1950s. One puzzling aspect of this emphasis has been that Canadian physicians regularly report finding the phenomenon to be less severe. A study at Toronto's Addiction Research Foundation, for example, indicated that skid-row alcoholics could have their symptoms suppressed in a supportive environment populated by other alcoholics who likewise did not experience withdrawal (Oki 1974). In a debate entitled "Is Inpatient Rehabilitation of the Alcoholic Cost Effective? (1984), Joseph Pursch, a clinician and medical director of the American CompCare Corporation, found the severely alcoholic patients he saw could rarely function outside the hospital. Helen Annis of the Canadian Addiction Research Foundation reported, on the other hand, that all the data indicated "outpatient treatment methods to have equal or even better chances of success" than inpatient care. She noted that well over 90 percent of Canadian patients weathered detoxification without need for hospitalization and in fact benefited from detoxifying in a social, rather than a medical setting ("Inpatient vs. Outpatient Treatment" 1984). Even given Dr. Pursch's pessimistic appraisal of the American alcohol detoxification experience, other researchers—such as Tarter et al. (1983)—have found that only a minority of alcoholics undergo severe withdrawal (the alcoholics in this study had exhibited numerous impairments on intellectual and neuropsychological tests and had histories of heavy drinking averaging over fifteen years).

Can We Treat Away the Drug Problem?

As detailed in chapter 5, the role of withdrawal in the maintenance of addictive behavior is secondary at most. Indeed, any cured addict will have withstood both withdrawal and periodic urges to return to addicted use even—as with the returned Vietnam Veteran—if they continue to use the drug periodically. When alcoholics, narcotics addicts, and smokers do relapse, it is seldom because they have experienced unusual physical symptoms or craving for a substance (Marlatt and Gordon 1980). Furthermore, indications are that people can fortify themselves quite well to resist relapse, often appearing to do so better without the aid of treatment. Wille (1983) found that heroin addicts who were the least confident in their ability to overcome their physical need for the drug and who required the most institutional support to do so were those who had the most difficulty creating a nonaddicted lifestyle following treatment.

Addicts who are convinced they cannot escape their addictions are those particularly unlikely to believe they can manage their own physical discomfort, at the same time that they display a heightened respect for medical manipulations. Consider that the subject in the Light and Torrance (1929) study who expressed the greatest physical need for heroin was the one whose symptoms were relieved by an injection of saline solution. The addict least prepared for remission is the one who dreads getting off the drug and requires the greatest medical and chemical support for doing so. As a drug counselor exasperatedly told me, after one of his clients requested she be put in a hospital with doctors standing by to give her Demerol should her withdrawal from methadone prove too painful, "It's only called withdrawal if people *stop* taking drugs." From a commonsense standpoint, would one expect greater success at quitting smoking for the person who purchases a set of filters to step down the amount of nicotine he inhales or for the one who declares, "I'm going to quit smoking even if it kills me"?

By convincing addicts that remission from drug abuse is a severe metabolic strain, that their addiction is either inbred or deeply a part of their constitution, and that periodic desires to return to the drug represent powerful (albeit conditioned) physiological cravings, medical, pharmacological, and psychological treatment attack the very feelings of self-efficacy addicts need to achieve remission. Rather then warning addicts about how difficult quitting drugs is—and how much assistance they will need—the very opposite approach seems to be called for. That is, patients would benefit from being told that however tough the experience of withdrawal will be, they are capable of handling it. In any case, there is no alternative for such addicts to the recognition that the only way out of addiction is for them to be able to control their own craving and their desire for relief of discomfort or pain.

Bandura (1977a) signaled a major direction for modern therapies with his analysis that whatever improvement occurred in therapy was inevitably the result of patients' increased feeling of self-efficacy. Improved health outcomes of many types have been connected with enhanced self-efficacy, such as preventing the negative consequences of aging and even postponing death (Rodin and Langer 1977). On the other hand, people's belief that their own efforts are inadequate to affect their outcomes creates depression (Seligman 1975) and what Langer (1978) and Langer and Benevento (1978) labeled "self-induced dependence." The addicts who found quitting heroin easiest in therapy in Wille's (1983) study were those who began the process with the greatest expectation of success. Condiotte and Lichtenstein (1981) made a similar discovery about those with the best outcomes in a smoking cessation program. When smokers attribute their immediate cessation of smoking in such programs to their own efforts rather than to the skill of the therapist or the efficacy of the therapy, they are more likely to maintain abstinence (Colletti and Kopel 1979; Fisher et al. 1982).

If those who quit addiction already have such feelings of self-efficacy, or must acquire them, does therapy help? Hodgson and Miller's (1982) text outlining a record-keeping and behavior modification procedure for treating addictions and compulsions described a single case of a man who quit smoking on his own after having a religious vision one night (cf. Marlatt 1981). What are we to make of the fact that about 20 million Americans quit smoking on their own in the decade from 1965 to 1975 ("Adult Use of Tobacco" 1975)? Surely most did so without employing elaborate behavioral techniques or undergoing religious experiences (Peele 1983a). The self-curers in Schachter's (1982) study of natural remission among smokers and overeaters appeared to take the most straightforward approaches: simply resolving to quit cigarettes or to eat less, cut out desserts, eat less fattening foods, and so forth (Gerin 1982). Schachter actually found those who had never been in therapy to have higher remission rates than those who had. Is it possible that the very act of turning oneself over to a treatment program is antagonistic to the feeling of self-efficacy necessary to succeed at cure? While the Schachter comparison of those who relied on treatment or not involved very small numbers, the 1982 Surgeon General's Report on Smoking, based on a survey of the research and a large data base, intriguingly summarized that "outcomes are sometimes better with less rather than more therapeutic contact" (p. 284).

Therapy works best when it requires clients to change attitudes, practice skills, and make life changes and when it attributes these changes to the client. Therapy that instead convinces clients they have inbred weaknesses that require the permanent intervention of the therapy attack the beliefs necessary for cure and effective self-management. All therapy is a mixed bag conveying, often simultaneously, elements of both messages. Yet disease views have at their core a vision of the intractability of the client's malady and of the essentialness of therapy's role. The strange story of Synanon epitomizes these attitudes. The best-known therapeutic community for drug addicts in the United States, Synanon (under its founder Charles Dederich) became obsessed with the idea that clients leaving the organization obviated their own cures and undercut the organization. Dederich employed a security force to coerce clients to stay in the treatment community, and he was eventually convicted of placing a rattlesnake in the mailbox of a lawyer representing dissident clients trying to leave the organization ("Synanon Founder . . . Convicted in Attack With a Snake" 1980).

Former Dederich supporters (like Jane Fonda and other luminaries of the entertainment industry) may regard Dederich's actions to be aberrations from Synanon's original philosophy. In fact, his response was the natural consequence of the Synanon credo that membership in the community is a lifetime proposition, a credo it shares with the most popular brand of alcoholism therapy: Alcoholics Anonymous. Popular stump speakers like Father Joseph Martin have been widely successful in promoting AA's own claims of near-infallibility into tenets of faith. In contrast, the only controlled comparison of AA with other treatments reported the highest dropout and relapse rate for those randomly assigned to AA (Brandsma et al. 1980; see Miller and Hester 1980). For therapies that involve alcoholics in nonreligious AA-type groups, the only two studies again favored the untreated comparisons (Pattison et al. 1967; Zimberg 1974). A survey of group therapies with nonalcoholic or drug-abusing college students found that the Synanon version of group therapy, called "the game," produced the most frequent cases of extremely negative outcomes (Lieberman et al. 1973).

Groups like Synanon and Alcoholics Anonymous have offered effective group support for abstinence for some people. At the same time, their demands for a consuming, full-time commitment have their own negative sequelae; for example, encouraging a totalitarian outlook that denies the possibility of self-cure or of pursuing other goals (such as cutting back drinking) or other therapies. Despite their considerable drawbacks, and no signs that they can work for other than self-selected populations, AA and related organizations completely dominate the U.S. treatment field, and their principles and policies are widely regarded to be the main hope for reducing drug and alcohol abuse in this country. Moreover, the religious absolutism of AA has been carefully melded with medical dogma. This modern synthesis is embodied in Harvard psychiatrist George Vaillant's acclaimed book, The Natural History of Alcoholism. In this remarkable work, Vaillant argued with his subjects against their claims that they could drink again nonaddictively or go it alone without AA (a majority of his subjects did both) and demanded that alcohol abusers be funneled through the health care system (while finding medical treatment did not improve the prognosis for severe alcoholism and was positively unnecessary for less severe alcohol abuse). Vaillant's research has been widely hailed as a defense of conventional treatments of alcoholism.

The Alcoholism and Chemical Dependence Industry

At the time the first edition of the Alcoholics Anonymous "Big Book" appeared in 1939, AA claimed no more than 100 active members. There was little public concern or awareness about the extent and the danger of alcoholism in the United States. The National Committee for Education on Alcoholism (the progenitor of the National Council on Alcoholism, created in 1944 by AA members with the aid of the faculty of the Yale University Center of Alcohol Studies) identified its mandate to be alerting the public to these dangers as well as helping alcoholics to understand the nature of their problem. Between 1942 and 1976, Room (1980) estimated, the number of people receiving treatment for alcoholism increased twentyfold. Yet an even more rapid growth in the delivery of alcoholism services has occurred since the mid-1970s, when funding for alcoholism treatment shifted from large public institutions to service contracts and third-party payments provided to private alcoholism organizations. A 1982 Gallup Poll revealed that fully one-third of U.S. families believed one of their members had a drinking problem, a figure that had doubled over the previous six years.

Industry spokespeople now indicate more than 15 million Americans require treatment for alcoholism (Hackler 1983). This is to be compared with estimates by NCA founder Marty Mann (1970) that there were 3 million alcoholics in the United States in 1943, 5 million in 1956, and 6.5 million in 1965. By reckoning that the relatives of alcoholics need treatment as urgently as alcoholics themselves, the treatment industry now considers perhaps one in three or four Americans a potential beneficiary of therapy for alcoholism. In the 1980s, for-profit alcoholism clinics have become a $400 million-a-year industry with stocks traded on the exchanges and with fees ranging from $2,500 to $13,000 a month (Hackler 1983). This is in addition to the nearly $900 million earmarked by the Reagan administration in its 1985 budget for programs in Alcohol, Drug Abuse, and Mental Health. The public inebriates and skid-row denizens who once typified the alcoholic for the average American have been replaced by prominent public figures who announce their alcoholism and enroll in elite private clinics.

The economic strength and public allure of this growth industry has been matched by its political clout. In the fall of 1983, Medicare proposed that reimbursement for hospital stays for alcoholism treatment be calculated on an average length of 8.1 days. Immediately, the NIAAA, NCA, and organizations of treatment centers and counselors inundated DHHS with protests. The standards were suspended. Particularly effective was said to have been Betty Ford's personal appeal to Health and Human Services secretary Margaret Heckler ("Anatomy of a Victory: The DRG Exemption" 1984). Lost in the ballyhoo were the recently released findings of the U.S. Congressional Office of Technology Assessment: "controlled studies have typically found no differences in outcomes according to intensity and duration of treatment . . . with respect to treatment setting, there is little evidence for the superiority of either inpatient or outpatient care alone . . ." (Saxe et al. 1983: 4–5).

With the shift in funding mechanisms for alcoholism has come the aggressive marketing of disease concepts and alcoholism treatment services and identification of new client groups (Weisner and Room 1984). In addition to middle-class drinkers and children of alcoholics, these groups include teenage problem drinkers, women, minorities, functioning workers, and so on. An important change has also taken place in the traditional AA attitude that only those who indicated a readiness could be helped in combatting their alcoholism. Instead, the emphasis is now on active intervention and confrontational strategies, so-called outreach approaches (Weisner and Room 1984). From this perspective denial has become the defining trait of alcoholism, with alcoholics being identifiable by their inability or unwillingness to acknowledge the nature of their problems. This view is opposed by evidence that alcoholics have a good notion of what their drinking problems are and that contradicting these self-conceptions *impedes* treatment (Miller 1983c).

Because alcoholics are considered incapable of deciding what is best for themselves, most patients are now mandated into treatment through either industrial employee assistance programs or the court system. The largest group of treatment clients are those who are offered therapy as an alternative to a jail sentence for drunk driving or for such other crimes as wife battery, child abuse, writing bad checks, and even robbery (Weisner 1983). The programs are nearly all AA-based and demand that participants acknowledge that they are alcoholics. This is despite the repeated finding that drunk drivers and others convicted of alcohol-related offenses do not conform to the typical alcoholic profile (Vingilis 1983). Such individuals are now likely to be instructed that they are alcoholics, but will this label help them? The one study to date comparing those sent to jail for driving while intoxicated with those assigned to treatment found a significantly lower recidivism rate for the incarcerated subjects (Salzberg and Klingberg 1983). An earlier study discovered that simply putting people on probation was superior to compelling them to attend either clinical treatment or AA meetings (Ditman and Crawford 1966; Ditman et al. 1967).

The awareness that treatment produces very small and inexact benefits for alcoholics points to the prevention of alcohol problems as the most effective means of dealing with alcoholism. What does prevention look like from a disease framework? The bulk of the research money spent by the Alcohol, Drug Abuse, and Mental Health Administration (ADAMHA) is for biological investigation; the major focus of this research is on identifying inherited biological traits that cause alcoholism and drug dependence. According to acting ADAMHA director Robert Trachtenberg, "This research will have great impact upon the prevention of alcoholism as well as the understanding of the biological mechanisms that determine the onset of this disease" ("Biomed Research Gets Top Priority" 1984). In his presidential message in the *Bulletin of the Society of Psychologists in Addictive Behaviors*, Marlatt (1984) sounded the cry that psychosocial and epidemiological research is in danger of being submerged entirely by "the emergent political strength of the biomedical researchers" (p. 2, quoting Robin Room). Ironically, the bulk of articles by the *psychologists* in this issue of the *Bulletin* concerned animal and human biological research.

The leading proponent of biological predispositions in alcoholism, Schuckit (1984), enthusiastically looked forward to the development of tests for a variety of potential biological markers for the malady, with the aim of being better able to indicate which young people should be told never to drink ("Alcoholism Not Inherited: Predisposition Does Exist" 1984). He added, "If we ever get to that point, where these kinds of tests are used to screen people [for example, for job applications], we're going to have to fight to make sure they don't get misused" (p. 15). Another proponent of this futuristic vision is the National Foundation for Prevention of Chemical Dependency Disease (1984), whose mission is:

> To sponsor scientific research and development of a simple biochemical test that can be administered to our young children to determine any predisposition for chemical dependency disease; to promote greater awareness, understanding and acceptance of the disease by the general public so prevention or treatment can be commenced at the age youngsters are most vulnerable.

What are the dangers of this method of prevention? The research and point of view behind this book indicate that (1) alcoholism and addiction do not exist at the level of biological determinants, so that no individual genetic predisposition indicates if addiction will or will not appear; (2) there is strong situational and lifespan variation in the appearance of addiction, so that those addicted at one time and place—and *particularly the young*— will often outgrow severe addiction; (3) the *belief* in one's susceptibility to addiction is itself a strong predisposing factor in addiction and that labeling oneself as an addict is the strongest guarantee of perpetuating an addiction; and (4) a cultural milieu in which the imminence, innateness, and inevitability of addiction are emphasized is associated with the highest addiction rates. In other words, the approach now favored by the official institutional leadership in the field is one whose only efficacy had been in the direction of creating addiction.

While the research program to uncover biological markers in alcoholism searches for ways to identify future alcoholics, active interventions with young people are already very much a part of the current treatment scene. Concern over epic rates of alcohol and drug abuse has prompted a huge public awareness campaign that emphasizes not only the dangers in drug use but the identification of children who use drugs as being chemically dependent (as exemplified by the two public television programs "Chemical People" shown nationally in November 1983). Like alcoholism, chemical dependence is seen to be a permanent condition requiring lifetime prophylactic measures. One program for diagnosing children as dependent involves gathering family members and others close to the child to confront the child about drug use and other aberrant behaviors. The aim of the intervention is to have the child acknowledge his or her illness and to enter treatment.

Residential treatments in which children are stripped of their possessions and other signs of their status in the outside world in order to eradicate their prior identities as drug users have received mixed ratings from the media. Many observers have been shocked by depictions of verbal and emotional abuse of the children in such get-tough or tough-love programs. The techniques the programs utilize borrow from the Synanon group therapy or "game" and resemble the process by which the individual is forced to admit previous ideological errors and to adopt a new, approved group identity that Schein (1961) described in his analysis of brainwashing techniques. Underlying all these methods is an AA—and a religious—concept termed *surrender*, or the sacrifice of the individual's critical self-awareness for a subservience to God or the treatment authorities. It is only at the point of total self-abnegation, this belief has it, that meaningful therapy can take place. The Addiction Recovery Corporation—a treatment center in Concord, Massachusetts—advertises itself to parents with the chilling claim: "We Hang On Until They Let Go."

Interventions with the young are not reserved for those who have actually used drugs or alcohol. One thrust of the idea that children of alcoholics are at a high risk to have drinking problems is the identification of such children for special attention even before they are teens. They may as children be educated about the nature of alcoholism, taught to abstain themselves, and made aware of the kinds of roles that family members are said to assume around the figure of a drunken parent. It is such roles that are the object of treatment for nonalcoholic relatives of alcoholics. The treatment of family members of alcoholics has exploded since the late 1970s. The National Association for Children of Alcoholics was established in 1983 with aims described by one of its founders, Dr. Timmen Cermak ("The Founding, Future and Vision of NACoA" 1983: 19):

> Children of alcoholics require and deserve treatment in and of themselves, not as mere adjuncts of alcoholics. . . . [T]hat entails . . . accepting the concept of co-alcoholism . . . [as being as legitimate] as the diagnosis of alcoholism.

These children include the adult children of alcoholics, themselves not presently living with alcoholics, who are still thought to bear the brunt of childhood identities fashioned by having grown up with a parent with a drinking problem (cf. Black 1982; Woititz 1983).

In his play *Our Town* (published the year before Alcoholics Anonymous was officially established), Thornton Wilder (1938: 931) recorded the following exchange:

> WOMAN IN THE BALCONY: Is there much drinking in Grover's Corners?
> MR. WEBB: Well, ma'am, I wouldn't know what you'd call *much.* Sattidy nights the farmhands meet down in Ellery Greenough's stable and holler some. Fourth of July I've been known to taste a drop myself—and Decoration Day, of course. We've got one or two town drunks [Grover's Corners' population is approximately 3,000], but they're always having remorses every time an evangelist comes to town.

From this off-hand, humorous image of alcoholism—in the person of the occasional town drunk who sobers up whenever an itinerant preacher arrives in town—the United States has developed a notion of alcoholism as an overwhelming specter that potentially clouds the lives of nearly every citizen. It might be said that the disease of alcoholism and related maladies have become a primary component of Americans' self-conception, one requiring constant vigilance, the segregation and re-education of many of our young—including some who have never had a drink—and the coerced treatment of many young and adult alike.

Spreading Diseases

The concept that adults who may never have been drunk warrant the same disease diagnosis and treatment as the alcoholic represents a monumental advance in the spread of alcoholism and disease in general. The concept has infinite ramifications: for example, if people need to be confronted about their unacknowledged drinking problems, then must others be confronted and treated for their unacknowledged relationship to an alcoholic or to a person who has failed to acknowledge his alcoholism? Although many more people will come under the purview of alcoholism treatment in this way, other trends signify that still larger numbers of people will be labeled as having a disease and as requiring medical attention.

The broadest view yet of the disease of alcoholism was offered by alcoholism researcher and psychiatrist Donald Goodwin (1984) when he argued that "One reason to believe alcoholism is a real disease—as real as a houseboat or a rose bush or double pneumonia—is that it has a natural history" (p. 1). For Goodwin, a disease is anything that can be identified and traced over time—even should it disappear! Apparently, for Goodwin, if some-thing exists at all, then it is a disease. The possibility that disease theoriz-ing would move in this direction was anticipated by Jules Masserman (1976), another alcohol researcher and psychiatrist, when he wrote that "Addiction to drink . . . is a 'disease' only in the sense that excessive eating, sleeping, smoking, gambling, wandering, or lechery may also be so classi-fied. All are attempts to deny conscious or unconscious insecurities and apprehensions, to challenge the milieu, and to escape onerous responsibil-ity" (p. 4).

Masserman could as well have added stealing, overwork, worrying, sadness, fear, incompetence, forgetfulness, stage fright, procrastination, an-ger, child abuse, murder, premenstrual tension, sloppiness, and the host of other problems people seek treatment for. What he quite correctly meant to indicate was that regarding alcoholism as a disease denuded that word of all its commonsensical meaning. Masserman's work—along with Szasz's (1974) and my own book, *Love and Addiction*—was part of a movement that indicated compulsive chemical use was no less subject to individual self-control and cognitive and social influence than was any other strongly felt urge. This whole line of reasoning has now been turned on its ear, so that all involvements that are broadly similar to alcoholism and drug addic-tion can be reclassified as diseases, as if in having thus labeled such activi-ties and states of being clinicians had made a scientific contribution akin to discovering a new planet or life form. In this way, as Masserman (1976) noted, what has historically been referred to as lechery can now be called "sexual addiction" (Carnes 1983), requiring that sufferers join groups con-structed along AA lines for its cure.

That more and more behaviors are being called diseases does not rule out a moralistic characterization of the same actions. In fact, as Marlatt (1983) observed, the modern disease model "is little more than the old 'moral model' (drinking as sinful behavior) dressed up in sheep's clothing (or at least a white coat)" (p. 1107), in which abstinence signifies repent-ance. When professional football player Art Schlichter, who had been sus-pended for gambling, was readmitted to the National Football League, NFL commissioner Pete Rozelle declared: "We . . . reviewed medical views of physicians qualified in the care of compulsive gambling . . . [and] the doc-tors believe Art's condition is under control" ("Schlichter Suspension Lifted by Rozelle" 1984: 31). Here is how Schlichter himself described his remis-sion on his reinstatement: "There are choices in everybody's lives. There is a bad side of the road and a good side of the road. The bad side is easier to take, but it will lead you into trouble. Do it the difficult, the good way" ("People" 1984: B9).

There is nothing the matter, of course, with people resolving to change the "side of the road" they travel on. The difficulty enters with considering this street crossing to be a medical matter. Those societies in which alcohol (or anything else) is seen to provide an explanation for uncontrolled behavior—be the explanation magical or medical—are those with the highest incidence of alcohol-related antisocial behavior. Telling drunk drivers they cannot control their drinking or be responsible for their actions once they have drunk is tantamount to allowing them to disregard the law and social regulation when they are drinking. Accepting drug and alcohol intoxication or withdrawal, premenstrual tension, love sickness, eating junk food, and so on as extenuating circumstances in the commission of a crime is to guarantee that more crimes will be committed under these circumstances (Peele 1982a). Consider, in this light, Schachter's (1980: 156–157) explanation for social disintegration as a result of nicotine withdrawal:

> When a large portion of an addicted population is attempting to quit smoking or switches to low nicotine brands, a very large number of people in that population will be in withdrawal. Given what we know of withdrawal, this means large numbers of people simultaneously in a state of irritability, irascibility, short temper, and so on. One could with reason anticipate high rates of divorce, assault, and general mayhem in such a population.

Diseases have made tremendous inroads not only in explaining crime but in defining the innermost feelings people, sometimes quite ordinary people, have. Depression has for some years been promoted as a disease (cf. Kline 1981). Now irrational love attractions (Liebowitz 1983) and phobias (Sheehan 1984)—the latter of which constitute the second-most common mental health problem (after alcoholism) in America—are called diseases. Unlike garden-variety sadness, attachment to a lover, and anxiety or fear, disease-based versions of these maladies are termed endogenous and conceived as biochemical or neurological anomalies requiring drug treatments. Oddly enough, given the quite different behavioral manifestations and settings of these diseases, all seem to respond best to the administration of antidepressant drugs. Just as with alcoholism and the metabolic disease of narcotic addiction, these latter-day maladies are seen to be lifetime characteristics of people that require them always to be aware of their illness and to be on guard against it. Since prescribed medications only arrest the problem without curing it, as in the case of methadone treatment for heroin addiction, such drugs are considered a necessary and permanent adjunct to the person's functioning.

The same course of discovery and the same scientific problems appear with the modern diseases of depression, love sickness, and phobias as with alcoholism and narcotic addiction. That is, clinicians remark on the severity and resistance to treatment of some cases of irrational behavior. In frustration, some physicians try different drugs until they find one that provides symptom relief. They then infer the existence of an endogenous biochemical source for the observed behaviors and feelings. The discoveries are in this way invariably made by exclusion, with neurological sources for a malady being deduced from the flagrance and persistence of its symptoms and its intractability to conventional psychotherapy. Never is the diagnosis of an individual case suggested by a biochemical analysis instead of by self-report, nor are hypotheses about the nature of the disease ever originally generated by neurochemical research.

The same baffling definitional problems remain for these contemporary diseases as have been noted for addiction. For example, they are all heavily linked to gender; more apparent among women than men are depression (by a 3:1 ratio, Weissman and Klerman 1977), severe phobias (4:1, Sheehan 1984) and love sickness or "hysteroid dysphoria" (10 +:1, Liebowitz and Klein 1979), while alcoholism remains the prototypical male disease (found ten or more times as often with men as women; Öjesjö 1984). In accounting for the greater frequency of a purportedly biological form of anxiety among women, Sheehan (1984) adopts a rather old saw by suggesting female hormones may be the culprit. In fact, no reasonable biological relationship has been shown to underlie all the sex-linked emotional diseases (cf., in the case of alcohol, Cloninger et al. 1978). Moreover, similar sex ratios are apparent in the milder versions of these same diseases, such as problem drinking and less severe anxiety and depression. It defies scientific rationality and parsimony to imagine that social causes create a set of problems, while an entirely different collection of factors comes into play for the same groups of people at the point at which their problems become diseases.

As with addictive diseases, notions about these new diseases rest on the feelings and self-conceptions of a relatively small group of individuals who seek therapeutic help. Missing in the analysis of the problem are surveys of broader populations, accounts by those who choose to treat their own symptoms, natural histories of young people and others whose difficulties fall away as their lives evolve, and the complicated feelings of all the other groups that consistently confound disease views of addiction. In the past, people who felt they were in the throes of an inescapable sickness were free to choose help on their own. Today, public health campaigns actively promote the existence of these emotional diseases and encourage doctors, teachers, and child-care providers to search for victims among the young. In schools and elsewhere, young people are identified as hyperkinetic, learning-disabled, maladjusted, abuse victims, offspring of alcoholics, and so forth, with the *purpose* of convincing them they are truly ill. The most ready means for dealing with all those who are different or who have problems is to label their diseases and submit them for treatment.

George Orwell's *1984* found nearly everyone voluntarily cooperating with a military dictatorship because they accepted its rendition of history and willingly policed themselves. In the historic 1984, we see a revised version of mind control. People eagerly seek out, or have forced upon them, self-designations that are even more comprehensive than the social and political roles in Orwell's futuristic society. These roles tell us not only how we feel and who we are, but how we *should* feel and how we *will* behave into the unlimited future. The nineteenth-century revolution in thinking about mental illness, analyzed by some as a social-control mechanism for the deviant and those who cannot be assimilated into society, has been supplanted by a far more thorough psychological categorization. Affecting practically everyone in one fashion or another, it is a vision of normal life as being rife with emotional disease.

The Cure for Addiction

> The nineteenth-century discovery [in Britain] that the [narcotic] addict is a suitable case for treatment is today an entrenched and unquestioned premise, with society unaware of the arbitrariness of this come-lately assumption. . . . Any suggestion that the current model is fundamentally mistaken in its assumption, that the treatment enterprise should be closed down and people with bad habits left to their own devices, would be dismissed only as outrageous and bizarre.
>
> (Berridge and Edwards 1981: 251)

Even with government and other reports showing minimal and sometimes double-edged benefits from therapy for addiction, there is no slowing down the rush to have all addicts treated. In imagining how the results of this gigantic enterprise can be maximized, it is good to recall an evaluation of treatment outcomes for an alcoholism program by Gerard et al. (1962) in which the authors noted that improvement was a consequence of "a change in the alcoholic's attitude toward the use of alcohol based on a person's own experiences, which in the vast majority of cases took place outside any clinical interactions" (p. 94). The insight these researchers had more than two decades ago has not been improved on by all the research on treatment cited in this book.

Whether in therapy or not, addicts improve when their relationships to work, family, and other aspects of their environment improve. Addicts have come to count on the regular rewards they get from their addictive involvement. They can give up these rewards when they believe they will find superior gratifications from other activities in the regular fiber of their lives. Therapy helps this process by focusing on external rewards and by assisting addicts in conceptualizing these rewards and obtaining them. Any rewards therapy itself produces must be regarded as intermediate and time-limited, as a passage to the stable, environmental rewards that are necessary to create a nonaddictive equilibrium in people's lives. Only when such everyday but potent reinforcements are firmly in place is an addiction cured. (See figure 6–1.)

Therapy—whether behavioral, group, or psychodynamic—errs when it designates its rewards and addicts' functioning in the therapeutic environment to be its goals. Similarly, by focusing solely on the addictive involvement as the object of change and not on addicts' life context, such therapy becomes too inward-focused to have real meaning or impact. For example, if conducted in splendid isolation within the laboratory, aversion training (or antabuse drug therapy or hypnotic suggestions) that attaches negative feelings to the addiction will be overwhelmed by outside pressures in addicts' lives. The idea that people can cease addictions by replacing them with so-called positive addictions like running or meditation is likewise a simplistic reduction of the role of addiction in people's lives. Like all-encompassing group involvements, activity substitution mainly holds out the opportunity for alternate addictions that may not be any less self-destructive than the original one (Peele 1981a).

Establishing systematic, ingrained rewards in people's lives is an imperfect, difficult process. The avoidance of this complexity marks addicts' pursuit and acceptance of addictive rewards in the first place. Preparation

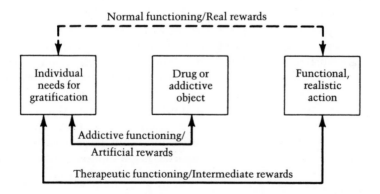

Addiction short-circuits a person's achievement of real-world rewards through normal functioning. Therapy must remove the barrier presented by an addiction so that a person can experience these real rewards. One way for therapy to do this is to provide intermediate rewards that lead to realistic action.

Source: Peele 1981a.

Figure 6–1. Breaking the Addiction Cycle

for a nonaddicted lifestyle includes an awareness that this imperfection exists, that negative feelings will return, that slips will occur, and that insoluble problems and a sense of inadequate rewards will never disappear entirely. The discovery that prior motivation is the most important element in predicting successful outcomes for addiction treatment is a restatement of the evident truth that only those who are willing to tolerate the uncertainty of a life without the addiction and who believe they can tolerate it will succeed at doing so. Therapy fails by causing addicts to imagine there is some way to short-circuit this fundamental self-reliance. It succeeds when it increases people's sense of their strength to withstand the uncertainty and discomfort as well as to generate positive rewards for themselves.

The summary of the steps out of an addiction that this book has highlighted—that people recover to the extent that they (1) believe an addiction is hurting them and wish to overcome it, (2) feel enough efficacy to manage their withdrawal and life without the addiction, and (3) find sufficient alternative rewards to make life without the addiction worthwhile—cannot make us optimistic about dramatic techniques for curing addiction. As an approach to our major problems of addiction, individual, therapeutic remedies obviously do not have the necessary breadth and depth of impact. Therapy is no more likely to eliminate addiction overall than is spontaneous recovery. While some seem to be aided to recovery through treatment, we can never get enough people to accept therapy, cure enough people through therapy, and keep enough people from relapsing after therapy to change fundamentally our society-wide levels of addiction.

More than anything, our failure at combatting addiction is due to our inability to prevent new addicts from being created. While use of major illicit drugs has receded somewhat for younger Americans in the 1980s, it is still greater than for the youth of any other Western nation (Johnston et al. 1981). Alcohol intoxication remains extremely common in this group, and both excessive alcohol and drug use by adolescents signal a dangerous future of addiction in our country. While the extremity of our response to these trends indicates how justifiably frightened we are, the efforts we have made over two decades have been futile. Indeed, extreme reactions to drug use and other addictive problems—such as the promotion of alternate compulsive activities as remedies—constitute major social and health problems in themselves.

Future generations of addicts—the enemy within—are the focus of a continual barrage of information about drugs and alcohol. My analysis in this book agrees with the assumption behind antidrug campaigns that there is something fundamentally wrong with the need many young people show—and some express consistently—for the modification of experience brought on by drugs and alcohol. However, I analyze the regular pursuit by many of an eradication of awareness to be an expression of mainstream cultural trends. There is no reason to assume that at any given time and place people are being prepared psychologically and practically by social institutions for what they must deal with. If addiction is a retreat from the attempt to attain a balanced set of gratifications in life, then its increase means that more people are finding their resources for coping to be insufficient relative to the benefits they believe an active involvement in this world will yield. This chronic deficiency can be traced to a lack of practice at self-reliance, of feelings of competence, of an ability to tolerate discomfort, and of self-confidence combined with the absence of positive values toward achievement, toward experience, toward society and community (and, in the most extreme cases of addictiveness, toward health and toward the self; cf. Peele 1983b). What we are missing in our culture today is a sense of our capacities, a moderation of our fear of the world, and positive expectations about what can be gained from life.

As I wrote with Archie Brodsky in 1975 (p. 145):

> The best antidotes to addiction are joy and competence—joy as the capacity to take pleasure in the people, activities, and things that are available to us; competence as the ability to master relevant parts of the environment and the confidence that our actions make a difference for ourselves and others.

Preparing people better to achieve joy and competence offers us our only substantial chance at affecting the incidence of addiction. It is certainly not a modest goal: Some might call it utopian or quixotic. Yet to the extent that our addiction theories avoid this realization—whether these theories come from pharmacologists, from clinicians and self-help groups who see themselves as combatting a disease, from sociologists, from psychologists—we will only obfuscate and exacerbate the addictive tendencies of our society.

Our current approaches to tackling addiction are defeated before they begin and stand no hope of success, since they misappraise the nature and the solution of the problem. What we need, in Henry Murray's (1981: 533–534) words, is "the conception of a better world composed of better societies composed of better persons" and a drive "to actualize it by self-transformations and social reconstructions." Yet often scientists dealing with behavior "prevent all development in this direction by shattering man's faith in the existence of the necessary potentialities within himself and reducing him to cynicism and despair" as though these scientists were "intending out of malice to reduce the concept of human nature to its lowest common denominators, and were gloating" about having done so. Nowhere is the description more apt than in our theories of addiction.

References

Addicted mothers and babies. 1984. *Journal,* Addiction Research Foundation (April): 12.

Adler, M.W.; Bendotti, C.; Ghezzi, D.; Samanin, R.; and Valzelli, L. 1975. Dependence to morphine in differentially housed rats. *Psychopharmacologia* 41:15–18.

Adult use of tobacco. 1975. Washington, DC: Center for Disease Control and National Cancer Institute.

Alcoholics Anonymous. 1939. *Alcoholics Anonymous.* New York: Works Publishing.

Alcoholism not inherited: Predisposition does exist. 1984. *U.S. Journal of Drug and Alcohol Dependence* (January): 1; 15.

Alexander, B.K.; Beyerstein, B.L.; Hadaway, P.F.; and Coambs, R.B. 1981. Effects of early and later colony housing on oral ingestion of morphine in rats. *Pharmacology Biochemistry and Behavior* 15:571–576.

Alexander, B.K.; Coambs, R.B.; and Hadaway, P.F. 1978. The effect of housing and gender on morphine self-administration in rats. *Psychopharmacology* 58:175–179.

Alexander, B.K., and Hadaway, P.F. 1982. Opiate addiction: The case for an adaptive orientation. *Psychological Bulletin* 92:367–381.

Allen, J. 1984. Correlates of success in health change efforts. Paper presented at Annual Conference of the American Psychological Association, Toronto, August.

American Psychiatric Association. 1980. *Diagnostic and statistical manual of mental disorders.* 3rd ed. Washington DC: American Psychiatric Association.

Anatomy of a victory: The DRG exemption. 1984. *U.S. Journal of Drug and Alcohol Dependence* (January): 3.

Aneshensel, C.S., and Huba, G.J. 1983. Depression, alcohol use, and smoking over one year. *Journal of Abnormal Psychology* 92:134–150.

Appenzeller, O.; Standefer, J.; Appenzeller, J.; and Atkinson, R. 1980. Neurology of endurance training V: Endorphins. *Neurology* 30:418–419.

Apsler, R. 1978. Untangling the conceptual jungle of "drug abuse." *Contemporary Drug Problems* 7:55–80.

Armor, D.J.; Polich, J.M.; and Stambul, H.B. 1978. *Alcoholism and treatment.* New York: Wiley.

Atkinson, J.W., and Feather, N.T., eds. 1966. *A theory of achievement motivation.* New York: Wiley.

Ausubel, D.P. 1961. Causes and types of narcotic addiction: A psychosocial view. *Psychiatric Quarterly* 35:523–531.

Baekeland, F.; Lundwall, L.; and Kissin, B. 1975. Methods for the treatment of chronic alcoholism: A critical appraisal. In *Research advances in alcohol and drug problems,* eds. R.J. Gibbons, Y. Israel, H. Kalant, R.E. Popham, W. Schmidt, and R.G. Smart. vol. 2. New York: Wiley.

Bales, R.F. 1946. Cultural differences in rates of alcoholism. *Quarterly Journal of Studies on Alcohol* 6:480–499.

Ball, J.C.; Smith, J.P.; and Graff, H., eds. 1977. International survey. *Addictive Diseases* 3 (1):entire issue.

Bandura, A. 1977a. Self-efficacy: Toward a unifying theory of behavioral change. *Pychological Review* 84:191–215.

———. 1977b. *Social learning theory.* Englewood Cliffs, NJ: Prentice-Hall.

Barnett, M.L. 1955. Alcoholism in the Cantonese of New York City: An anthropological study. In *Etiology of chronic alcoholism,* ed. O. Diethelm. Springfield, IL: Charles C Thomas.

Beauchamp, D.E. 1980. *Beyond alcoholism: Alcoholism and public health policy.* Philadelphia, PA: Temple University Press.

Beauchamp, D.E., et al. 1980. Comments on "Patterns of Alcoholism over Four Years"; and a response. *Journal of Studies on Alcohol* 41:760–796.

Becker, H.S. 1953. Becoming a marijuana user. *American Journal of Sociology* 59:235–242.

———. 1963. *Outsiders.* London: Free Press of Glencoe.

Becker, M., ed. 1974. *The health belief model and personal health behavior.* Thorofare, NJ: Charles B. Slack.

Beckman, L.J. 1978. The psychosocial characteristics of alcoholic women. *Drug abuse and alcoholism review* (September/December): 1–12.

Beecher, H.K. 1959. *Measurement of subjective responses: Quantitative effects of drugs.* New York: Oxford University Press.

The behaviorists. 1984. *Journal,* Addiction Research Foundation (February): 9–10.

Bejerot, N. 1980. Addiction to pleasure: A biological and social-psychological theory of addiction. In *Theories on drug abuse,* eds. D.J. Lettieri, M. Sayers, and H.W. Pearson. Research Monograph 30. Rockville, MD: National Institute on Drug Abuse.

Bem, D.J., and Funder, D.C. 1978. Predicting more of the people more of the time: Assessing the personality of situations. *Psychological Review* 85:485–501.

Bem, D.J., and Lord, C.G. 1979. The template-matching technique. *Journal of Personality and Social Psychology* 37:833–846.

Bennett, R.; Batenhorst, R.L.; Graves, D.; Foster, T.S.; Bauman, T.; Griffen, W.O.; and Wright, B.D. 1982. Morphine titration in positive laparotomy patients using patient-controlled analgesia. *Current Therapeutic Research* 32:45–51.

Bennett, W., and Gurin, J. 1982. *The dieter's dilemma.* New York: Basic Books.

Benson, C.S., and Wilsnack, S.C. 1983. Gender differences in alcoholic personality characteristics and life experiences. In *Identifying and measuring alcoholic personality characteristics,* ed. W. M. Cox. San Francisco: Jossey-Bass.

Berridge, V., and Edwards, G. 1981. *Opium and the people: Opiate use in nineteenth-century England.* New York: St Martin's.

Best, J.A., and Bloch, M. 1979. Compliance in the control of cigarette smoking. In *Compliance in health care,* eds. R.E. Haynes, D.W. Taylor, and D.L. Sackett. Baltimore: John Hopkins University Press.

Best, J.A., and Hakstian, A.R. 1978. A situation-specific model for smoking behavior. *Addictive Behaviors* 3:79–92.

Biomed research gets top priority. 1984. *U.S. Journal of Drug and Alcohol Dependence* (May): 1; 21.

Birney, R.C.; Burdick, H.; and Teevan, R.C. 1969. *Fear of failure.* New York: Van Nostrand.

Black, C. 1982. *It will never happen to me.* Denver: M.A.C.

Blum, R.H. 1969. On the presence of demons. In *Drugs I: Drugs and society,* eds. R.H. Blum et al. San Francisco: Jossey-Bass.

Blum, R.H., and associates. 1969. *Drugs I: Society and drugs.* San Francisco: Jossey-Bass.

Blum, R.H., and Blum, E.M. 1969. A cultural case study. In *Drugs I: Drugs and society,* eds. R.H. Blum et al. San Francisco: Jossey-Bass.

Boland, F.J. 1983. Open letter concerning failure to replicate with new colony Wistar rats. Queen's University, Kingston, Canada, June 30.

Boskind-White, M., and White, W.C. 1983. *Bulimarexia: The binge/purge cycle.* New York: Norton.

Boyd, W. 1976. Excitement: The gambler's drug. In *Gambling and society,* ed. W.R. Eadington. Springfield, IL: Charles C Thomas.

Brandsma, J.M.; Maultsby, M.C.; and Welsh, R.J. 1980. *The outpatient treatment of alcoholism: A review and comparative study.* Baltimore: University Park Press.

Brecher, E.M. 1972. *Licit and illicit drugs.* Mount Vernon, NY: Consumers Union.

Brown, S.A.; Goldman, M.S.; Inn, A.; and Anderson, L.R. 1980. Expectations of reinforcement from alcohol: Their domain and relation to drinking patterns. *Journal of Consulting and Clinical Psychology* 48:419–426.

Bruch, H. 1973. *Eating Disorders.* New York: Basic Books.

Brunke, M.L.; Bowman, M.; Alexander, B.K.; and Coambs, R.B. 1980. Failure to find an effect of catheterization on oral morphine consumption in rats. *Psychological Reports* 47:444–446.

Brunswick, A.F. 1979. Black youth and drug use behavior. In *Youth drug abuse: Problems, issues and treatment,* eds. G. Beschner and A. Friedman. Lexington, MA: Lexington.

Burke, H., and Marcus, R. 1977. MacAndrew MMPI alcoholism scale: Alcoholism and drug addictiveness. *Journal of Psychology* 96:141–148.

Burnett, M. 1979. Understanding and overcoming addictions. In *Helping clients with special concerns,* eds. S. Eisenberg and L.E. Patterson. Chicago: Rand McNally.

Cahalan, D. 1970. *Problem drinkers: A national survey.* San Francisco: Jossey-Bass.

Cahalan, D.; Cisin, I.H.; and Crossley, H.M. 1969. *American drinking practices.* Monograph 6. New Brunswick, NJ: Rutgers Center of Alcohol Studies.

Cahalan, D., and Room, R. 1974. *Problem drinking among American men.* Monograph 7. New Brunswick, NJ: Rutgers Center of Alcohol Studies.

Califano, J.E. 1983. *The 1982 report on drug abuse and alcoholism.* New York: Warner.

Cameron, D.C. 1971a. Abuse of alcohol and drugs: Concepts and planning. *World Health Organization Chronicle* 25:8–16.

———. 1971b. Facts about drugs. *World Health* (April): 4–11.

Caplan, R.D.; Cobb, S.; and French, J.R.P., Jr. 1975. Relationships of cessation of smoking with job stress, personality, and social support. *Journal of Applied Psychology* 60:211–219.

Cappell, H., and Herman, C.P. 1972. Alcohol and tension reduction—a review. *Quarterly Journal of Studies on Alcohol* 33:33–64.

Carnes, P. 1983. *The sexual addiction.* Minneapolis: CompCare.

Caudill, B.D., and Marlatt, G.A. 1975. Modeling influences in social drinking: An experimental analogue. *Journal of Consulting and Clinical Psychology* 43:405–415.

Chaney, E.F.; O'Leary, M.R.; and Marlatt, G.A. 1978. Skill training with alcoholics. *Journal of Consulting and Clinical Psychology* 46:1092–1096.

Chein, I. 1969. Psychological functions of drug use. In *Scientific basis of drug dependence,* ed. H. Steinberg. London: Churchill.

Chein, I.; Gerard, D.L.; Lee, R.S.; and Rosenfeld, E. 1964. *The road to H.* New York: Basic Books.

Chernick, V.; Childiaeva, R.; and Ioffe, S. 1983. Effects of maternal alcohol intake and smoking on neonatal electroencephalogram and anthropometric measurements. *American Journal of Obstetrics and Gynecology* 146:41–47.

Chipkin, R.E. 1976. Aversiveness of oral methadone in rats. Doctoral dissertation, Medical College of Virginia, Richmond, VA.

Christiansen, B.A., and Goldman, M.S. 1983. Alcohol-related expectancies versus demographic/background variables in the prediction of adolescent drinking. *Journal of Consulting and Clinical Psychology* 51:249–257.

Clark, W.B. 1976. Loss of control, heavy drinking and drinking problems in a longitudinal study. *Journal of Studies on Alcohol* 37:1256–1290.

———. 1982. Public drinking contexts: Bars and taverns. In *Social drinking contexts,* eds. T.C. Harford and L.S. Gaines. Research Monograph 7. Rockville, MD: National Institute on Alcohol Abuse and Alcoholism.

Clark, W.B., and Cahalan, D. 1976. Changes in problem drinking over a four-year span. *Addictive Behaviors* 1:251–260.

Clausen, J.A. 1961. Drug addiction. In *Contemporary social problems,* eds. R.K. Merton and R.A. Nisbet. New York: Harcourt.

Cloninger, C.R.; Christiansen, K.O.; Reich, T.; and Gottesman, I.I. 1978. Implications of sex differences in the prevalences of antisocial personality, alcoholism, and criminality for family transmission. *Archives of General Psychiatry* 35:941–951.

Coambs, R.B. 1977. The effect of environment on morphine consumption in opiate naive rats. Honors essay, Simon Fraser University, Burnaby, BC.

———. 1980. Aversiveness of orally administered morphine in rats. Masters thesis, Simon Fraser University, Burnaby, BC.

Coambs, R.B.; Alexander, B.K.; Davis, C.M.; Hadaway, P.F.; and Tressel, W.K. 1980.

A drug dispenser to measure individual drinking in rat colonies. *Pharmacology Biochemistry and Behavior* 13:593–595.

Cocaine: middle class high. 1981. *Time* (July 6):56–63.

Cohen, S. 1983. Current attitudes about the benzodiazepines: Trial by media. *Journal of Psychoactive Drugs* 15:109–113.

Colletti, G., and Kopel, S.A. 1979. Maintaining behavior change: An investigation of three maintenance strategies and the relationship of self-attribution to the long-term reduction of cigarette smoking. *Journal of Consulting and Clinical Psychology* 47:614–617.

Collier, P., and Horowitz, D. 1976. *The Rockefellers: An American dynasty.* New York: New American Library.

The collision of prevention and treatment. 1984. *Journal,* Addiction Research Foundation (February):16.

Colt, E.W.D.; Wardlaw, S.L.; and Frantz, A.G. 1981. The effect of running on plasma β-endorphin. *Life Sciences* 28:1637–1640.

Condiotte, M.M., and Lichtenstein, E. 1981. Self-efficacy and relapse in smoking cessation programs. *Journal of Consulting and Clinical Psychology* 49:648–658.

Coppolillo, H.P. 1975. Drug impediments to mothering behavior. *Addictive Diseases* 2:201–208.

Costello, R.M. 1975. Alcoholism treatment and evaluation II: Collation of two year follow-up studies. *International Journal of Addictions* 10:857–867.

Courtwright, D.T. 1982. *Dark paradise: Opiate addiction in America before 1940.* Cambridge, MA: Harvard University Press.

Csikszentmihalyi, M., and Kubey, R. 1981. Television and the rest of life. *Public Opinion Quarterly* 45:317–328.

Cummings, N.A. 1979. Turning bread into stones: Our modern antimiracle. *American Psychologist* 34:1119–1124.

Cushner, I.M. 1981. Maternal behavior and perinatal risks: Alcohol, smoking, and drugs. *Annual Review of Public Health* 2:201–218.

Davies, D.L. 1962. Normal drinking in recovered alcohol addicts. *Quarterly Journal of Studies on Alcohol* 23:94–104.

Davis, M., and Shanks, B. 1975. Neurological aspects of perinatal narcotic addiction and methadone treatment. *Addictive Diseases* 2:213–226.

Debate rages on 1973 Sobell study. 1982. *Monitor,* American Psychological Association (November):8–9.

DeFeudis, F.V.; DeFeudis, P.A.; and Samoza, E. 1976. Altered analgesic responses to morphine in differentially housed mice. *Psychopharmacology* 49:117–118.

Desmond, M.M., and Wilson, G.S. 1975. Neonatal abstinence syndrome: Recognition and diagnosis. *Addictive Diseases* 2:113–121.

Dickens, B.M.; Doob, A.N.; Warwick, O.H.; and Winegard, W.C. 1982. *Report of the Committee of Enquiry into Allegations Concerning Drs. Linda and Mark Sobell.* Toronto: Addiction Research Foundation.

Dielman, T.E. 1979. Gambling: A social problem? *Journal of Social Issues* 35:36–42.

Ditman, K.S., and Crawford, G.G. 1966. The use of court probation in the management of the alcohol addict. *American Journal of Psychiatry* 122:757–762.

Ditman, K.S.; Crawford, G.G.; Forgy, E.W.; Moskowitz, H.; and MacAndrew, C. 1967. A controlled experiment on the use of court probation for drunk arrests. *American Journal of Psychiatry* 124:160–163.

Dole, V.P. 1972. Narcotic addiction, physical dependence and relapse. *New England Journal of Medicine* 286:988–992.

———. 1980. Addictive behavior. *Scientific American* (June): 138–154.

Dole, V.P., and Nyswander, M.E. 1967. Heroin addiction: A metabolic disease. *Archives of Internal Medicine* 120:19–24.

———. 1976. Methadone maintenance treatment: A ten-year perspective. *Journal of the American Medical Association* 235:2117–2119.

Donegan, N.H.; Rodin, J.; O'Brien, C.P.; and Solomon, R.L. 1983. A learning theory approach to commonalities. In *Commonalities in substance abuse and habitual behavior,* eds. P.K. Levison, D.R. Gerstein, and D.R. Maloff. Lexington, MA: Lexington.

Drink/smoke combo significant risk to fetus. 1983. *Journal,* Addiction Research Foundation (May):3.

Drinking problem dispute. 1980. *New York Times* (January 30):20.

Dunwiddie, T. 1983. Neurobiology of cocaine and opiate abuse. *U.S. Journal of Drug and Alcohol Dependence* (December):17.

Eddy, N.B.; Halbach, H.; Isbell, H.; and Seevers, M.H. 1965. Drug dependence: Its significance and characteristics. *Bulletin of the World Health Organization* 32:721–733.

Eddy, N.B., and May, E.L. 1973. The search for a better analgesic. *Science* 181:407–414.

Edwards, G., and Gross, M.M. 1976. Alcohol dependence: Provisional description of a clinical syndrome. *British Medical Journal* 1:1058–1061.

Efron, V.; Keller, M.; and Gurioli, C. 1974. *Statistics on consumption of alcohol and on alcoholism.* New Brunswick, NJ: Rutgers Center of Alcohol Studies.

Emrick, C.D. 1975. A review of psychologically oriented treatment of alcoholism II: The relative effectiveness of different treatment approaches and the effectiveness of treatment versus no treatment. *Journal of Studies on Alcohol* 36:88–109.

Emrick, C.D., and Hansen, J. 1983. Assertions regarding effectiveness of treatment for alcoholism: Fact or fantasy? *American Psychologist* 38:1078–1088.

Engle, K.B., and Williams, T.K. 1972. Effect of an ounce of vodka on alcoholics' desire for alcohol. *Quarterly Journal of Studies on Alcohol* 33:1099–1105.

Epstein, E.J. 1977. *Agency of fear: Opiates and political power in America.* New York: Putnam.

Falk, J.L. 1981. The environmental generation of excessive behavior. In *Behavior in excess,* ed. S.J. Mulé. New York: Free Press.

———. 1983. Drug dependence: Myth or motive? *Pharmacology Biochemistry and Behavior* 19:385–391.

Falk, J.L.; Dews, P.B.; and Schuster, C.R. 1983. Commonalities in the environmental control of behavior. In *Commonalities in substance abuse and habitual behavior,* eds. P.K. Levison, D.R. Gerstein, and D.R. Maloff. Lexington, MA: Lexington.

Ferguson, G.A. 1981. *Statistical analysis in psychology and education.* 5th ed. New

York: McGraw-Hill.

Fillmore, K.M. 1975. Relationships between specific drinking problems in early adulthood and middle age: An exploratory 20 year follow-up study. *Journal of Studies on Alcohol* 36:882–907.

Fishburne, P.M.; Abelson, H.I.; and Cisin, I. 1980. *National survey on drug abuse, main findings: 1979.* Rockville, MD: National Institute on Drug Abuse.

Fisher, E. 1981. *Eddie: My life, my loves.* New York: Harper & Row.

Fisher, E.B., Jr.; Levenkron, J.C.; Lowe, M.R.; Loro, A.D., Jr.; and Green, L. 1982. Self-initiated self-control in risk reduction. In *Adherence, compliance and generalization in behavioral medicine*, ed. R.B. Stuart. New York: Brunner/Mazel.

Fisher, J.C.; Mason, R.L.; and Fisher, J.V. 1976. A diagnostic formula for alcoholism. *Journal of Studies on Alcohol* 37:1247–1255.

For drug prosecutor, a sense of frustration. 1984. *New York Times* (May 22): B4.

Foucault, M. 1973. *Madness and civilization: A history of insanity in the age of reason.* New York: Random House.

The founding, future and vision of NACoA. 1983. *U.S. Journal of Drug and Alcohol Dependence* (December): 19.

Fuentes, V.O.; Hunt, W.B.; and Crossland, J. 1978. The production of morphine tolerance and physical dependence by the oral route in the rat. *Psychopharmacology* 59:65–69.

Garcia, J.; Hankins, W.G.; and Rusniak, K.W. 1974. Behavioral regulation of the milieu interne in man and rat. *Science* 185:824–831.

Garn, S.M.; Bailey, S.M.; and Cole, P.E. 1980. Continuities and changes in fatness and obesity. In *Nutrition, physiology and obesity*, ed. R. Schemmel. Palm Beach, FL: CRC Press.

Garn, S.M.; Bailey, S.M.; and Higgins, T.T. 1980. Effects of socioeconomic status, family line, and living together on fatness and obesity. In *Childhood prevention of atherosclerosis and hypertension*, eds. R.M. Lauer and R.B. Shekelle. New York: Raven.

Garn, S.M.; Cole, P.E.; and Bailey, S.M. 1979. Living together as a factor in family-line resemblances. *Human Biology* 51:565–587.

Garn, S.M.; LaVelle, M.; and Pilkington, J.J. 1984. Obesity and living together. *Marriage and Family Review* 7:33–47.

Garn, S.M.; Pilkington, J.J.; and LaVelle, M. 1984. Relationship between initial fatness level and long-term fatness change. *Ecology of Food and Nutrition* 14:85–92.

Gay, G.R.; Senay, E.C.; and Newmeyer, J.A. 1973. The pseudo-junkie: Evolution of the heroin lifestyle in the nonaddicted individual. *Drug Forum* 2:279–290.

Gerard, D.L., and Saenger, G. 1966. *Out-patient treatment of alcoholism: A study of outcome and its determinants.* Toronto: University of Toronto Press.

Gerard, D.L.; Saenger, G.; and Wile, R. 1962. The abstinent alcoholic. *Archives of General Psychiatry* 6:83–95.

Gerin, W. 1982. (No) accounting for results. *Psychology Today* (August): 32.

Gilbert, D.G. 1979. Paradoxical tranquilizing and emotion-reducing effects of nicotine. *Psychological Bulletin* 86:643–661.

Gilbert, R.M. 1981. Drug abuse as excessive behavior. In *Classic contributions in the addictions*, eds. H. Shaffer and M.E. Burglass. New York: Brunner/Mazel.

Glaser, F.B. 1974. Psychologic vs. pharmacologic heroin dependence. *New England Journal of Medicine* 290:231.

Glassner, B. and Berg, B. 1980. How Jews avoid alcohol problems. *American Sociological Review* 45:647–664.

Glazer, N. 1952. Why Jews stay sober. *Commentary* 13:181–186.

Glickman, S.E., and Schiff, B.B. 1967. A biological theory of reinforcement. *Psychological Review* 74:81–109.

Goldblatt, P.B.; Moore, M.E.; and Stunkard, A.J. 1965. Social factors in obesity. *Journal of the American Medical Association* 192:1039–1044.

Goldstein, A. 1972. Heroin addiction and the role of methadone in its treatment. *Archives of General Psychiatry* 26:291–297.

———. 1976a. Heroin addiction: Sequential treatment employing pharmacological supports. *Archives of General Psychiatry* 33:353–358.

———. 1976b. Opioid peptides (endorphins) in pituitary and brain. *Science* 193:1081–1086.

Goldstein, A.; Kaizer, S.; and Whitby, O. 1969. Psychotropic effects of caffeine in man IV: Quantitative and qualitative differences associated with habituation to coffee. *Clinical Pharmacology and Therapeutics* 10:489–497.

Goldstein, J.W., and Sappington, J.T. 1977. Personality characteristics of students who become heavy drug users: An MMPI study of an avant-garde. *American Journal of Drug and Alcohol Abuse* 4:401–412.

Gomberg, E.L. 1980. Drinking and problem drinking among the elderly. *Alcohol, drugs and aging: Usage and problems series.* I. Institute of Gerontology, University of Michigan, Ann Arbor.

Goode, E. 1972. *Drugs in American society.* New York: Knopf.

Goodwin, D.W. 1976. *Is alcoholism hereditary?* New York: Oxford University Press.

———. 1979. Alcoholism and heredity. *Archives of General Psychiatry* 36:57–61.

———. 1980. The bad-habit theory of drug abuse. In *Theories on drug abuse,* eds. D.J. Lettieri, M. Sayers, and H.W. Pearson. Research Monograph 30. Rockville, MD: National Institute on Drug Abuse.

———. 1984. A paean to the follow-up. In *Longitudinal research in alcoholism,* eds. D.W. Goodwin, K.T. van Dusen, and S.A. Mednick. Boston: Kluwer-Nijhoff.

Goodwin, D.W.; Crane, J.B.; and Guze, S.B. 1971. Felons who drink: An 8-year follow-up. *Quarterly Journal of Studies on Alcohol* 32:136–147.

Goodwin, D.W.; Schulsinger, F.; Hermansen, L.; Guze, S.B.; and Winokur, G. 1973. Alcohol problems in adoptees raised apart from biological parents. *Archives of General Psychiatry* 28:238–243.

Gordis, E.; Dorph, D.; Sepe, V.; and Smith, H. 1981. Outcome of alcoholism treatment among 5578 patients in an urban comprehensive hospital-based program: Application of a computerized data system. *Alcoholism: Clinical and Experimental Research* 5:509–522.

Gordon, B. 1979. *I'm dancing as fast as I can.* New York: Harper & Row.

Grant, E.C. 1963. An analysis of the social behavior of the male laboratory rat. *Behavior* 21:260–281.

Gray, J.A. 1978. Anxiety. *Human Nature* (July): 38–45.

Greaves, G. 1974. Toward an existential theory of drug dependence. *Journal of*

Nervous and Mental Disease 159:263–274.

———. 1980. An existential theory of drug dependence. In *Theories on drug abuse,* eds. D.J. Lettieri, M. Sayers, H.W. Pearson. Research Monograph 30. Rockville, MD: National Institute on Drug Abuse.

Greeley, A.M.; McCready, W.C.; and Theisen, G. 1980. *Ethnic drinking subcultures.* New York: Praeger.

Greenough, W.T. 1975. Experimental modification of the developing brain. *American Scientist* 63:37–46.

Griffiths, R.R.; Brady, J.V.; and Bradford, L.D. 1979. Predicting the abuse liability of drugs with animal drug self-administration procedures: Psychomotor stimulants and hallucinogens. In *Advances in behavioral pharmacology,* eds. T.T. Thompson and P.B. Dews. vol. 2. New York: Academic.

Gross, M.M. 1977. Psychobiological contributions to the Alcohol Dependence Syndrome: A selective review of recent literature. In *Alcohol related disabilities,* eds. G. Edwards et al. WHO Offset Publication 32. Geneva: World Health Organization.

Gusfield, J.R. 1963. *Symbolic crusade: Status politics and the American temperance movement.* Urbana: University of Illinois Press.

———. 1981. *The culture of public problems: Drinking-driving and the symbolic order.* Chicago: University of Chicago Press.

Hackler, T. 1983. The road to recovery. *United Airlines Magazine* (September): 39–42.

Hadaway, P.F.; Alexander, B.K.; Coambs, R.B.; and Beyerstein, B. 1979. The effect of housing and gender on preference for morphine-sucrose solutions in rats. *Psychopharmacology* 66:87–91.

Hansen, J., and Emrick, C.D. 1983. Whom are we calling "alcoholic"? *Bulletin of the Society of Psychologists in Addictive Behaviors* 2:164–178.

Hanson, J.W.; Jones, K.L.; and Smith, D.W. 1976. Fetal alcohol syndrome: Experience with 41 patients. *Journal of the American Medical Association* 235:1458–1460.

Harding, W.M.; Zinberg, N.E.; Stelmack, S.M.; and Barry, M. 1980. Formerly-addicted-now-controlled opiate users. *International Journal of the Addictions* 15:47–60.

Harford, T.C. 1979. Ecological factors in drinking. In *Youth, alcohol and social policy,* eds. H.T. Blane and M.E. Chafetz. New York: Plenum.

Harford, T.C., and Gaines, L.S., eds. 1982. *Social drinking contexts.* Research Monograph 7. Rockville, MD: National Institute on Alcohol Abuse and Alcoholism.

Hatterer, L. 1980. *The pleasure addicts.* New York: A.S. Barnes.

Hawley, L.M., and Butterfield, G.E. 1981. Exercise and the endogenous opioids. *New England Journal of Medicine* 305:1591.

Heather, N., and Robertson, I. 1981. *Controlled drinking.* London: Methuen.

———. 1983. Why is abstinence necessary for the recovery of some problem drinkers? *British Journal of Addiction* 78:139–144.

Heather, N.; Rollnick, S.; and Winton, M. 1983. A comparison of objective and subjective measures of alcohol dependence as predictors of relapse following treatment. *British Journal of Clinical Psychology* 22:11–17.

Heather, N.; Winton, M.; and Rollnick, S. 1982. An empirical test of "a cultural delusion of alcoholics." *Psychological Reports* 50:379–382.

Herman, C.P., and Polivy, J. 1975. Anxiety, restraint and eating behavior. *Journal of Abnormal Psychology* 84:666–672.

———. 1980. Restrained eating. In *Obesity*, ed. A.J. Stunkard, Philadelphia: Saunders.

Heroin in West a 'widening crisis': INCB. 1981. *Journal*, Addiction Research Foundation (March): 1.

Heroin trade rising despite U.S. efforts. 1981. *New York Times* (February 15): 1; 32.

Hingson, R., et al. 1982. Effects of maternal drinking and marijuana use on fetal growth and development. *Pediatrics* 70:539–546.

Hodgson, R., and Miller, P. 1982. *Self-watching: Addictions, habits, compulsions; what to do about them.* London: Century.

Hodgson, R.; Rankin, H.; and Stockwell, T. 1979. Alcohol dependence and the priming effect. *Behavior Research and Therapy* 17:379–387.

Hodgson, R.; Stockwell, T.; Rankin, H.; and Edwards, G. 1978. Alcohol dependence: The concept, its utility and measurement. *British Journal of Addiction* 73:339–342.

Hooper, H.E., and Santo, Y. 1980. Use of propoxyohene (Darvon) by adolescents admitted to drug abuse programs. *Contemporary Drug Problems* 9:357–368.

Horn, G.; Rose, S.P.R.; and Bateson, P.P.G. 1979. Experience and plasticity in the central nervous system. *Science* 203:75–78.

Huidobro, F. 1964. Studies on morphine VI: Ingestion of morphine solutions in normal mice and rats and in animals with chronic morphinism. *Archives Internationales de Pharmacodynamie et de Therapie* 151:299–312.

Hull, J.G., and Young, R.D. 1983. The self-awareness reducing effects of alcohol: Evidence and implications. In *Psychological perspectives on the self*, eds. J. Suls and A.G. Greenwald. vol. 2. Hillsdale, NJ: Erlbaum.

Inpatient vs. outpatient treatment. 1984. *U.S. Journal of Drug and Alcohol Dependence* (May): 3.

Is inpatient rehabilitation of the alcoholic cost effective? 1984. Session at Conference on Controversies in Alcoholism and Substance Abuse, National Association on Drug Abuse Problems, New York, March.

Isbell, H. 1958. Clinical research on addiction in the United States. In *Narcotic drug addiction problems*, ed. R.B. Livingston. Bethesda, MD: Public Health Service.

Istvan, J., and Matarazzo J.D. 1984. Tobacco, alcohol, and caffeine use: A review of their interrelationships. *Psychological Bulletin* 95:301–326.

Jacobson, R.C., and Zinberg, N.E. 1975. *The social basis of drug abuse prevention.* Publication SS-5. Washington, DC: Drug Abuse Council.

Jaffe, J.H. 1980. Drug addiction and drug abuse. In *Goodman and Gilman's The pharmacological basis of therapeutics*, eds. A.G. Gilman, L.S. Goodman, and B.A. Gilman. 6th ed. New York: Macmillan.

Jaffe, J.H., and Harris, T.G. 1973. As far as heroin is concerned, the worst is over. *Psychology Today* (August): 68–79, 85.

Jaffe, J.H., and Martin, W.R. 1980. Opioid analgesics and antagonists. In *Goodman and Gilman's The pharmacological basis of therapeutics*, eds. A.G. Gilman, L.S. Goodman, and B.A. Gilman. 6th ed. New York: Macmillan.

Jarvik, M.E. 1973. Further observations on nicotine as the reinforcing agent in smoking. In *Smoking behavior: Motives and incentives,* ed. W.L. Dunn, Jr. Washington, DC: Winston.

Jarvik, M.E.; Glick, S.D.; and Nakamura, R.K. 1970. Inhibition of cigarette smoking by orally administered nicotine. *Clinical Pharmacology and Therapeutics* 11:574–576.

Jellinek, E.M. 1946. Phases in the drinking history of alcoholics: Analysis of a survey conducted by the official organ of Alcoholics Anonymous. *Quarterly Journal of Studies on Alcohol* 7:1–88.

———. 1952. Phases of alcohol addiction. *Quarterly Journal of Studies on Alcohol* 13:637–684.

———. 1960. *The disease concept of alcoholism.* New Haven: Hillhouse Press.

Jessor, R. 1979. Marijuana: A review of recent psychosocial research. In *Handbook on drug abuse,* eds. R.L. Dupont, A. Goldstein, and J. O'Donnell. Rockville, MD: National Institute on Drug Abuse.

Jessor, R.; Chase, J.; and Donovan, J. 1980. Psychosocial correlates of marijuana use and problem drinking in a national sample of adolescents. *American Journal of Public Health* 70:604–613.

Jessor, R., and Jessor, S.L. 1975. Adolescent development and the onset of drinking. *Journal of Studies on Alcohol* 36:27–51.

———. 1977. *Problem behavior and psychosocial development: A longitudinal study of youth.* New York: Academic.

Johanson, C.E., and Uhlenhuth, E.H. 1981. Drug preference and mood in humans: Repeated assessment of d-amphetamine. *Pharmacology Biochemistry and Behavior* 14:159–163.

Johnson, C., and Larson, R. 1982. Bulimia: An analysis of moods and behavior. *Psychosomatic Medicine* 44:341–351.

Johnston, L.D.; Bachman, J.G.; and O'Malley, P.M. 1981. *Highlights from "Student Drug Use in America 1975–1981."* Rockville, MD: National Institute on Drug Abuse.

Johnston, L.; O'Malley, P.; and Eveland, L. 1978. Drugs and delinquency: A search for causal connections. In *Longitudinal research on drug issues,* ed. D.B. Kandel. Washington, DC: Hemisphere.

Jones, H.B., and Jones, H.C. 1977. *Sensual drugs.* Cambridge, England: Cambridge University Press.

Jones, E., and Berglas, S. 1978. Control of attributions about the self through self-handicapping strategies: The appeal of alcohol and the role of underachievement. *Personality and Social Psychology Bulletin* 4:200–206.

Jones, K.L., and Smith, D.W. 1973. Recognition of the fetal alcohol syndrome in early infancy. *Lancet* 2:999–1001.

Jorquez, J.S. 1983. The retirement phase of heroin using careers. *Journal of Drug Issues* 13:343–365.

Kalant, H. 1982. Drug research is muddied by sundry dependence concepts. Paper presented at the Annual Meeting of the Canadian Psychological Association, Montreal, June (cited in *Journal,* Addiction Research Foundation [September 1982]: 12).

Kalant, O.J., and Kalant, H. 1976. Death in amphetamine users: Causes and estimates of mortality. In *Research advances in alcohol and drug problems*, eds. R.J. Gibbins, Y. Israel, H. Kalant, R.E. Popham, W. Schmidt, and R.G. Smart. vol. 3. New York: Wiley.

Kales, A.; Bixler, E.O.; Tjiauw-Ling, T.; Scharf, M.B.; and Kales, J.D. 1974. Chronic hypnotic-drug use: Ineffectiveness, drug-withdrawal insomnia, and dependence. *Journal of the American Medical Association* 227:513–517.

Kandel, D.B. 1978. Homophily, selection, and socialization in adolescent friendships. *American Journal of Sociology* 84:427–436.

———. 1980. Drug and drinking behavior among youth. In *Annual review of sociology*, eds. J. Coleman, A. Inkeles, and M. Smelser. vol. 6. Palo Alto, CA: Annual Reviews.

———. 1984. Marijuana users in young adulthood. *Archives of General Psychiatry* 41:200–209.

Kandel, D.B.; Kessler, R.C.; and Margulies, R.Z. 1978. Antecedents of adolescent initiation into stages of drug use: A developmental analysis. In *Longitudinal research on drug use*, ed. D.B. Kandel. Washington, DC: Hemisphere.

Kaplan, E.H., and Wieder, H. 1974. *Drugs don't take people, people take drugs*. Secaucus, NJ: Lyle Stuart.

Katz, D.M., and Steinberg, H. 1970. Long term isolation in rats reduces morphine response. *Nature* 228:469–471.

Kay, E.; Lyons, A.; Newman, W.; Mankin, D.; and Loeb, R. 1978. A longitudinal study of the personality correlates of marijuana use. *Journal of Counsulting and Clinical Psychology* 46:470–477.

Keller, M. 1969. Some views on the nature of addiction. First E.M. Jellinek Memorial Lecture presented at 15th International Institute on the Prevention and Treatment of Alcoholism, Budapest, Hungry, June (available from Publications Division, Rutgers Center of Alcohol Studies, New Brunswick, NJ).

———. 1970. The great Jewish drink mystery. *British Journal of Addiction* 64:287–295.

———. 1975. Problems of epidemiology in alcohol problems. *Journal of Studies on Alcohol* 36:1442–1451.

———. 1981. Perspective on medicine and alcoholism. Paper delivered at National Council on Alcoholism–American Medical Society on Alcoholism Medical-Scientific Luncheon, New Orleans, April 13.

Kendell, R.E. 1979. Alcoholism: A medical or a political problem? *British Medical Journal* 1:367–371.

Kern, M. 1984. Arousal modification in preferential drug use. Paper presented at meeting of Western Psychological Association, Los Angeles, April.

Khantzian, E.J. 1975. Self selection and progression in drug dependence. *Psychiatry Digest* 36:19–22.

Khantzian, E.J.; Mack, J.E.; and Schatzberg, A.F. 1974. Heroin use as an attempt to cope: Clinical observations. *American Journal of Psychiatry* 131:160–164.

Khavari, K.A.; Peters, T.C.; and Baity, P.L. 1975. Voluntary morphine ingestion, morphine dependence, and recovery from withdrawal signs. *Pharmacology Biochemistry and Behavior* 3:1093–1096.

Kilpatrick, D.G.; Sutker, P.B.; and Smith, A.D. 1976. Deviant drug and alcohol use:

The role of anxiety, sensation seeking, and other personality variables. In *Emotions and anxiety,* eds. M. Zuckerman and C.D. Speilberger. Hillsdale, NJ: Erlbaum.

King, A. 1958. *Mine enemy grows older.* New York: Simon and Schuster.

King, R. 1972. *The drug hang-up.* New York: Norton.

Kissin, B.; Lowinson, J.H.; and Millman, R.B. 1978. *Recent developments in chemotherapy of narcotic addiction.* New York: New York Academy of Sciences.

Klaus, M.H., and Kennell, J.H. 1981. *Parent-infant bonding.* 2d ed. St. Louis: C.V. Mosby.

Klausner, S.Z.; Foulks, E.F.; and Moore, M.H. 1980. The Inupiat, economics and alcohol on the Alaskan North Slope. Center for Research on the Acts of Man, University of Pennsylvania, Philadelphia, PA.

Kline, N.S. 1981. *From sad to glad.* New York: Ballantine.

Knop, J.; Goodwin, D.W.; Teasdale, T.W.; Mikkelsen, U.; and Schulsinger, F. 1984. A Danish prospective study of young males at high risk for alcoholism. In *Longitudinal research in alcoholism,* eds. D.W. Goodwin, K.T. van Dusen, and S.A. Mednick. Boston: Kluwer-Nijhoff.

Knupfer, G. 1972. Ex-problem drinkers. In *Life history research in psychopathology,* eds. M.A. Roff, L.N. Robins, and M. Pollack. vol. 2. Minneapolis: University of Minnesota Press.

Kolata, G.B. 1981. Fetal alcohol advisory debated. *Science* 214:642–645.

Kolb, L. 1958. Factors that have influenced the management and treatment of drug addicts. In *Narcotic drug addiction problems,* ed. R.B. Livingston. Bethesda, MD: Public Health Service.

———. 1962. *Drug addiction: A medical problem.* Springfield, IL: Charles C Thomas.

Kosterlitz, H.W. 1979. Endogenous opioid peptides and the control of pain. *Psychological Medicine* 9:1–4.

Kostowski, W.; Czlonkowski, A.; Rewerski, W.; and Piechocki, T. 1977. Morphine action in grouped and isolated rats and mice. *Psychopharmacology* 53:191–193.

Kraft, D.P. 1982. Public drinking practices of college youths: Implications for prevention programs. In *Social drinking contexts,* eds. T.C. Harford and L.S. Gaines. Research Monograph 7. Rockville, MD: National Institute on Alcohol Abuse and Alcoholism.

Krasnegor, N.A., ed. 1979. *Cigarette smoking as a dependence process.* Research Monograph 23. Rockville, MD: National Institute on Drug Abuse.

Kron, R.E.; Kaplan, S.L.; Finnegan, L.P.; Litt, M.; and Phoenix, M.D. 1975. The assessment of behavior change in infants undergoing narcotic withdrawal. *Addictive Diseases* 2:257–275.

Krystal, H., and Raskin, H.A. 1970. *Drug dependence: Aspects of ego function.* Detroit: Wayne State University.

Kumar, R., and Stolerman, I.P. 1977. Experimental and clinical aspects of drug dependence. In *Handbook of psychopharmacology,* eds. L.L. Iverson, S.D. Iverson, and S.H. Snyder. vol. 7. New York: Plenum.

Lang, A.R. 1983. Addictive personality: A viable construct? In *Commonalities in substance abuse and habitual behavior,* eds. P.K. Levison, D.R. Gerstein, and

D.R. Maloff. Lexington, MA: Lexington.

Lang, A.R.; Goeckner, D.J.; Adesso, V.J.; and Marlatt, G.A. 1975. Effects of alcohol on aggression in male social drinkers. *Journal of Abnormal Psychology* 84:508–518.

Lang, A.R.; Searles, J.; Lauerman, R.; and Adesso, V. 1980. Expectancy, alcohol, and sex guilt as determinants of interest in and reaction to sexual stimuli. *Journal of Abnormal Psychology* 89: 644–653.

Langer, E.J. 1978. The illusion of incompetence. In *Choice and perceived control,* eds. L. Perlmuter and R. Monty. Hillsdale, NJ: Erlbaum.

Langer, E.J., and Benevento, A. 1978. Self-induced dependence. *Journal of Personality and Social Psychology* 36:886–893.

Lasagna, L. 1981. Heroin: A medical "me too." *New England Journal of Medicine* 304:1539–1540.

Lasagna, L.; Mosteller, F.; von Felsinger, J.M.; and Beecher, H.K. 1954. A study of the placebo response. *American Journal of Medicine* 16:770–779.

Lasagna, L.; von Felsinger, J.M.; and Beecher, H.K. 1955. Drug-induced mood changes in man. *Journal of the American Medical Association* 157:1006–1020. 1020.

Lazarus, R. 1966. *Psychological stress and the coping process.* New York: McGraw-Hill.

Lear, M.W. 1974. All the warnings, gone up in smoke. *New York Times Magazine* (March 10): 18–19, 86–91.

LeFlore, R., and Hawkins, J. 1978. Stealing was my speciality. *Sports Illustrated* (February 6): 62–74.

Lender, M.E., and Martin, J.K. 1982. *Drinking in America: A history.* New York: Free Press.

Lennard, H.L.; Epstein, L.J.; Bernstein, A.; and Ransom, D. 1971. *Mystification and drug misuse.* San Francisco: Jossey-Bass.

Lennard, H.L.; Epstein, L.J.; and Rosenthal, M.S. 1972. The methadone illusion. *Science* 176:881–884.

Leventhal, H. 1980. Toward a comprehensive theory of emotion. In *Advances in experimental social psychology,* ed. L. Berkowitz. vol. 13. New York: Academic.

Leventhal, H., and Cleary, P.D. 1980. The smoking problem: A review of the research and theory in behavioral risk modification. *Psychological Bulletin* 88:370–405.

Leventhal, H., and Nerenz, D. 1983. A model for stress research and some implications for the control of stress disorders. In *Stress prevention and management,* eds. D. Meichenbaum and M. Jaremko. New York: Plenum.

Levine, H.G. 1978. The discovery of addiction: Changing conceptions of habitual drunkenness in America. *Journal of Studies on Alcohol* 39:143–174.

Lewis, A. 1969. Introduction: Definitions and perspectives. In *Scientific basis of drug dependence,* ed. H. Steinberg. London: Churchill.

Lewis, C.E.; Cloninger, C.R.; and Pais, J. 1983. Alcoholism, antisocial personality, and drug use in a criminal population. *Alcohol and Alcoholism* 18:53–60.

Lewontin, R.C.; Rose, S.; and Kamin, L.J. 1984. *Not in our genes.* New York: Pantheon.

Lidz, C.W., and Walker, A.L. 1980. *Heroin, deviance and morality.* Beverley Hills,

CA: Sage.

Lieberman, M.; Yalom, I.; and Miles, M. 1973. *Encounter groups: First facts.* New York: Basic Books.

Liebowitz, M.R. 1983. *The chemistry of love.* Boston: Little-Brown.

Liebowitz, M.R., and Klein, D.F. 1979. Hysteroid dysphoria. *Psychiatric Clinics of North America* 2:555–575.

Light, A.B., and Torrance, E.G. 1929. Opiate addiction VI: The effects of abrupt withdrawal followed by readministration of morphine in human addicts, with special reference to the composition of the blood, the circulation and the metabolism. *Archives of Internal Medicine* 44:1–16.

Lindblad, R.A. 1977. Self-concept of white, middle socioeconomic status addicts: A controlled study. *International Journal of the Addictions* 12:137–151.

Lindesmith, A.R. 1968. *Addiction and opiates.* Chicago: Aldine.

Lipscomb, T.R., and Nathan, P.E. 1980. Blood alcohol level discrimination: The effects of family history of alcoholism, drinking pattern, and tolerance. *Archives of General Psychiatry* 37:571–576.

Lolli, G.; Serianni, E.; Golder, G.M.; and Luzzatto-Fegiz, P. 1958. *Alcohol in Italian culture.* Glencoe, IL: Free Press.

Lore, R., and Flannelly, K. 1977. Rat societies. *Scientific American* (May): 106–116.

Lovibund, S.H., and Caddy, G. 1970. Discriminative aversive control in the moderation of alcoholics' drinking behavior. *Behavior Therapy* 1:437–444.

Lukoff, I.F., and Brook, J.S. 1974. A sociocultural exploration of reported heroin use. In *Sociological aspects of drug dependence,* ed. C. Winick. Cleveland: CRC Press.

MacAndrew, C. 1965. The differentiation of male alcoholic outpatients from non-alcoholic psychiatric outpatients. *Quarterly Journal of Studies on Alcohol* 26:238–246.

———. 1981. What the MAC scale tells us about alcoholic men: An interpretative review. *Journal of Studies on Alcohol* 42:604–625.

MacAndrew, C., and Edgerton, B. 1969. *Drunken comportment: A social explanation.* Chicago: Aldine.

Maddux, J.F., and Desmond, D.P. 1981. *Careers of opioid users.* New York: Praeger.

Magnusson, D., ed. 1981. *Toward a psychology of situations.* Hillsdale, NJ: Erlbaum.

Mangin, W. 1957. Drinking among the Andean Indians. *Quarterly Journal of Studies on Alcohol.* 18:55–66.

Mann, M. 1970. *Marty Mann answers your questions about drinking and alcoholism.* New York: Holt, Rinehart & Winston.

Many addicts have family alcoholism history. 1983. *Journal,* Addiction Research Foundation (November):3.

Markoff, R.; Ryan, P.; and Young, T. 1982. Endorphins and mood changes in long distance running. *Medicine and Science in Sports and Exercise* 14:11–15.

Marlatt, G.A. 1976. Alcohol, stress, and cognitive control. In *Stress and anxiety,* eds. I.G. Sarason and C.D. Speilberger. vol. 3. Washington, DC: Hemisphere.

———. 1978. Craving for alcohol, loss of control, and relapse: A cognitive-behavioral analysis. In *Alcoholism: New directions in behavioral research and treatment,* eds. P.E. Nathan, G.A. Marlatt, and T. Loberg. New York: Plenum.

———. 1981. Perception of "control" and its relation to behavior change. *Behav-*

ioral Psychotherapy 9:190–193.

———. 1982. Relapse prevention: A self-control program for the treatment of addictive behaviors. In *Adherence, compliance and generalization in behavioral medicine,* ed. R.B. Stuart. New York: Brunner/Mazel.

———. 1983. The controlled-drinking controversy: A commentary. *American Psychologist* 38:1097–1110.

———. 1984. President's message. *Bulletin of the Society of Psychologists in Addictive Behaviors* 3:2.

Marlatt, G.A.; Demming, B., and Reid, J.B. 1973. Loss of control drinking in alcoholics: An experimental analogue. *Journal of Abnormal Psychology* 81:223–241.

Marlatt, G.A., and Gordon, J.R. 1980. Determinants of relapse: Implications for the maintenance of behavior change. In *Behavioral medicine: Changing health lifestyles,* eds. P.O. Davidson and S.M. Davidson. New York: Brunner/Mazel.

Marlatt, G.A., and Rohsenow, D.J. 1980. Cognitive processes in alcohol use: Expectancy and the balanced placebo design. In *Advances in substance abuse,* ed. N.K. Mello. vol. 1. Greenwich, CT: JAI Press.

Masserman, J.H. 1976. Alcoholism: Disease or dis-ease? *International Journal of Mental Health* 5:3–15.

Mayer, W. 1983. Alcohol abuse and alcoholism: The psychologist's role in prevention, research, and treatment. *American Psychologist* 38:1116–1121.

McAuliffe, W.E., and Gordon, R.A. 1974. A test of Lindesmith's theory of addiction: The frequency of euphoria among long-term addicts. *American Journal of Sociology* 79:795–840.

———. 1980. Reinforcement and the combination of effects: Summary of a theory of opiate addiction. In *Theories on drug abuse,* eds. D.J. Lettieri, M. Sayers, and H.W. Pearson. Research Monograph 30. Rockville, MD: National Institute on Drug Abuse.

McClelland, D.C.; Davis, W.N.; Kalin, R.; and Wanner, E. 1972. *The drinking man.* New York: Free Press.

McGuire, M.T.; Stein, S.; and Mendelson, J.H. 1966. Comparative psychosocial studies of alcoholic and nonalcoholic subjects undergoing experimentally induced ethanol intoxication. *Psychosomatic Medicine* 28:13–25.

McIntosh, T.K.; Vallano, M.L.; and Barfield, R.J. 1980. Effects of morphine, β-endorphin and naloxone on catecholamine levels and sexual behavior in the male rat. *Pharmacology Biochemistry and Behavior* 13:435–441.

McMurray, R.G.; Sheps, D.S.; and Guinan, D.M. 1984. Effects of naloxone on maximal stress testing in females. *Journal of Applied Physiology* 56:436–440.

Mello, N.K., and Mendelson, J.H. 1971. A quantitative analysis of drinking patterns in alcoholics. *Archives of General Psychiatry* 25:527–539.

———. 1972. Drinking patterns during work-contingent and non-contingent alcohol acquisition. *Psychosomatic Medicine* 34:1116–1121.

———. 1977. Clinical aspects of alcohol dependence. In *Handbook of psychopharmacology.* vol. 45/I. Berlin: Springer-Verlag.

———. 1978. Alcohol and human behavior. In *Handbook of psychopharmacology,* eds. L.L. Iverson, S.D. Iverson, and S.H. Snyder. vol. 12. New York: Plenum.

Mendelson, J.H., and Mello, N.K. 1979a. Biological concomitants of alcoholism. *New England Journal of Medicine* 301:912–921.

———. 1979b. One unanswered question about alcoholism. *British Journal of Ad-*

diction 74:11–14.

Merry, J. 1966. The "loss of control" myth. *Lancet* 4:1257–1258.

Mexico making progress in war on cultivation of opium poppies. 1980. *New York Times* (February 24): 12.

Milkman, H., and Sunderwirth, S. 1983. The chemistry of craving. *Psychology Today* (October): 36–44.

Miller, W.R. 1976. Alcoholism scales and objective assessment methods: A review. *Psychological Bulletin* 83:649–674.

———. 1983a. Controlled drinking: A history and critical review. *Journal of Studies on Alcohol* 44:68–83.

———. 1983b. Haunted by the Zeitgeists: Reflections on contrasting treatment goals and concepts of alcoholism in Europe and America. Paper presented at Conference on Alcohol and Culture, Farmington, CT, May.

———. 1983c. Motivational interviewing with problem drinkers. *Behavioral Psychotherapy* 11:147–172.

Miller, W.R., and Hester, R.K. 1980. Treating the problem drinker: Modern approaches. In *The addictive behaviors: Treatment of alcoholism, drug abuse, smoking, and obesity*, ed. W.R. Miller. Oxford: Pergamon.

Miller, W.R., and Muñoz, R.F. 1976. *How to control your drinking*. Englewood Cliffs, NJ: Prentice-Hall.

———. 1982. *How to control your drinking*. rev. ed. Albuquerque, NM: University of New Mexico Press.

Miller, W.R., and Saucedo, C.F. 1983. Neuropsychological impairment and brain damage in problem drinkers: A critical review. In *Behavioral effects of neurological disorders*, eds. C.J. Golden et al. New York: Grune & Stratton.

Mischel, W. 1974. Process in delay of gratification. In *Advances in experimental social psychology*, ed. L. Berkowitz. vol. 7. New York: Academic.

———. 1979. On the interface of cognition and personality: Beyond the person-situation debate. *American Psychologist* 34:740–754.

———. 1984. Convergences and challenges in the search for consistency. *American Psychologist* 39:351–364.

Mohatt, G. 1972. The sacred water: The quest for personal power through drinking among the Teton Sioux. In *The drinking man*, eds. D. McClelland, W.N. Davis, R. Kalin, and E. Wanner. New York: Free Press.

Moos, R.H., and Finney, J.W. 1982. New directions in program evaluation: Implications for expanding the role of alcoholism researchers. Paper presented at Conference on New Directions in Alcohol Abuse Treatment Research, Newport, Rhode Island, October.

Morgan, W.P. 1979. Negative addiction in runners. *Physician and Sportsmedicine* 7(2):55–70.

Mumford, L., and Kumar, R. 1979. Sexual behavior of morphine-dependent and abstinent male rats. *Psychopharmacology* 65:179–185.

Murray, H.A. 1981. *Endeavors in psychology*, ed. E.S. Shneidman. New York: Harper & Row.

Musto, D.F. 1973. *The American disease: Origins of narcotic control*. New Haven: Yale University Press.

Nathan, P.E. 1980. Ideal mental health services for alcoholics and problem drinkers: An exercise in pragmatics. In *Behavioral medicine: Changing health lifestyles*, eds. P.O. Davidson and S.M. Davidson. New York: Brunner/Mazel.

Nathan, P.E., and O'Brien, J.S. 1971. An experimental analysis of the behavior of alcoholics and nonalcoholics during prolonged experimental drinking: A necessary precursor of behavior therapy? *Behavior Therapy* 2:455–476.

Nathan, P.E.; Titler, N.A.; Lowenstein, L.M.; Solomon, P.; and Rossi, A.M. 1970. Behavioral analysis of chronic alcoholism. *Archives of General Psychiatry* 22:419–430.

National Foundation for Prevention of Chemical Dependency Disease. 1984. Mission statement, March 1, Omaha.

Nesbitt, P.D. 1972. Chronic smoking and emotionality. *Journal of Applied Social Psychology* 2:187–196.

New insights into alcoholism. 1983. *Time* (April 25):64, 69.

Newman, J.M. 1970. Peer pressure hypothesis for adolescent cigarette smoking. *School Health Review* 1:15–18.

Nichols, J.R.; Headlee, C.P.; Coppock, H.W. 1956. Drug addiction I: Addiction by escape training. *Journal of the American Pharmacological Association* 45:788–791.

Nisbett, R.E. 1968. Taste, deprivation, and weight determinants of eating behavior. *Journal of Personality and Social Psychology* 10:107–116.

———. 1972. Hunger, obesity, and the ventromedial hypothalamus. *Psychological Review* 79:433–453.

Nurco, D.N.; Cisin, I.H.; and Balter, M.B. 1981. Addict careers III: Trends across time. *International Journal of the Addictions* 16:1353–1372.

Oates, W. 1971. *Confessions of a workaholic.* New York: World.

O'Brien, C.P. 1975. Experimental analysis of conditioning factors in human narcotic addiction. *Pharmacological Reviews* 27:533–543.

O'Brien, C.P.; Nace, E.P.; Mintz, J.; Meyers, A.L.; and Ream, N. 1980. Follow-up of Vietnam veterans I: Relapse to drug use after Vietnam service. *Drug and Alcohol Dependence* 5:333–340.

O'Brien, C.P.; Testa, T.; O'Brien, T.J.; Brady, J.P.; and Wells, B. 1977. Conditioned narcotic withdrawal in humans. *Science* 195:1000–1002.

O'Donnell, J.A. 1969. *Narcotic addicts in Kentucky.* Chevy Chase, MD: National Institute of Mental Health.

O'Donnell, J.A.; Voss, H.; Clayton R.; Slatin, G.; and Room, R. 1976. *Young men and drugs: A nationwide survey.* Research Monograph 5. Rockville, MD: National Institute on Drug Abuse.

Öjesjö, L. 1984. Risks for alcoholism by age and class among males. In *Longitudinal research in alcoholism,* eds. D.W. Goodwin, K.T. van Dusen, and S.A. Mednick. Boston: Kluwer-Nijhoff.

Oki, G. 1974. Alcohol use by Skid Row alcoholics I: Drinking at Bon Accord. Substudy 612. Toronto: Addiction Research Foundation.

Orford, J., and Edwards, G. 1977. *Alcoholism.* New York: Oxford University Press.

Ostrea, E.M.; Chavez, C.J.; and Strauss, M.E. 1975. A study of factors that influence the severity of neonatal narcotic withdrawal. *Addictive Diseases* 2:187–199.

Ouellette, E.M.; Rosett, H.L.; Rosman, N.P.; and Weiner, L. 1977. Adverse effects on offspring of maternal alcohol abuse during pregnancy. *New England Journal of Medicine* 297:528–530.

Panksepp, J. 1980. Brief isolation, pain responsivity, and morphine analgesia in young rats. *Psychopharmacology* 72:111–112.

Panksepp, J.; Najam, N.; and Soares, F. 1979. Morphine reduces social cohesion in rats. *Pharmacology Biochemistry and Behavior* 11:131–134.

Paredes, A.; Hood, W.R.; Seymour, H.; and Gollob, M. 1973. Loss of control in alcoholism. *Quarterly Journal of Studies on Alcoholism* 34:1141–1161.

Pargman, D., and Baker, M.C. 1980. Running high: Enkephalin indicated. *Journal of Drug Issues* 10:341–349.

Patai, R. 1977. *The Jewish mind.* New York: Scribners.

Pattison, E.M.; Brissenden, A.; and Wohl, T. 1967. Assessing specific effects of inpatient group psychotherapy. *International Journal of Group Psychotherapy* 17:283–297.

Pattison, E.M.; Sobell, M.B.; and Sobell, L.C. 1977. *Emerging concepts of alcohol dependence.* New York: Springer.

Peele, S. 1977. Redefining addiction I: Making addiction a scientifically and socially useful concept. *International Journal of Health Services* 7:103–124.

———. 1978. Addiction: The analgesic experience. *Human Nature* (September): 61–67.

———. 1979. Redefining addiction II: The meaning of addiction in our lives. *Journal of Psychedelic Drugs* 11:289–297.

———. 1980. Addiction to an experience: A social-psychological-pharmacological theory of addiction. In *Theories on drug abuse,* eds. D.J. Lettieri, M. Sayers, and H.W. Pearson. Research Monograph 30. Rockville, MD: National Institute on Drug Abuse.

———. 1981a. *How much is too much: Healthy habits or destructive addictions.* Englewood Cliffs, NJ: Prentice-Hall.

———. 1981b. Reductionism in the psychology of the eighties: Can biochemistry eliminate addiction, mental illness, and pain? *American Psychologist* 36:807–818.

———. 1982a. Love, sex, drugs and other magical solutions to life. *Journal of Psychoactive Drugs* 14:125–131.

———. 1982b. What caused John Belushi's death? *U.S. Journal of Drug and Alcohol Dependence* (April): 7.

———. 1982c. When governments get tough on drugs. *U.S. Journal of Drug and Alcohol Dependence* (July): 7.

———. 1983a. Behavior therapy, the hardest way: Natural remission in alcoholism and controlled drinking. Discussant's remarks on the Panel of Controlled Drinking, 4th World Congress on Behavior Therapy, Washington, DC, December.

———. 1983b. *Don't panic: A parent's guide to understanding and preventing alcohol and drug abuse.* Minneapolis: CompCare.

———. 1983c. Is alcoholism different from other substance abuse? *American Psychologist* 38:963–964.

———. 1983d. Out of the habit trap. *American Health* (September/October): 42–47.

———. 1983e. *The science of experience: A direction for psychology.* Lexington, MA: Lexington.

———. 1983f. Through a glass darkly: Can some alcoholics learn to drink in moderation? *Psychology Today* (April): 38–42.

———. 1984a. The internal–external model and beyond: Reductionist approaches to smoking and obesity in the context of social psychological theory. Unpublished manuscript, Morristown, NJ.

———. 1984b. The media and the latest glamor drug. In *The human side of addiction: Unpopular ideas on the drug and alcohol scene*, S. Peele. Morristown, NJ: Author.

———. 1984c. *Sixty Minutes'* report on the Sobell–Pendery controlled drinking dispute. In *The human side of addiction: Unpopular ideas on the drug and alcohol scene*, S. Peele. Morristown, NJ: Author.

Peele, S., with Brodsky, A. 1975. *Love and addiction*. New York: Taplinger, 1975.ʹ

Pelton, L.H., ed. 1981. *The social context of child abuse and neglect*. New York: Human Sciences Press.

Pendery, M.L.; Maltzman, I.M.; and West, L.J. 1982. Controlled drinking by alcoholics? New findings and a reevaluation of a major affirmative study. *Science* 217:169–174.

People. 1984. *New York Times* (June 28): B9.

Platt, J., and Labate, C. 1976. *Heroin addiction: Theory, research, and treatment*. New York: Wiley.

Polich, J.M.; Armor, D.J.; and Braiker, H.B. 1981. *The course of alcoholism: Four years after treatment*. New York: Wiley.

Polivy, J., and Herman, C.P. 1983. *Breaking the diet habit: The natural weight alternative*. New York: Basic Books.

Pollock, V.E.; Volavka, J.; Mednick, S.A.; Goodwin, D.W.; Knop, J.; and Schulsinger, F. 1984. A prospective study of alcoholism: Electroencephalographic findings. In *Longitudinal research in alcoholism*, eds. D.W. Goodwin, K.T. van Dusen, and S.A. Mednick. Boston: Kluwer-Nijhoff.

Porjesz, B., and Begleiter, H. 1982. Evoked brain potential deficits in alcoholism and aging. *Alcoholism: Clinical and Experimental Research* 6:53–63.

Prep schools in a struggle to curb spread of cocaine. 1984. *New York Times* (May 27): 1; 50.

Prescott, J.W. 1980. Somatosensory affectional deprivation (SAD) theory of drug and alcohol use. In *Theories on drug abuse*, eds. D.J. Lettieri, M. Sayers, and H.W. Pearson. Research Monograph 30. Rockville, MD: National Institute on Drug Abuse.

Prial, F.J. 1984. Criticism of the alcohol industry has grown lately. *New York Times* (February 22): C13.

Primm, B.J. 1977. Pseudoheroinism. In *Drug abuse: Clinical and basic aspects*, eds. S. N. Pradhan and S.N. Dutta. St. Louis, MO: C.V. Mosby.

Public Health Service. 1979. Change in cigarette smoking and current smoking practices among adults: United States, 1978. *Advance Data* 52:1–16.

Rado, S. 1933. The psychoanalysis of pharmacothymia (drug addiction). *Psychoanalytic Quarterly* 2:1–23.

Restak, R. 1979. *The brain*. Garden City, NY: Doubleday.

Riggs, C.E. 1981. Endorphins, neurotransmitters, and/or neuromodulators and exercise. In *Psychology of running*, ed. M.H. Sacks and M.L. Sachs. Champaign, IL: Human Kinetics.

Robbins, J.M., and Joseph. P. 1982. Behavioral components of exercise addiction. Unpublished manuscript, Jewish General Hospital, Montreal.

Robertson, I.H., and Heather, N. 1982. A survey of controlled drinking treatment in Britain. *British Journal on Alcohol and Alcoholism* 17:102–105.

Robins, L.N. 1978. The interaction of setting and predisposition in explaining novel behavior: Drug initiations before, in, and after Vietnam. In *Longitudinal research on drug use*, ed. D.B. Kandel. Washington, DC: Hemisphere.

———. 1980. The natural history of drug abuse. In *Theories on drug abuse: Selected contemporary perspectives*, eds. D.J. Lettieri, M. Sayers, and H.W. Pearson. Research Monograph 30. Rockville, MD: National Institute on Drug Abuse.

Robins, L.N.; Davis, D.H.; and Goodwin, D.W. 1974. Drug use by U.S. army enlisted men in Vietnam: A follow-up on their return home. *American Journal of Epidemiology* 99:235–249.

Robins, L.N.; Davis, D.H.; and Wish, E. 1977. Detecting predictors of rare events: Demographic, family, and personal deviance as predictors of stages in the progression toward narcotic addiction. In *The origins and course of psychopathology*, eds. J.S. Straug, B. Haroutun, and M. Roff. New York: Plenum.

Robins, L.N.; Helzer, J.E.; and Davis, D.H. 1975. Narcotic use in Southeast Asia and afterward. *Archives of General Psychiatry* 32:955–961.

Robins, L.N.; Helzer, J.E.; Hesselbrock, M.; and Wish, E. 1980. Vietnam veterans three years after Vietnam: How our study changed our view of heroin. In *The yearbook of substance use and abuse*, eds. L. Brill and C. Winick. vol. 2. New York: Human Sciences Press.

Robins, L.N., and Murphy, G.E. 1967. Drug use in a normal population of young Negro men. *American Journal of Public Health* 57:1580–1596.

Rodin, J. 1981. Current status of the internal-external hypothesis for obesity: What went wrong? *American Psychologist* 36:361–372.

Rodin, J., and Langer, E.J. 1977. Long-term effects of a control-relevant intervention with the institutionalized aged. *Journal of Personality and Social Psychology* 35:897–902.

Rohsenow, D.J. 1983. Alcoholics' perceptions of control. In *Identifying and measuring alcoholic personality characteristics*, ed. W.M. Cox. San Francisco: Jossey-Bass.

Roizen, R. 1978. Comment on the Rand Report. In *Alcoholism and treatment*, eds. D.J. Armor, J.M. Polich, and H.B. Stambul. New York: Wiley.

Roizen, R.; Cahalan, D.; and Shanks, P. 1978. "Spontaneous remission" among untreated problem drinkers. In *Longitudinal research on drug use*, ed. D.B. Kandel, Washington, DC: Hemisphere.

Rollnick, S., and Heather, N. 1982. The application of Bandura's self-efficacy theory to abstinence-oriented alcoholism treatment. *Addictive Behaviors* 7:243–250.

Room, R. 1976. Ambivalence as a sociological explanation: The case of cultural explanations of alcohol problems. *American Sociological Review* 41:1047–1065.

———. 1977. Measurement and distribution of drinking patterns and problems in general populations. In *Alcohol related disabilities*, eds. G. Edwards et al. WHO Offset Publication 32. Geneva: World Health Organization.

———. 1980. Treatment seeking populations and larger realities. In *Alcoholism treatment in transition*, eds. G. Edwards and M. Grant. London: Croom Helm.

———. 1983. Sociological aspects of the disease concept of alcoholism. In *Research advances in alcohol and drug problems,* eds. R.G. Smart, F.B. Glaser, Y. Israel, H. Kalant, R.E. Popham, and W. Schmidt. vol. 7. New York: Plenum.

———. 1984. Alcohol control and public health. *Annual Review of Public Health* 5:293–317.

Rosensweig, M.R. 1971. Effects of environment on development of brain and of behavior. In *The biopsychology of development,* eds. E. Tobach, L. Aronson, and E. Shaw. New York: Academic.

Roston, R.A. 1961. Some personality characteristics of compulsive gamblers. Unpublished doctoral dissertation, University of California, Los Angeles.

Rothman, D.J. 1971. *The discovery of the asylum.* Boston: Little, Brown.

Rubington, E. 1967. Drug addiction as a deviant career. *International Journal of the Addictions* 2:3–20.

Russell, J.A., and Bond, C.R. 1980. Individual differences in beliefs concerning emotions conducive to alcohol use. *Journal of Studies on Alcohol* 41:753–759.

Sachs, M.L., and Pargman, D. 1984. Running addiction. In *Running as therapy,* eds. M.L. Sachs and G.W. Buffone. Lincoln: University of Nebraska Press.

Salzberg, P.M., and Klingberg, C.L. 1983. The effectiveness of deferred prosecution for driving while intoxicated. *Journal of Studies on Alcohol* 44:299–306.

Sanchez-Craig, M. 1980. Random assignment to abstinence or controlled drinking in a cognitive-behavioral program: Short term effects on drinking behavior. *Addictive Behaviors* 5:35–39.

———. 1983. The role of the drinker in determining how much is too much: In search of nonobjective indices. Paper presented at International Alcohol Research Seminar, National Institute on Alcohol Abuse and Alcoholism, Washington, DC, October.

Sanchez-Craig, M.; Annis, H.M.; Bornet, A.R.; and MacDonald, K.R. 1984. Random assignment to abstinence and controlled drinking: Evaluation of a cognitive-behavioral program for problem drinkers. *Journal of Consulting and Clinical Psychology* 52:390–403.

Sarason, I.G., and Sarason, B.R. 1981. The importance of cognition and moderator variables in stress. In *Toward a psychology of situations,* ed. D. Magnusson. Hillsdale, NJ: Erlbaum.

Saxe, L.; Dougherty, D.; and Esty, J. 1983. *The effectiveness and costs of alcoholism treatment.* Washington, DC: Congressional Office of Technology Assessment.

Schachter, S. 1968. Obesity and eating. *Science* 161:751–756.

———. 1971. Some extraordinary facts about obese humans and rats. *American Psychologist* 26:129–144.

———. 1977. Nicotine regulation in heavy and light smokers. *Journal of Experimental Psychology: General* 106:13–19.

———. 1978. Pharmacological and psychological determinants of smoking. *Annals of Internal Medicine* 88:104–114.

———. 1980. Non-psychological explanations of behavior. In *Retrospections on social psychology,* ed. L. Festinger. New York: Oxford University Press.

———. 1982. Recidivism and self-cure of smoking and obesity. *American Psychologist* 37:436–444.

Schachter, S., and Rodin, J. 1974. *Obese humans and rats.* Washington, DC: Erlbaum.

Schachter, S., and Singer, J.E. 1962. Cognitive, social, and physiological determinants of emotional state. *Psychological Review* 69:379–399.

Schaefer, H.H. 1971. A cultural delusion of alcoholics. *Psychological Reports* 29:587–589.

———. 1972. Twelve-month follow-up of behaviorally trained ex–alcoholic social drinkers. *Behavior Therapy* 3:286–289.

Schein, E.H. 1961. *Coercive persuasion.* New York: Norton.

Schlichter suspension lifted by Rozelle. 1984. *New York Times* (June 23): 31.

Schuckit, M.A. 1984. Prospective markers for alcoholism. In *Longitudinal research in alcoholism,* eds. D.W. Goodwin, K.T. van Dusen, and S.A. Mednick. Boston: Kluwer-Nijhoff.

Schur, E.M. 1962. *Narcotic addiction in Britain and America.* Bloomington: Indiana University Press.

Seevers, M.H. 1936. Opiate addiction in the monkey I: Methods of study. *Journal of Pharmacology and Experimental Therapeutics* 56:147–156.

———. 1963. Laboratory approach to the problem of addiction. In *Narcotic drug addiction problems,* ed. R.B. Livingston. Public Health Service Publication 1050. Bethesda, MD: National Institute of Mental Health.

Segal, B. 1977. Reasons for marijuana use and personality: A canonical analysis. *Journal of Alcohol and Drug Education* 22:64–67.

Seligman, M.E.P. 1975. *Helplessness.* San Francisco: Freeman.

Selzer, M.L.; Vinokur, A.; and Wilson, T.D. 1977. A psychosocial comparison of drunken drivers and alcoholics. *Journal of Studies on Alcohol* 38:1294–1312.

Shaffer, H., and Burglass, M.E., eds. 1981. *Classic contributions in the addictions.* New York: Brunner/Mazel.

Shaw, S. 1979. A critique of the concept of the alcohol dependence syndrome. *British Journal of Addiction* 74:339–348.

Sheehan, D.V. 1984. *The anxiety disease and how to overcome it.* New York: Scribner.

Siegel, R.K. 1979. Natural animal addictions: An ethological perspective. In *Psychopathology in animals,* ed. J.D. Keehn. New York: Academic.

Siegel, R.K., and Jarvik, M.E. 1980. DMT self-administration by monkeys in isolation. *Bulletin of the Psychonomic Society* 16:117–120.

Siegel, S. 1975. Evidence from rats that morphine tolerance is a learned response. *Journal of Comparative and Physiological Psychology* 89:498–506.

———. 1979. The role of conditioning in drug tolerance and addiction. In *Psychopathology in animals: Research and treatment implications,* ed. J.D. Keehn. New York: Academic.

———. 1983. Classical conditioning, drug tolerance, and drug dependence. In *Research advances in alcohol and drug problems,* eds. R.G. Smart, F.B. Glasser, Y. Israel, H. Kalant, R.E. Popham, and W. Schmidt. vol. 7. New York: Plenum.

Skinner, H.A.; Glaser, F.B.; and Annis, H.M. 1982. Crossing the threshold: Factors in self-identification as an alcoholic. *British Journal of Addiction* 77:51–64.

Skinner, H.A.; Holt, S.; Allen, B.A.; and Haakonson, N.H. 1980. Correlation between medical and behavioral data in the assessment of alcoholism. *Alcoholism: Clinical and Experimental Research* 4:371–377.

Slater, P. 1980. *Wealth addiction.* New York: Dutton.

Slochower, J.A. 1983. *Excessive eating: The role of emotions and environment.* New York: Human Sciences Press.

Smith, D. 1981. The benzodiazepines and alcohol. Paper presented at Third World Congress of Biological Psychiatry, Stockholm, July.

Smith, D.E., ed. 1983. The benzodiazepines: Two decades of research and clinical experience. *Journal of Psychoactive Drugs* 15(1–2):entire issue.

Smith, D.E., and Wesson, D.R. 1983. Benzodiazepine dependency syndromes. *Journal of Psychoactive Drugs* 15:85–95.

Smith, G.M., and Beecher, H.K. 1962. Subjective effects of heroin and morphine in normal subjects. *Journal of Pharmacology and Experimental Therapeutics* 136:47–52.

Snyder, S.H. 1977. Opiate receptors and internal opiates. *Scientific American* (March): 44–56.

Sobell, M.B., and Sobell, L.C. 1973. Alcoholics treated by individualized behavior therapy: One year treatment outcomes. *Behavior Research and Therapy* 11:599–618.

———. 1976. Second year treatment outcome of alcoholics treated by individualized behavior therapy: Results. *Behavior Research and Therapy* 14:195–215.

———. 1982. Controlled drinking: A concept coming of age. In *Self-control and self-modification of emotional behavior*, eds. K.R. Blanstein and J. Polivy. New York: Plenum.

———. 1984. The aftermath of heresy: A response to Pendery et al.'s (1982) critique of "Individualized Behavior Therapy for Alcoholics." *Behavior Research and Therapy* 22:413–447.

Solomon, F.; White, C.C.; Parron, D.L.; and Mendelson, W.B. 1979. Sleeping pills, insomnia and medical practice. *New England Journal of Medicine* 300:803–808.

Solomon, R. 1977. The evolution of non-medical opiate use in Canada II: 1930–1970. *Drug Forum* 6:1–25.

Solomon, R.L. 1980. The opponent-process theory of acquired motivation: The costs of pleasure and the benefits of pain. *American Psychologist* 35:691–712.

Solomon, R.L., and Corbit, J.D. 1973. An opponent-process theory of motivation II: Cigarette addiction. *Journal of Abnormal Psychology* 81:158–171.

———. 1974. An opponent-process theory of motivation I: Temporal dynamics of affect. *Psychological Review* 81:119–145.

Sonnedecker, G. 1958. Emergence and concept of the addiction problem. In *Narcotic drug addiction problems*, ed. R.B. Livingston. Bethesda, MD: Public Health Service.

Spotts, J.V., and Shontz, F.C. 1982. Ego development, dragon fights, and chronic drug abusers. *International Journal of the Addictions* 17:945–976.

———. 1983. Psychopathology and chronic drug use: A methodological paradigm. *International Journal of the Addictions* 18:633–680.

Stafford, R.A. 1980. Alcoholics' perception of the internal–external locus of their drinking problem. *Journal of Studies on Alcohol* 41:300–309.

Steiner, C. 1971. *Games alcoholics play.* New York: Grove.

Stewart, O. 1964. Questions regarding American Indian criminality. *Human Organization* 23:61–66.

Stockwell, T.; Hodgson, R.; and Rankin, H. 1982. Tension reduction and the effects of prolonged alcohol consumption. *British Journal of Addiction* 77:65–73.

Stone, N.; Fromme, M.; and Kagan, D. 1984. *Cocaine: Seduction and solution.* New York: Potter.

Stunkard, A.J. 1958. The results of treatment for obesity. *New York State Journal of Medicine* 58:79–87.

———. 1967. Obesity. In *Comprehensive textbook of psychiatry*, eds. A.M. Freedman and W.I. Kaplan. Baltimore: Williams & Wilkins.

Stunkard, A.J., ed. 1980. *Obesity.* Philadelphia: Saunders.

Stunkard, A.J.; d'Aquili, E.; Fox, S.; and Filion, R.D.L. 1972. Influence of social class on obesity and thinness in children. *Journal of the American Medical Association* 221:579–584.

Surgeon General. 1982. *The health consequences of smoking: Cancer.* Rockville, MD: U.S. Department of Health and Human Services.

Synanon founder and two guards convicted in attack with a snake. 1980. *New York Times* (July 16): 1; 20.

Szasz, T.S. 1961. *The myth of mental illness.* New York: Hoeber–Harper.

———. 1974. *Ceremonial chemistry.* Garden City, NY: Anchor Press.

Tang, M.; Brown, C.; and Falk, J. 1982. Complete reversal of chronic ethanol polydipsia by schedule withdrawal. *Pharmacology Biochemistry and Behavior* 16:155–158.

Tarter, R.E.; Goldstein, G.; Alterman, A.; Petrarulo, E.W.; and Elmore, S. 1983. Alcoholic seizures: Intellectual and neuropsychological sequelae. *Journal of Nervous and Mental Disease* 171:123–125.

Teasdale, J.D. 1972. The perceived effect of heroin on the interpersonal behavior of heroin-dependent patients, and a comparison with stimulant dependent patients. *International Journal of the Addictions* 7:533–548.

———. 1973. Conditioned abstinence in narcotic addicts. *International Journal of the Addictions* 8:273–292.

Tennov, D. 1979. *Love and limerence.* New York: Stein and Day.

Tobacco use as an addiction. 1982. Special report on symposium sponsored by Merrell Dow Pharmaceuticals, New York City, March 12. *U.S. Journal of Drug and Alcohol Dependence.*

Tokar, J.T.; Brunse, A.J.; Stefflre, V.J.; and Napior, D.A. 1973. Emotional states and behavioral patterns in alcoholics and non-alcoholics. *Quarterly Journal of Studies on Alcohol* 34:133–143.

Trebach, A.S. 1982. *The heroin solution.* New Haven, CT: Yale University Press.

Trice, H.M., and Roman, P.M. 1970. Delabeling, relabeling, and Alcoholics Anonymous. *Social Problems* 17:538–546.

Tuchfeld, B.S. 1981. Spontaneous remission in alcoholics: Empirical observations and theoretical implications. *Journal of Studies on Alcohol* 42:626–641.

Tuchfeld, B.S.; Lipton, W.L.; and Lile, E.A. 1983. Social involvement and the resolution of alcoholism. *Journal of Drug Issues* 13–323–332.

U.S. is seen as losing war on cocaine smuggling as planes get through. 1984. *New York Times* (May 18): 12.

U.S. social tolerance of drugs found on rise. 1983. *New York Times.* (March 21): 1; B5.

Vaillant, G.E. 1966. A 12-year follow-up of New York addicts IV: Some characteristics and determinants of abstinence. *American Journal of Psychiatry* 123:573–584.

———. 1977. *Adaptation to life.* Boston: Little, Brown.

———. 1983. *The natural history of alcoholism.* Cambridge, MA: Harvard University Press.

Vaillant, G.E., and Milofsky, E.S. 1982. The etiology of alcoholism: A prospective viewpoint. *American Psychologist* 37:494–503.

Van Dyke, C., and Byck, R. 1982. Cocaine. *Scientific American* (March): 128–141.

Vingilis, E. Drinking drivers and alcoholics: Are they from the same population? In *Research advances in alcohol and drug problems,* eds. R.G. Smart, F.B. Glaser, Y. Israel, H. Kalant, R.E. Popham, and W. Schmidt. vol. 7. New York: Plenum.

Vogler, R.E., and Bartz, W.R. 1982. *The better way to drink.* New York: Simon & Schuster.

Vogler, R.E.; Compton, J.V.; and Weissbach, J.A. 1975. Integrated behavior change techniques for alcoholism. *Journal of Consulting and Clinical Psychology* 43:233–243.

Waldorf, D. 1973. *Careers in dope.* Englewood Cliffs, NJ: Prentice-Hall.

———. 1983. Natural recovery from opiate addiction: Some social-psychological processes of untreated recovery. *Journal of Drug Issues* 13:237–280.

Waldorf, D., and Biernacki, P. 1981. The natural recovery from opiate addiction: Some preliminary findings. *Journal of Drug Issues* 11:61–74.

Wallerstein, R.S.; Chotlos, J.W.; Friend, M.B.; Hammersley, D.W.; Perlswig, E.A.; and Winship, G.M. 1957. *Hospital treatment of alcoholism: A comparative experimental study.* New York: Basic Books.

Washton, A. 1983. Diagnostic and treatment strategies. Paper presented at Cocaine Update Conference, New York, December.

Weeks, J.R., and Collins, R.J. 1968. Patterns of intravenous self-injection by morphine-addicted rats. In *The addictive states,* ed. A.H. Wikler. Baltimore: Williams and Wilkins.

———. 1979. Dose and physical dependence as factors in the self administration of morphine by rats. *Psychopharmacology* 65:171–177.

Weisner, C. 1983. The alcohol treatment system and social control: A study in institutional change. *Journal of Drug Issues* 13:117–133.

Weisner, C., and Room, R. 1984. *Financing and ideology in human services: The alcohol treatment system as a case study.* Berkeley, CA: Alcohol Research Group.

Weissman, M.M., and Klerman, G.L. 1977. Sex differences and the epidemiology of depression. *Archives of General Psychiatry* 34:98–111.

Weisz, D.J., and Thompson, R.F. 1983. Endogenous opioids: Brain-behavior relations. In *Commonalities in substance abuse and habitual behavior,* eds. P.K. Levison, D.R. Gerstein, and D.R. Maloff. Lexington, MA: Lexington.

Wiener, C. 1981. *The politics of alcoholism: Building an arena around a social problem.* New Brunswick, NJ: Transaction Books.

Wikler, A. 1973. Dynamics of drug dependence. *Archives of General Psychiatry* 28:611–616.

———. 1980. *Opioid dependence.* New York: Plenum.

Wikler, A., and Pescor, F.T. 1967. Classical conditioning of a morphine abstinence phenomenon, reinforcement of opioid-drinking behavior and "relapse" in morphine-addicted rats. *Psychopharmacologia* 10:255–284.

Wilder, T. 1938. Our town. In *Best plays of 1937–38.*, ed. B. Mantle. New York: Dodd Mead.

Wilkinson, R.W. 1970. *The prevention of drinking problems: Alcohol control and cultural influences.* New York: Oxford University Press.

Wille, R. 1983. Processes of recovery from heroin dependence: Relationship to treatment, social changes and drug use. *Journal of Drug Issues* 13:333–342.

Williams, T. 1971. Summary and implications of review of literature related to adolescent smoking. National Clearinghouse for Smoking and Health, U.S. Department of Health, Education and Welfare, Bethesda, MD.

Wilsnack, S.C. 1976. The impact of sex roles and women's alcohol use and abuse. In *Alcoholism problems in women and children*, eds. M. Greenblatt and M.A. Schuckit. New York: Grune & Stratton.

Wilson, G.T. 1981. The effect of alcohol on human sexual behavior. In *Advances in substance abuse*, ed. N.K. Mello. vol. 2. Greenwich, CT.

Wilson, G.T., and Lawson, D.M. 1978. Expectancies, alcohol, and sexual arousal in women. *Journal of Abnormal Psychology* 85:489–497.

Wingard, J.A.; Huba, J.V.; and Bentler, P.M. 1979. The relationship of personality structure to patterns of adolescent substance use. *Multivariate Behavioral Research* 14:131–143.

Winick, C. 1961. Physician narcotic addicts. *Social Problems* 9:174–186.

———. 1962. Maturing out of narcotic addiction. *Bulletin on Narcotics* 14:1–7.

Wishnie, H. 1977. *The impulsive personality.* New York: Plenum.

Woititz, J.G. 1983. *Adult children of alcoholics.* Hollywood, FL: Health Communications.

Woods, J.H. 1978. Behavioral pharmacology of drug self-administration. In *Psychopharmacology: A generation of progress*, eds. M.A. Lipton, A. DiMascio, and K.F. Killam. New York: Raven.

Woods, J.H., and Schuster, C.R. 1971. Opiates as reinforcing stimuli. *Stimulus properties of drugs*, eds. T. Thompson and R. Pickens. New York: Appleton-Century-Crofts.

World Health Organization Expert Committee on Mental Health. 1957. *Addiction producing drugs: 7th report of the WHO Expert Committee.* WHO Technical Report Series 116. Geneva: World Health Organization.

Wray, I., and Dickerson, M.G. 1981. Cessation of high frequency gambling and "withdrawal" symptoms. *British Journal of Addiction* 76:401–405.

Wright, J.T., et al. 1983. Alcohol consumption, pregnancy, and low birth-weight. *Lancet* 8326(1):663–665.

Wurmser, L. 1978. *The hidden dimension: Psychodynamics in compulsive drug use.* New York: Jason Aronson.

Yanagita, T. 1970. Self-administration studies on various dependence-producing agents in monkeys. *University of Michigan Medical Center Journal* 36(4, pt. 2):216–224.

Yates, A.; Leehey, K.; and Shisslak, C.M. 1983. Running: An analogue of anorexia? *New England Journal of Medicine* 308:251–255.

Zelson, C. 1975. Acute management of neonatal addiction. *Addictive Diseases* 2:159–168.

Zentner, J.L. 1979. Heroin: Devil drug or useful medicine? *Journal of Drug Issues* 9:333–340.

Zimberg, S. 1974. Evaluation of alcoholism treatment in Harlem. *Quarterly Journal of Studies on Alcohol* 35:550–557.

Zinberg, N.E. 1972. Heroin use in Vietnam and the United States. *Archives of General Psychiatry* 26:486–488.

———. 1974. The search for rational approaches to heroin use. In *Addiction*, ed. P.G. Bourne. New York: Academic Press.

———. 1979. Nonaddictive opiate use. In *Handbook on drug abuse*, eds. R.L. Dupont, A. Goldstein, J. O'Donnell. Rockville, MD: National Institute on Drug Abuse.

———. 1981. "High" states: A beginning study. In *Classic contributions in the addictions*, eds. H. Shaffer and M.E. Burglass. New York Brunner/Mazel.

———. 1984. *Drug, set, and setting: The basis for controlled intoxicant use.* New Haven, CT: Yale University Press.

Zinberg, N.E., and Fraser, K.M. 1979. The role of the social setting in the prevention and treatment of alcoholism. In *The diagnosis and treatment of alcoholism*, eds. J.H. Mendelson and N.K. Mello. New York: McGraw-Hill.

Zinberg, N.E., and Harding, W.M., eds. 1982. *Control over intoxicant use: Pharmacological, psychological, and social considerations.* New York: Human Sciences Press.

Zinberg, N.E.; Harding, W.M.; and Apsler, R. 1978. What is drug abuse? *Journal of Drug Issues* 8:9–35.

Zinberg, N.E.; Harding, W.M.; and Winkeller, M. 1977. A study of social regulatory mechanisms in controlled illicit drug users. *Journal of Drug Issues* 7:117–133.

Zinberg, N.E., and Jacobson, R.C. 1976. The natural history of chipping. *American Journal of Psychiatry* 133:37–40.

Zinberg, N.E., and Lewis, D.C. 1964. Narcotic usage I: A spectrum of a difficult medical problem. *New England Journal of Medicine* 270:989–993.

Zinberg, N.E., and Robertson, J.A. 1972. *Drugs and the public.* New York: Simon & Schuster.

Zismer, D.K., and Holloway, R.L. 1984. The development and validation of an alcohol reinforcement value measure. Unpublished manuscript, Health Services Research Center, Minneapolis.

Zucker, R.A. 1976. Parental influence on the drinking patterns of their children. In *Alcoholism problems in women and children*, eds. M. Greenblatt and M.A. Schuckit. New York: Grune & Stratton.

Author Index

190 • *The Meaning of Addiction*

Subject Index

Abstinence: cure for alcoholism, 30–31, 34, 38, 41, 42, 43, 49, 104, 123, 145, 149, 151; cure for smoking, 144; recommendation for pregnant women, 77; recovery without treatment and return to nonproblematic drinking, 29, 34, 35–45, 49, 122, 123. *See also* Controlled drinking; Moderation

Achievement, 17, 96, 107, 108, 119, 130, 157

Adaptation theories, 47, 69–72; adaptation to internal and external needs, 70; meekness of theorists inappropriate, 72; physiological mechanisms needed, 71

Addiction, causes: among animals, 88–94; any potent experience, 25, 55, 94–96, 97; avoidance of withdrawal (denied), 98; biological factors (inadequate), 12, 18, 54–62, 128, 147–148; cognitive factors, 17, 68–70, 95, 103, 106–110, 128, 138, 148; developmental factors, 15–16, 103, 122–128; exposure to narcotics (denied), 57, 94; personality factors, 1, 3, 9, 16–17, 43, 72, 95–98, 103, 111, 113–122, 127–128; pleasure (denied), 64, 98; ritualistic factors, 14–15, 33, 66, 103, 106, 107, 119, 122, 129; situational factors, 14, 19, 34, 47, 51, 63, 66, 71–73, 84, 90, 94, 96, 97, 103, 110–113, 128, 135, 148; social factors, 1, 2, 13–14, 19, 21, 23, 34, 52–54, 56, 79, 80, 85, 87, 95, 97, 103, 104–106, 127, 128, 130, 131, 135, 148, 151; susceptibility or disposition (psychosocial causes), 95, 96, 98, 104–128

Addiction, nature: adaptation to internal and external needs, 70; animal (no exact equivalent to human), 73, 77–96; behavioral pattern, 1, 2, 5, 10, 18–19, 20–21, 24, 26, 72, 75, 79, 94, 113–114, 127, 128, 133; compulsive, self-destructive activity, 12; concept, 1, 2, 3, 12, 17–26, 72; control issue, 5, 18, 108, 112, 121, 133, 139, 143–144, 151; cure (fundamental self-reliance), 154–157; cycle, 75, 128–132, 155; disease (disputed), 2, 3, 5–6, 47, 55, 57, 59, 72, 128, 133–134, 139, 152–154; drug dependence (denied), 2, 16–25, 39, 57, 60, 136; experience, 12, 25–26, 55, 94–95, 97–132; extreme on continuum of feeling and behavior, 2, 20, 25, 99, 103, 109; formula, 130; given to habit or vice, 3, 12; heroin model for medical definition, 2, 5, 6, 10, 26, 69; illustration, 130; infant (no exact equivalent to adult), 7, 73–77, 94–96; Jaffe's definition, 20–21; label for those who behave in socially unacceptable ways (perpetuating addiction), 21, 26, 56, 109, 134, 147–148, 151, 153; lack of control, 5, 18, 29, 31, 121, 129; overwhelming involvement, 20–21, 26, 47, 97, 98, 132; overworked term, 20; pathological, self-destructive, harmful nature, 1, 2, 26, 47, 95–97, 104, 129; Peele's

Environment *(continued)*
    also Adaptation theories;
    Conditioning theories; Setting;
    Situational factors
Escape from reality, 16, 71, 99, 101,
    103, 113, 119–120, 125, 129
Eskimo attitude toward alcohol, 13,
    33, 50, 106, 109
Ethnic patterns of drug use, 13, 33–34,
    44–45, 48–50, 62, 70, 115
Etonitazene, 88, 91
Euphoria, 63–65, 99; alcohol, 64; allure
    of narcosis, 95; heroin, 64;
    motivation for use of addictive
    drugs, 64; not produced by addictive
    drugs, 95
Experience: normal life, 26, 55, 70, 72,
    94–96, 103, 106, 120, 132; potent,
    25–26, 49, 55, 95, 96, 97, 110, 129.
    See also Addictive experience;
    Behavior; Situational factors
Exposure theories, 56–69, 133. *See also*
    Conditioning theories; Metabolic
    theories

Fear of failure, 118–120
Federal Bureau of Narcotics, 7, 108,
    135
Feeling: and addiction, 1, 2, 66, 101,
    109, 120, 129; state of being, 129.
    See also Emotional factors;
    Experience; Euphoria; Guilt
Fetal alcohol syndrome (FAS), 75–77
Fisher, Eddie, 115
Funding, 134, 146, 147

Gambling, 4, 21, 25, 63, 98, 100, 120,
    134, 151
Genetic theories, 48–56, 133, 139, 148;
    biological mechanism not found,
    49; endorphin deficiency
    exceptional, 51; ethnicity not
    controlled for, 48; genetic factor in
    alcoholism, 11, 18, 27, 29, 45, 47–
    50, 58, 139, 148; greater risk from
    certain biological abnormalities,
    49–50; love not due to chemical
    imbalances, 54; obesity due to
    social factors, 52–54; one biological
    factor cannot explain myriad

addictions, 55
Gratification, 2, 16, 66, 98, 113, 129,
    130, 154, 155, 157
Guilt, 101, 131

Heroin, nature: analgesic, 10, 99;
    compared to alcohol (addictive), 27–
    28; depressant, 99; and euphoria,
    63–66, 99; interchangeable with
    morphine, 80; legal suppression, 4–
    5, 135–140; medical prescription
    prohibited, 135, 140; most sinister
    drug of abuse (conventionally), 12,
    27, 109, 117, 135; origin, 4, 10, 99;
    sources (Turkey, Mexico, Asia), 136;
    worse because "worse" people use
    it, 9, 74, 140. *See also* Opiates;
    Narcotics
Heroin, use: animals, 77–78; humans
    (addicting), 3, 10, 16, 27, 109, 122,
    124; humans (controlled), 8–10, 16,
    28, 67, 68, 100, 101, 109, 123, 139;
    pregnant women (effect on baby),
    73–75
Heroin addiction, causes: association
    with deviant social groups, 13, 71,
    74; diversion and entertainment,
    101; escape from reality, 16, 71, 99,
    101, 103, 113, 119–120, 125, 129;
    euphoria (disputed), 63–68, 99;
    feelings of personal inadequacy,
    102, 121, 142–143; pleasure
    (debunked), 98; relief from
    unpleasant consciousness of life,
    99; rite of self-injection, 14, 71, 103;
    withdrawal (debunked), 98
Heroin addiction, nature: 2, 3, 8, 9, 16,
    78, 103, 118; "American disease,"
    12–13; among outsiders, 115;
    compared to dependent love
    relationships, 98; controlled use, 8–
    10, 16, 28, 67, 68, 100–101, 123;
    cure, 125, 140; degraded lifestyle,
    74; "hooked" (dependent), 122;
    metabolic disease (disputed), 57;
    model for medical definition of all
    addictions, 2, 5–6, 9–10, 26, 69, 98,
    100–101, 109, 117, 133–134;
    numbers of addicts (1920), 27, 135,
    136; (1982), 28, 136, 137; quitting

the habit, 51, 67, 125–126, 128, 143; in Vietnam, 8–9, 14, 51, 110–111; youthful habit, 15, 122. *See also* Addicts; Alcoholism; Narcotic addiction; Nonnarcotic addiction
Hallucinogens, 21, 22, 63, 78, 79, 88
Harrison Act (1914), 4–5, 135
Health: moderating value, 96, 116, 130; positive value, 74, 104, 125, 157
History of drug use: alcohol, 12–13, 27, 30–32, 38, 145–146, 150; heroin, 4, 10, 14, 99, 134, 135; legal suppression, 135–140; opium, 3–5, 12, 27, 75, 108, 135
"Hooked," 122

Identity, 121, 127, 128
Illicit drugs, 3, 9, 74, 75, 105, 115, 123, 137, 139, 141, 150; degraded lifestyle, 74; feelings of guilt and shame, 131; nonconformity and independence predictors of use, 10, 117; peer and parental influence, 105; quitting, 123. *See also* Drug abuse; Drugs; Law
Indians, American: attitude toward alcohol, 13, 33, 50, 106–107, 109
Insanity, 120. *See also* Mental illness
Institute for the Study of Drug Dependence (ISDD), xi
Internal-external model of overeating, 52–54, 100, 121
Interpersonal addiction, 47, 54, 110, 121. *See also* Love
Irish attitude toward alcohol, 33, 34, 44–45, 48, 106, 109
Italian attitude toward alcohol, 13, 33, 45, 107, 109

Jaffe, J.K.: definition of addiction, 20–21
Japanese attitude toward alcohol, 13, 33, 50, 106–107
Jellinek, E.M.: disease theory of alcoholism, 29, 59
Jewish attitude toward alcohol, 13, 33, 62, 106, 109, 115
Joy, 157

Laudanum, 4, 7
Law: effort to suppress drug trade, 135–140; failure for focusing on supply, not demand, 137; invasion of everyday life to mandate treatment, 147; role in definition of addiction, 3, 4, 5, 7, 10, 27, 35, 115, 130, 134. *See also* Medicine; Police; Policies
Legalization, 138
"Limerant" people, 54
Liquor. *See* Alcohol
Loss of control, 1, 5, 6, 11, 13, 17, 21, 53, 62; sign of alcoholism, 18, 29, 30, 31, 32, 49, 53, 108, 109, 120, 121, 122, 128, 129, 149. *See also* Control; Compulsive behavior; Drug abuse
Love: and addiction, 12, 16, 47, 54, 65–66, 98, 109–110, 120, 126, 134; compared to heroin addiction, 98; and disease, 152, 153. *See also* Interpersonal addiction; Nonnarcotic addiction
Lower class factor, 4, 8, 16, 34, 101, 104, 122, 135, 140
LSD, 21

Magic, mystification, and myth, 1, 25, 98, 120, 130, 134, 152
Marijuana, 13–14, 21, 22, 63, 76, 105, 117, 118, 123, 138
Maturing out, 15, 97, 122, 125, 134. *See also* Age factor
Media: depiction of therapies that attack individuality, 149; role to discourage heroin use, 9. *See also* Television
Medicine, organized: role in changing definition of addiction, 4, 6, 7, 21–23, 28–30, 31, 32, 34, 38, 108, 123, 134, 145; treatment, 5–6, 32, 134, 140–157. *See also* Policy; Therapy; Treatment
Meditation, 155
Men, 4, 30, 50, 101, 102, 107, 112, 116, 117, 122, 123, 153. *See also* Women
Mental illness, 1, 120, 129, 134, 154. *See also* Disease theories; Medicine
Metabolic theories, 50, 51, 56–62, 141, 152; alcohol supply model does not

About the Author

Stanton Peele is a psychologist who has worked in the field of addiction since 1969, when he began the research for his well-known book, *Love and Addiction.* Dr. Peele has taught at the Harvard Business School, Columbia University Teachers College, and the addiction programs of the University of California at Los Angeles and Berkeley. He has written for popular publications such as *Psychology Today* and *American Health*, for publishers in the drug and alcohol abuse field such as Hazelden and the National Institute on Drug Abuse, and for academic journals such as *American Psychologist* and *Public Opinion Quarterly*. His most recent book, also published by Lexington, was *The Science of Experience: A Direction for Psychology*.